ROUTLEDGE LIBRARY EDITIONS: WW2

Volume 3

BRITAIN'S FOOD SUPPLIES IN PEACE AND WAR

BRITAIN'S FOOD SUPPLIES IN PEACE AND WAR

CHARLES SMITH

LONDON AND NEW YORK

This edition first published in 2022
by Routledge
2 Park Square, Milton Park, Abingdon, Oxon OX14 4RN

and by Routledge
605 Third Avenue, New York, NY 10158

Routledge is an imprint of the Taylor & Francis Group, an informa business

First published in 1940 by George Routledge & Sons, Ltd.

All rights reserved. No part of this book may be reprinted or reproduced or utilised in any form or by any electronic, mechanical, or other means, now known or hereafter invented, including photocopying and recording, or in any information storage or retrieval system, without permission in writing from the publishers.

Trademark notice: Product or corporate names may be trademarks or registered trademarks, and are used only for identification and explanation without intent to infringe.

British Library Cataloguing in Publication Data
A catalogue record for this book is available from the British Library

ISBN: 978-1-03-201217-9 (Set)
ISBN: 978-1-00-319367-8 (Set) (ebk)
ISBN: 978-1-03-208004-8 (Volume 3) (hbk)
ISBN: 978-1-03-208006-2 (Volume 3) (pbk)
ISBN: 978-1-00-321247-8 (Volume 3) (ebk)

DOI: 10.4324/9781003212478

Publisher's Note
The publisher has gone to great lengths to ensure the quality of this reprint but points out that some imperfections in the original copies may be apparent.

Disclaimer
The publisher has made every effort to trace copyright holders and would welcome correspondence from those they have been unable to trace.

BRITAIN'S FOOD SUPPLIES

IN PEACE AND WAR

A Survey prepared for the Fabian Society

By
CHARLES SMITH

LONDON
GEORGE ROUTLEDGE & SONS, LTD.
BROADWAY HOUSE 68-74 CARTER LANE, E.C.

First published 1940

PRINTED IN GREAT BRITAIN BY
STEPHEN AUSTIN AND SONS, LTD., HERTFORD.

CONTENTS

Note	. . . .	vii
Preface by John Morgan MP	. . .	ix
1.	The Need for a Food Policy . . .	1
2.	Bread	14
3.	Milk and Milk Products	32
4.	Eggs	64
5.	Meat	78
6.	Bacon	114
7.	Sea Fish	129
8.	Vegetables and Fruit	155
9.	Tea	192
10.	Sugar	203
11.	British Agriculture and Food Supply .	219
12.	The Problem of Distribution . . .	239
13.	Food Problems in Wartime . . .	253
14.	The Improvement of Nutrition . .	271
	Index	283

To A. B. T. and M. T.

NOTE

This study of food supply and food policy was prepared during the tenure of a post as Research Assistant to the Fabian Society. Its preparation and drafting were made possible by the great generosity of an anonymous member of the Society. I should like to express my thanks to the numerous members of the Society and others who assisted me to procure information on the food trades or who read portions of the manuscript.

The book was completed in the early days of war. The new conditions of food control and rationing made its subject of even more pressing importance and interest, and it has consequently been revised to include a survey of the effect of the first six months of war on the food trades. As will be apparent, the final proofs were passed before the invasion of Denmark and Holland, so that the passages referring to those countries must be read in the light of later developments. This contribution to the discussion of food problems is offered in the hope that the facts which it assembles and the lines of policy it sketches may during the war prove of some use to the Labour movement, and after the war may assist in that reconstruction which the working people alone can carry out.

The Fabian Society has of course no collective responsibility for the views here expressed, but confines itself to approving the report as one worthy of consideration by the Labour movement and the public generally.

C. S.

Fabian Society,
11 Dartmouth Street,
London, S.W. 1.

PREFACE

This study is a most original, commendable, and timely piece of research work. Hitherto there has not existed an account of the sources of the principal food supplies of this country and of the methods by which they are distributed to the people. It is a story which was complicated in peace time by restriction schemes, quota arrangements and international agreements, all of which were designed to reduce the quantities of food made available. It is especially appropriate that this book should appear now. War conditions necessitate a specially serious consideration of all questions associated with food supply. And new restrictions, in the form of governmental controls, have been put upon the food trades. In some cases these are intended to be permanent, but more usually the idea is that they shall be replaced by the former methods of distribution when peace returns.

The study starts, as all studies of food supply should, from the need of additional food in which so large a proportion of our fellow countrymen are obliged to live, in peace as in war. It attempts to calculate the total quantities of food which would be required to feed the whole nation properly. But it also sets out to discover why these supplies are not forthcoming at reasonable prices, and the sources from which they might be secured.

Both home produced and imported foods are covered in this survey. The author makes clear the part which a revived British agriculture could play in improving the health and diet of the people. War conditions should underline this lesson for us. But for agriculture to be restored two things are needed—money must be available to invest in the land for development, and the marketing of agricultural produce must be made more efficient and so cheaper. If these can be secured and a market for foodstuffs provided in our towns, there will be no more talk of depression in agriculture. The health-giving foods, milk, vegetables, oats, are home-grown foods. A well-fed nation means a prosperous rural community.

In peace or war malnutrition is one of the challenging problems which we have at present to face. For attack on its insidious ravages, ranging from rickets to premature senile decay, a thorough survey of the sources and distribution of our present food supplies is essential to all serious and constructive socialists and students of social well-being. As providing this as well as providing the material for a bold and comprehensive programme which should form a valuable basis of discussion, I commend this volume.

JOHN MORGAN
MP

6.6.40

BRITAIN'S FOOD SUPPLIES

1 THE NEED FOR A FOOD POLICY

Soon after the war broke out there was a rumour that the Ministry of Information had put a ban on the word 'malnutrition'. No doubt it was a baseless rumour—but the spread of it shows a readiness to believe that the authorities would gladly discourage discussion of so inconvenient a topic. Such discouragement, however, would be disastrously shortsighted even from a military point of view, for modern wars, in which whole civilian populations no less than armies are engaged, are won by food supply. 'The food question ultimately decided the issue of this war,' wrote Lloyd George of the war of 1914–18.[1] The Spanish war taught the same lesson. It was food shortage that broke the morale of the Republicans and gave the victory to General Franco.

The war of 1914–18 indeed provided a powerful impetus to the scientific study of nutrition. Governments wanted to know from the experts how much—or rather how little—a man must eat in order to be able to work and fight. Scientific study of diet had been developing in the first few years of the century, but the experts in the subject did not then enjoy sufficient prestige to ensure that their advice would always be taken or that there would not be occasions on which the authorities in their ignorance would issue broadcast directions on feeding which were not only misleading but dangerous.[2] As late as 1912 the word vitamins was coined to describe the elements in food which had been the subject of close investigation and careful experiment in

---

[1] In general the effect of food shortage was felt most directly by the civilian population. Military experts, however, recognise as one of the major causes of the Italian rout at Caporetto the reduction in the cereal ration of the Italian soldier some months earlier.

[2] For example, the 'meatless day' campaign launched in April 1917, by Lord Devonport, then Food Controller, was attacked by scientists on the ground that it would lead to a reduction of the consumption of home produced food at the expense of imported grain. Earlier a memorandum by the Royal Society had criticised the official Food Economy Handbook for such wild statements as, 'if you are eating meat you are better without bread; starch and meat together double the stomach's work.' (See J. C. Drummond and Anne Wilbraham, *The Englishman's Food*, 1939.)

the preceding years. Proteins, fats and carbohydrates had already been studied, and it had become to some extent recognised that they were essential to a satisfactory diet.

The strain of war and the restriction of food supplies which war involved were imposed upon a population which was poorly nourished and which showed this physically. The Inspector General of Recruiting in 1903 had given an unpleasant shock to the optimism of Edwardian Britain by drawing attention to 'the gradual deterioration of the physique of the working classes from which the bulk of the recruits must always be drawn'. When in 1917-18 conscription involved medical examination of $2\frac{1}{2}$ million men of military age, the result was summed up as follows :—

> Of every nine men of military age in Great Britain on the average three were perfect, fit, and healthy; two were on a definitely inferior plane of health and strength, whether from some disability or some failure of development; three were incapable of undergoing more than a very moderate degree of physical exertion, and could almost (in view of their age) be described with justice as physical wrecks; and the remaining man was a chronic invalid with a precarious hold on life.

Even allowing for the fact that this was not altogether a fair sample since it was made up of those who were not in the army by 1917 and therefore included all those of military age who were in bad health and only a proportion of those in good health, the results of the examination were alarming. The lowered resistance and vitality which resulted from war conditions were shown in the epidemics which spread through Britain and the Continent after the Armistice and proved almost as devastating as warfare itself.

The scientific study of diet which took its origin from the practical attempts of doctors to remedy the deficiency diseases—as they would be called to-day—from which sailors and others whose occupations restricted their food supplies suffered, grew gradually and, given an impetus by the Great War, has provided in the last few years an altogether new background for the discussions of poverty and ill health. Inquiry and discussion have gone along two lines—what should be eaten for health and welfare, and what in fact is eaten.

THE NEED FOR A FOOD POLICY

The first is a specialised question; and experts are now able to return an answer on the broad lines of which they are agreed. Advances in the study of nutrition have established the need for a varied and balanced diet. The need for proteins, fats and energy-giving carbohydrates has been recognised for some time. Recent advances have shown the need for vitamins and minerals in a healthy diet.

A stimulus to the study of diet has been the desire of governments to know the minimum amount on which a family can live. The whole conception of minimum scales of diet has actually very little meaning. Individuals are very different in their requirements; and any minimum scales based on experiment are likely to be too low because they depend on observations covering a comparatively short period during which a man may live on a diet which would be quite inadequate if he tried to subsist upon it permanently. Moreover, knowledge of nutrition is not yet complete (although experts are sufficiently agreed upon the broad outlines for far greater use to be made of what they say). In the present state of medical knowledge it is not safe even to say of any diet that it cannot be improved; the more 'abundant, mixed and varied' it can be made the better.[1] On the basis of this nutritional knowledge, however, the British Medical Association drew up a set of minimum diets for men, women and children. They were very bare minima; in the case of a man there was not sufficient food for him to carry on moderately hard work; in the case of a woman the scales were inadequate to maintain health, and of a child insufficient for health and proper development. Particularly small was the ration of milk included in these scales—far below that recommended by the Government Advisory Committee. These diets do not make allowance for the food wasted in preparation even by the most careful manager, and assume that the housewife will always buy in the cheapest market in the case of every item. Thus these

---

[1] A table of the nutrients required for perfect health which may be taken as summarising expert opinion has been drawn up by Stiebeling of the Government Bureau of Home Economics, U.S.A., and is printed in the League of Nations Report *The Problem of Nutrition*, 1937.

scales may be said to represent a bare minimum on which it is possible to exist without very apparent deficiency.[1]

So much for what people should eat. No less important

	Group I	Group II	Group III	Group IV	Group V	Group VI
Proportion of the population	10%	20%	20%	20%	20%	10%
Average food expenditure per week	4/–	6/–	8/–	10/–	12/–	14/–
Beef and veal, oz	10·5	14·5	17·2	18·9	19·5	18·9
Mutton and lamb, oz	3·1	5·6	7·2	9·4	11·6	13·9
Bacon and ham, oz	4·3	6·3	6·8	7·3	7·8	9·4
Other meat, oz	5·2	5·2	5·9	5·9	5·9	7·2
Total meat, oz	23·1	31·6	37·1	41·5	44·8	49·4
Bread and flour (including biscuits and cakes) (a), oz.	66·0	68·0	68·0	67·0	65·0	60·0
Milk, fresh, pints	1·1	2·1	2·6	3·1	4·2	5·5
Milk, condensed (b), pints	0·7	0·6	0·55	0·5	0·4	0·3
Eggs, number	1·5	2·1	2·6	3·2	3·6	4·5
Butter, oz	3·0	6·5	7·5	8·5	9·5	11·0
Cheese, oz	1·8	2·5	3·1	3·6	3·6	2·6
Margarine, oz	4·5	3·5	2·5	2·0	1·6	1·3
Tea, oz	2·2	2·7	2·9	3·0	2·9	2·7
Potatoes, oz	53·0	56·0	57·0	57·0	57·0	54·0
Lard, suet, and dripping, oz	2·7	3·6	4·2	4·4	4·3	3·5
Fish, oz	2·7	5·5	8·2	10·4	12·2	13·5
Sugar, purchased as such, oz	13·5	16·0	18·0	19·0	19·5	19·5
Jams, jellies, syrup, etc., oz	4·3	5·3	5·2	5·4	5·8	5·5
Sugar consumed in other forms	6·5	7·5	8·5	9·5	10·5	11·5
Fruit (c)	14·0	21·7	25·8	27·9	30·5	39·3
Vegetables (excluding potatoes) (c)	16·0	20·0	27·2	30·6	32·3	34·0

(a) In terms of flour : 130 bread is equal to 100 flour.
(b) In terms of liquid milk equivalent. Allowance has been made for consumption of condensed milk in complex foodstuffs.
(c) Group quantities for fruit and vegetables have been estimated from expenditure after allowing for quality variations, but the figures are subject to a wide margin of error.

[1] In November 1933 the cost of the BMA minima for a family consisting of a man, his wife, and three children was between 23/3 and 25/–. In November 1937 the cost of giving them these minimum diets had risen to between 29/6 and 31/6, and in December 1939 the costs varied from 33/6 to 36/–.

THE NEED FOR A FOOD POLICY

is an account of what they do eat. The completest and clearest general statement on that as far as this country is concerned is to be found in Orr's *Food, Health and Income*.[1] He divided the families whose budgets he studied into six income groups according to the income per head; then on the basis of an analysis of the budgets themselves he calculated how much was spent on food and what was bought. The results (p. 73) were as shown in table opposite.

The average quantity of foodstuffs eaten in the different groups was then set beside Stiebeling's standard of quantity of nutrients required for the maintenance of perfect health. This comparison showed—

> that the average diet of Group I was inadequate for health in all constituents considered; Group II was adequate only in total protein; Group III was adequate in energy value, protein and fat, but below standard in minerals and vitamins; Group IV was adequate in iron, phosphorus and vitamins, but probably below standard in calcium; Group V had ample margin of safety in everything with the possible exception of calcium; in Group VI the standard requirements are exceeded in every case.[2]

The numbers of the population who fell into the income groups were as follows :—

Group	Percentage of population	Total Number	Percentage of Children under 14
I	13·7	6,439,000	25·3
II	16·9	7,990,000	26·7
III	16·5	7,755,000	20·0
IV	25·3	11,870,000	19·0
V	18·4	9,130,000	7·3
VI	8·1	3,760,000	1·5

(Based on Colin Clark, *National Income and Outlay*)

There are some criticisms which may be made of Orr's calculations. For example, he worked on a basis of not many more than a thousand budgets, and took a large proportion of these from the industrial north of England. The later researches of Sir William Crawford, however, published in *The People's Food*,[3] confirm Orr's principal point—that

---
[1] First published, London, 1936.
[2] Orr, *Food, Health and Income*, 2nd edition, p. 42.
[3] London, 1938.

almost half the population are living on diets inadequate to maintain them in health.[1]

The budgets on which Sir John Orr originally worked were for the years 1932–34, and later surveys which he made in 1937–39 showed some improvement. More milk was being drunk and various health and welfare services had raised the standard of living of the very poor. Roughly the position on the outbreak of war was that

> The average dietary of about one-third of the population is above the standard required for health, the diet of about one-third nearly right, and the diet of the remaining third below the standard.[2]

The results of these surveys have not yet been published in detail so that it is not possible to make an exact comparison with the earlier position. In any case the sharp rise in prices since September 1939 will have brought new difficulties for the family and it may well be that the broad conclusions of Sir John Orr's *Food, Health and Income* are still true.

Now look at the cases of some special groups within the population; take first the families of long unemployed men. A recent inquiry gives an indication of their condition.[3] The standard by which their well-being was judged was R. F. George's 'poverty line'. Not only is this standard based on the B.M.A. minimum diet, but it makes no allowance for small miscellaneous expenditure on such things as football pools or cigarettes, which an unemployed man, very understandably, will often force himself to afford; thus it can be said to represent in fact a very low standard of life indeed. The inquiry showed that three out of every ten of these households were living below the George poverty line. '44% of the families were living at what Mr. George would reckon to be bare subsistence level or below it.'

The report further hints that even when a family appears to be above the subsistence level some of the individual

---

[1] Since Crawford's calculations of consumption are quoted subsequently in the case of separate commodities it is worth noting that from the very nature of his investigations the results for the lower income groups have more meaning than those for the higher income groups.

[2] Sir John Orr and D. Lubbock, *Feeding the People in War-Time*, 1940.

[3] *Men Without Work*. Report to the Pilgrim Trust, 1938.

THE NEED FOR A FOOD POLICY

members may for one reason or another be below it. Those members who actually bring in wages are felt to be entitled to a better diet than those who do not, and actually receive it. Again the report showed that in most unemployed families the parents, and particularly the wives, bore the burden of poverty as far as they could themselves, and ' in many cases were literally starving themselves in order to feed and clothe the children reasonably '.

Many of those falling within Orr's lowest income group may be getting even less food than would appear from the figures. Poverty of this kind with its inevitable accompaniment of malnutrition is not confined to the families of the long unemployed nor to the depressed areas. The Social Surveys of Liverpool, London and Southampton showed that a considerable proportion of the population, even in relatively prosperous parts of the country, is living below the poverty line. More recent evidence comes from Bristol,[1] where the general standard of living is high and the city, dependent upon a large variety of industries, enjoys a fairly steady prosperity. The survey was taken in 1937 at the peak of the business revival and covered four-fifths of the population of the city—all those in fact whose incomes fell below middle class levels. In this examination one family in ten was found to be below ' the poverty line ' (which was approximately the same as George's poverty standard). This does not mean to say that the remainder had enough to spend on food—for the George standard is a very meagre one—but it does show that one family in ten definitely had not got enough. When the figures are looked at more closely it emerges that of the families with four or more children, slightly over half fell below the poverty line and most of the rest were only slightly above it. Of families with three children a quarter were below. To put it another way, one child in every five under fourteen years of age came from a family which was living below the poverty line—that is, in extreme poverty.

There are some well-known and spectacular examples of a

[1] *The Standard of Living in Bristol*, published by the University of Bristol Social Survey, 1938.

clear and unmistakable connection between poverty and public health. There is for example the wide variation between infant and maternal mortality rates in depressed and in comparatively prosperous areas. Barrow in Furness has an infant mortality rate of 98 per thousand while Hastings has one of 35.[1] Again, take as an example of inequality the figures of the heights of working class, middle class and public school boys at different ages.[2] Thousands of observations over a number of years show that boys from Christ's Hospital, mainly drawn from the middle classes, were from the age of 10 onwards an average of 2–3 inches taller than elementary school boys; and that boys from public schools were on an average 1·5 to 3 inches taller than those of the same age from Christ's Hospital.

The food which people can afford to buy is not the sole factor responsible for their health; but how important it is even when compared with housing is shown by the observations of McGonigle at Stockton on Tees.[3] There a slum area was demolished and the inhabitants rehoused in a new estate; but the medical records showed quite clearly when allowance had been made for the different age composition of the populations that the death rate in the new housing estate went up while in the town as a whole and in the slum areas which still existed it went down. The rise could not be due to bad sanitation or bad living conditions; the new estate was modern and well planned. But an analysis of family budgets showed that the much higher rents which were charged in the new houses had forced the transferred families severely to cut their expenditure on food. The effects of poverty and underfeeding on an individual are not always obvious nor easy to measure by figures. A man's health is not so often destroyed by severe accidents as by

[1] To quote R. M. Titmuss, *Poverty and Population* (1938), 'if the same conditions and the same infant mortality rates that existed in 1936 in many towns of a " depressed " nature such as Jarrow and Gelligaer (South Wales), etc., had obtained throughout the whole of England and Wales the nation would have lost in that year approximately 25,000 more infants.' This book assembles all the information available on the relationship between poverty and health.
[2] See Orr, *Food, Health and Income.*
[3] See G. E. W. McGonigle and J. Kirby, *Poverty and Public Health*, 1936.

persistent and often unrecognised causes, of which one of the most important is a badly composed diet. Imperfect physical development, lack of endurance, lack of vitality, lack of resistance to disease and a tendency to age prematurely—all these follow from malnutrition.

Striking as an indication of the relations of nutrition and health are the results of Lady Williams' work in South Wales and Durham. Between the beginning of 1935 and the middle of 1937 she was able to provide extra nourishment from various funds for 10,000 expectant mothers. There were at the same time 18,000 others living under substantially the same conditions who could not receive the extra nourishment because the funds were limited.

In the case of mothers who received the additional food the puerperal death rate dropped to 1·63 per thousand. In the case of the other 18,854 the death rate was 6·15 per thousand. Moreover the extra provision influences to a marked extent the mortality of infants dying under one year of age (including stillbirths). In the first instance the rate was only 57 per thousand as compared with 59 for England and Wales as a whole in 1936; for the second group, i.e. those not receiving the extra nourishment—the rate was no less than 102, one of the worst figures recorded in any part of the country.[1]

The effects of malnutrition are likely to be specially severe in the long run because of the large number of children now being brought up in families where there is not enough to eat. A good deal of official optimism has been based upon figures derived from the medical examination of school children; but where the examinations have been thorough (as in the case of those carried out by McGonigle in Stockton on Tees, where he found that only 6% of the school children were altogether free from rickets) the results have been less reassuring.[2]

[1] *Bulletin* of Committee Against Malnutrition.
[2] The general figures for the health of school children are vitiated by a lack of any general consistent and objective standard. Thus in a given year 74·1% of the children are said to be of 'normal' nutrition; but standards of normality vary—in one district, for example, a local doctor points out, to be normal meant to have two carious teeth—and at best are based upon average standards. To say that three-quarters of the children reached the standard of health of the majority of the children does not get us far or tell us much. The matter is discussed fully in the book *Nutrition* published by the British Association for Labour Legislation.

The attitude of the Government as revealed in pre-war debates in the House of Commons was complacent. Much was made of the complexity of the problem of nutrition and of the improvement in public health standards in the course of the last half century. Such complacency reached its height when Mr. Walter Elliot, then Minister of Agriculture, declared—

> There are 22½ million people in this country in receipt of an optimum diet, a figure never before reached in any period of society . . . to have raised half the people to such a point that no further improvement of any kind or description can be made in their diet is a claim which is at any rate worth regard.

What, in the light of this public discussion and investigation which has been going on for the past few years, can be said to be established about the public health and standards of nutrition in this country? On the one hand certain standards of diet have been provisionally established as desirable, well buttressed by medical authority. The idea of an optimum diet has been developed and provides a basis for any positive work on nutrition. On the other hand it is established that the habitual diet of as much as one half of the population does not reach this necessary standard. Within that half of the population there are groups who not only fall short of the optimum diet, but do not even enjoy the bare minimum requirements. 13% of the population including one in four of all children under 14 fall within Sir John Orr's lowest income group, whose diet is defective in every particular. This widespread deficiency means that large numbers of the people are in varying degrees subject to the handicap of poor physique and reduced vitality in every activity they undertake—an intolerable situation, inconsistent with a democratic society.

Such inequality leaves no room for official optimism, and confirms the cautiously expressed view of the Ministry of Health Advisory Committee on Nutrition.

> Although much has been done, much still remains to be done before the general health and physique of the population reach the optimum level. It must not, for example, be overlooked that in 1935 tuberculosis was still responsible for 32,903 deaths (England, Scotland, and Wales), 6·1% of the total mortality,

THE NEED FOR A FOOD POLICY

or that the mortality rate from all causes in children aged one to four years, favourable as is its trend, is distinctly higher than that of certain other countries, notably Norway, Sweden, and the Netherlands.

While this malnutrition exists throughout the world, the production of foodstuffs has been increasing; in many producing countries markets have been glutted and ruin stares producers in the face. These difficulties, of which the British farmers have their share, make all the more necessary a comprehensive policy which will remedy the contradiction. Such a food policy must not be considered out of relation to other measures—such as wage advances won by trade union pressure or increases in unemployment benefit and assistance rates which would raise working class purchasing power. The benefits of these measures would be entirely lost if their enactment were allowed to coincide with a sharp rise in the price of food such as might be caused by the manœuvres of the speculators or, if plans were not worked out beforehand, by a genuine shortage of supplies of certain foodstuffs.

What is as important as a knowledge of present standards is some indication of what is likely to be bought with increased wages. Whatever theoretically perfect diets experts may devise it is certain that people will continue to eat broadly speaking what they like. The only way to discover the additional quantities required to give the whole population an optimum diet is to study present food consumption habits (as shown by the researches of Orr and Crawford). These give a basis for estimating the quantities of food which would be demanded if the purchasing power of the worst paid section of the working class were increased and prices remained unchanged. Food habits, as recent experience has shown, can to some extent be modified by propaganda in the form of poster advertising, recipe books, stalls at housewives' exhibitions and so on; and it may be desirable to make particular efforts to stimulate the consumption of particular foodstuffs which for one reason or another are not regarded with favour.

According to Sir John Orr the diet of his Group IV

whose members spend an average of 10/- per head per week on food, is on the whole adequate, although it may be deficient in calcium. Provided then that it is supplemented by an additional allowance of milk this may be taken as a minimum which it should be the aim to secure for the whole population; and it has the supreme advantage over other scales that it follows from a study of food habits. It provides a basis for calculating roughly the additional quantities of foodstuffs which will be required to bring the whole population to a comparatively satisfactory state of nutrition—although of course allowance must be made for the fact that a large section of the population already live at a standard above this proposed minimum and will continue to do so even if the remainder of the population is raised to this minimum.

If this qualification is borne in mind, and an allowance is made for wastage in distribution, a very rough estimate of the total quantities required of the principal foodstuffs may be made as follows:—

Food	Quantity required	Peace-time consumption	% increase
Butter	600,000 tons	513,000 tons	16
Eggs	9,000 million	7,200 million	25
Fish	1,120,000 tons	900,000 tons	25
Vegetables (excluding potatoes)	2,500,000 ,,	2,100,000 ,,	20
Fruit	3,300,000 ,,	2,380,000 ,,	50
Meat	3,375,000 ,,	3,000,000 ,,	12

The formulation of a policy for reducing prices and increasing supplies requires a detailed account of the sources of supply and methods of distribution of essential foodstuffs. It involves discussion of import trade, agriculture and distribution which have been too little discussed in their relations to one another and to the nutritional condition of the people. The plan of this book is to treat in detail each of the main commodities consumed in this country and then to draw some general conclusions on the organisation of their supply and distribution in conditions both of peace and war.

Pre-War Supplies and Retail Value of Foods

Commodity	Supplies in Thousand Tons			Retail Value in £ million
	Home produced	Imported	Total	
Wheat as flour	767	3,197	3,964	151
Sugar	469	1,618	2,087	37
Butter	45	472	517	70
Cheese	37	146	183	18
Eggs	409	190	599	46
Milk	4,556	—	4,556	98
Beef and mutton	918	1,007	1,925	175
Bacon and ham	151	325	476	114
Fruit and nuts	661	1,948	2,609	102
Potatoes	4,400	145	4,545	45
Other vegetables	1,206	644	1,850	42
Fish	774	186	960	66
Tea	—	206	206	44
Miscellaneous	753	1,055	1,808	151
Total	15,146	11,139	26,285	1,159

Note.—This table is intended to provide a rough comparison of different foods. The figures of supplies are for 1937–38 and are based on a table in Orr and Lubbock: *Feeding the People in War Time*. The figures of retail value are the estimate of A. E. Feavearyear for the year 1936. The figure of retail value given opposite wheat includes flour, bread, biscuits, and cakes. The value given for bacon and hams includes pork. The total includes an allowance of £35 million for the preparation of manufactured food.

2 BREAD

As Britain grew richer and its standard of living rose, the consumption of bread tended to decrease, not only by comparison with other foods, but even absolutely.[1] This tendency for the *per capita* consumption of bread to decline has been partially offset by an expensive 'Eat More Bread' campaign; but unless there is a sharp fall in the standard of living of a large section of the population, consumption will not rise to the figure at which it stood during the last century. Vegetables, fruit and breakfast foods replace bread in the diet of those who can afford them.

The better off a family is, the less it will spend on bread. Sir William Crawford's investigations give the following result:—

Family Income	Expenditure per head per week in pence	Quantity purchased per head per week in ounces
£500 and over	7·5	48·0
£250–£499	7·8	49·6
£125–£249	8·1	54·9
Under £125	8·7	62·4

Clearly bread accounts for a very much larger share of the food budget of the poor than of the rich; and for the very poor, the long-unemployed, the old age pensioner, and the wife of the low-paid worker with a large family, it does in fact remain the staff of life, and with tea and margarine may form the foundation of the customary diet.

If Crawford's figures are taken as a basis of calculation the total consumption must amount to about 3,600,000 tons in a year. The total retail value of this according to Feavearyear's estimate was £51 million in 1934 and £58 million in 1936. Most of this is white bread; indeed,

---

[1] This is generally the case in those few countries where bread is the staple food. In other countries, such as India and China, which base their diets upon rice, the consumption of wheat-bread increases as the community grows in wealth and is higher among the rich than among the poor.

30 or 40% of the families of the country never buy brown, and very many of the remainder taste it only occasionally. Some 14% of the total consumption is reckoned to be brown.[1]

From the point of view of nutrition, the popularity of white bread is bad. The changeover from grinding mills to roller mills in the 1880's meant that the process was quicker and cheaper; but the flour produced, although the desired whiteness, lost in the milling process many of the highly nutritious substances — proteins, mineral salts, fats and vitamins—in the germ of the wheat.

The Baker's Part

A great deal of our bread is baked in retail bakeries, employing an average of two or three men. There are some 20,000 of these. In addition there are a little under 3,000 larger establishments with five or more employees; and 1,750 wholesale bakehouses employing on an average 19 or 20 men. These large bakeries cater mainly for hospitals, schools and other institutions, but some distribute to grocers and other retailers and in some exceptional cases avail themselves of three or four thousand of such retail outlets.[2] There are a few breads (of which Neville's is the most important) which are made by large scale bakers, marketed through independent retailers and nationally advertised.

Until recently the conditions of labour in the smaller bakeries were definitely bad. Before the war average earnings for a man were 46/- and for a woman 23/- for a week of just over 50 hours.[3] So unsatisfactory are the conditions that a Trade Board has been set up. In the past undertakings about hours, particularly those given at local meetings of master bakers, have been lightheartedly broken.[4] A leading trade paper commented on the decision to set up a Trade Board that—

[1] These two sentences are based on a survey of the Bread Trade published in the *Advertising World*, August 1939.
[2] *Report of the Departmental Committee on Night Baking*, 1937.
[3] 1935 figures quoted in *Output, Employment and Wages in the UK, 1924, 1930, 1935*.
[4] See, for example, article by A. R. Daniel in *British Baker*, 27 January 1939.

if the employers have no reason to rejoice the operatives certainly have. As a body they have their hours of labour reduced, their wages increased and payment for all hours worked as overtime—that is beyond 48 in the week.[1]

For some years the price which the housewife pays has varied with the price of flour—in accordance with a scale recommended by the Food Council (although that body, which apparently was suspended on the outbreak of war, had no power to impose any regulations on bakers). The scale nominally applied only to London, but was in fact observed by bakers in many parts of the country. The 1932 Scale was revised in 1938 and again on the outbreak of war :—

Price of Quartern Loaf should not exceed	When the price of standard straight run flour per sack of 280 lb was between :		
	1932 Scale	1938 Scale	1939 Scale
9½d	43/- and 47/-	39/- and 43/-	37/- and 41/-
9d	39/- and 43/-	35/- and 39/-	33/- and 37/-
8½d	35/- and 39/-	31/- and 35/-	29/- and 33/-
8d	31/- and 35/-	27/- and 31/-	25/- and 29/-

Flour is the largest single item in the baker's costs as the comparative costs of different types of bakery show. (See table on facing page.)

The Food Council has emphasised the variations between the costs of different firms; in particular so far as distribution is concerned. The figure given above for this does not seem to be unrepresentative and shows that there has been a considerable increase in delivery expenses in the last five years, for in 1933 the costs of delivery and selling were about 10/- to 11/- per sack.[2]

Since there are these variations in cost and since no law prevents one baker from selling cheaper bread than another, it would seem likely that prices of bread would be cut very drastically and the less efficient firms bankrupted. What happens, however, is that bread prices—usually based on

---

[1] Editorial of *Baker and Confectioner*, 6 January 1939.
[2] According to information given by Colin Clark in a communication to the Fabian Society.

BREAD

BAKING COSTS (IN SHILLINGS PER SACK OF FLOUR OF 280 LB WEIGHT)

	Large Cooperative Bakery (1938)	Large Army Bakery (July, 1939)	Small Hand Bakery [1] (Sept.–Oct., 1939)
Flour (delivered price)	27/11·4 }	21/5·0	22/9
Wheat quota payment	2/9·6 }		3/6
Yeast and other materials.	3/8·8	/8·5	2/11
Total Materials	34/3·8	22/1·5	29/2
Bakehouse wages	4/2·0	4/9·5	7/6
Management and administration.	1/4·0	/5·0	1/8
Fuel	1/5·0	/8·5	1/6
Depreciation and maintenance.	3/6·4	1/8·5	7/11
Total Baking Costs.	10/5·4	7/7·5	18/7·3
Delivery	15/4·2	—	8/9·7
Grand Total	60/3·4	29/9·0	56/7
Selling price	Probably 66/– to 70/–	—	69/–

the Food Council scale—are fixed and enforced by local bakers' associations which exist in every part of the country.

The weapon which they use is the threat that the millers will withhold supplies of flour from any baker who sells under the agreed rate. Government Commissions have on more than one occasion condemned this practice, but it continues. The latest condemnation came from the Food Council itself, which was, however, not able to get further than recommending to the Board of Trade that an independent tribunal should be set up to which a baker could appeal before his supplies were actually cut off. As the Council suggested, this weapon was not being used merely to prevent some bakers from selling temporarily below cost :—

[1] This is based on some costs of production of bread collected by Plymouth Food Control Committee (see *Milling*, 11 November 1939). The figure for depreciation and maintenance is made up as follows: Rent 5/4 ; Rates 1/7·2d ; Lighting 5·3d ; Interest on Capital 6·5d. There is an item of 3/4 per sack on account of 'shop and clerical assistance and wages of errand boy'. This has been divided between 'Administration' and 'Delivery'.

When the bakers in some areas had persuaded the millers to insert a clause in their flour contracts by which flour could be cut off if the purchaser sold his bread below a certain price, they adopted as their minimum prices which were very close to the maximum prices of the Food Council, and in the north-eastern area the minimum prices dictated by the bakers and millers were actually above the Council's maximum prices.

The effect of this system is to fix a retail margin which will allow the less efficient concerns to continue to exist; and since baking, as has been shown, is largely done by small concerns, this margin is a fairly considerable one.

In the course of time, moreover, this system of fixing standard prices has had the effect of raising the scales themselves. Since the bakers could not cut prices against one another, competition between them took the form of greater expenditure on shop fittings and on distributive services.

In November 1937 the Food Council received a request from the Joint Price Committee of the two chief bakers' societies in London for an increase in the scale of maximum bread prices because costs of production and distribution had gone up since the scale was last revised in 1932. What the bakers wanted was an immediate increase of 3/- per sack pending a careful examination of baking and distributing costs with a possible further increase to 4/- per sack. The bakers' request was granted and a new scale of maximum prices was accordingly issued. The investigation into costs then took place, and the Food Council took the opportunity of making a number of valuable remarks on the state of retail baking. It was in this report that the Council emphasised the variations in cost and particularly in distributive costs between one firm and another.

So impressed were the Council with the heavy distributive costs that they tried to persuade bakers to charge less for bread bought over the counter than for that delivered at the door; but the bakers insisted that high rents made this impossible. The Food Council, although they continued to urge the point for some months, finally expressed agreement with this point of view and withdrew their recommendation.

The effect of the restriction of retail prices has been that the general technical level of the bakery trade is low, despite the technical advances which have lowered costs in some large bakeries. The Trade Board has forced upon the trade the need for overhauling their equipment and their methods; trade papers have recently devoted a lot of space to advice to small master bakers on lowering their costs so that the need to give better conditions to their workers shall not throw them out of business. The first article of one of these series [1] contains convincing evidence that there is room for greater efficiency; and that in fact in many cases this greater efficiency is essential if profits are to be made under Trade Board conditions :—

> I have noticed so much waste of time, material, and energy in so many bakeries in the past. These wastages do not mean just the obvious things that the words themselves imply, but also many wastages that are not immediately apparent. Up to now in quite a large percentage of cases that have come to my notice it has been usual for a week's wages to be paid for a 'week's' work. But whilst the wages have always been a fixed quantity, the week's work has implied getting a list of goods completed each day with no very definite amount of time allowed for the job. Hence it does not matter whether the bakery is a convenient or an inconvenient one to work in; whether there is or is not a sufficiency of tools or equipment or whether, for that matter, the employees are ten minutes late returning from meals or not. So long as the work is completed, nothing is said.

The articles in the series go on to suggest ways in which labour can be saved—by careful planning of the bakery to avoid waste of time in delivery of materials and collection of bread by roundsmen; by storing flour in a separate loft, hoisting it there by a pulley and chain and dropping it as required by a chute instead of having it carried up and down ladders—and so on.

It seems likely that the happy-go-lucky attitude of so many master bakers is due less to the system of paying a week's wages for a definite amount of work than to the protection which minimum retail prices have afforded, and to the compliance which the Food Council has shown in moving their whole scale of bread prices upward on the

---

[1] 'Trade Rearmament,' by A. R. Daniel, in *The British Baker*, 27 January 1939.

request of the bakers; but the articles nevertheless afford authoritative evidence of the room there is for modernising bakery equipment and routine.

The Flour Milling Industry

Just over half the country's supply of flour is used for making bread. The last authoritative figures of the utilisation of flour, quoted in the Report of the Wheat Commission (published in 1938), are taken from the Final Report of the Board of Trade on the Census of Production for 1930.[1] The total supply of flour was then 4,260,000 tons, and it was used as follows :—

	%
For bread baking	51
For cakes and pastries, etc.	6
For biscuits for human consumption	3
For all other purposes, including use for home bread-making, industrial purposes, and in manufacture of other kinds of food, e.g. meat pies	40

The supply of flour over the past three cereal years has been derived as follows :—

	1936–7	1937–8	1938–9
Imported	417	390	392
Home milled	3,730	3,727	3,814
Total	4,147	4,117	4,206

Figures in thousands of tons.

Of the home milled flour it is probable that less than one fifth was derived from home grown wheat. The rest was derived from imported grain.

In recent years and to a growing extent the supply of bread has been dominated not by the farmers who provide the grain or by the bakers who pass the bread on to the consumer, but by the millers who grind the wheat into flour. As the table above shows, the bulk of flour made

---

[1] It is unfortunate that no more recent figures are available. Since 1930, the Weston combine has grown up to supply the market for cheap biscuits so that the percentage of flour used for biscuit-making is probably now larger.

up into bread in this country passes through the hands of this highly organised industry. The ratio of extraction of flour from wheat was 66% before 1914, and is now reckoned at 70%.

The millers of Britain are in a particularly strong position. Wheat, although more bulky, is safer and easier to transport than flour, so it is an advantage for the miller to be fairly near the point of consumption and so avoid sea voyages or a number of changes for the flour. Again there is in Britain a good market for the by-products of milling ; the offals (30% by weight of the wheat) which are sold for cattle feed bring the miller some 10% of his receipts.

But the greatest strength of the milling industry in Britain lies in its high state of organisation. The members of the Millers Mutual Association produce 80% of the flour output of the country—practically the whole supply if we set aside that milled by the cooperative societies.

The main cause of the establishment of the Millers Mutual in 1929 was the surplus capacity of the industry and the cut throat competition between milling concerns. There had been in the previous sixty years a very marked increase in the efficiency of milling machinery and in the size of milling units, while the industry had become more and more concentrated in a few districts. The Linlithgow Report [1] stated that in 1923 about half the total flour requirements of the country could be met from the four principal port areas—(1) London, (2) Liverpool, Manchester and Ellesmere district, (3) the York and Hull district, and (4) Bristol and the Bristol Channel ports.[2] At the same time that new plant had been installed (especially under the stimulus of wartime conditions, when in order to economise on transport there was a ban on the transport of flour more than a 100

---

[1] *The Report of the Departmental Committee on the Distribution and Prices of Agricultural Produce*, 1923. This Committee, which was presided over by Lord Linlithgow, issued Interim Reports on the Marketing of Vegetables, Livestock, Cereals, and Milk and Milk Products. These are still of some value as descriptions of the machinery of agricultural marketing and food distribution.

[2] Complaints are frequent in the trade press that the tendency in recent years has been to close down inland mills and to concentrate milling at the ports to a degree which is likely to be dangerous in war.

miles), old and out-of-date plant had not been put out of use. Thus, after the 1914–18 war, whereas most economical production could be obtained in a mill working about 6,350 hours per annum, all the country's requirements could be met by running all the existing mills for an average of less than 5,000 hours per annum. Again, it was later calculated that the aggregate capacity of all the mills was about 6,500 sacks per hour, whereas the demand could be supplied by plants of a capacity of 5,500–5,700 sacks per hour working full time.

The bigger milling firms took the initiative in forming the Millers Mutual Association in 1929. The details of its operations are not available to the public; but it appears that in form it is an insurance company which by a system of fines and bonuses restricts the production of members on a datum period basis. The effect is said to be to maintain profits about the level of 2/6 to 3/- per sack (280 lb). If this is the case the millers are considerably better off than in the years before 1929, when profits were about a shilling a sack and any attempt to enforce higher prices by agreement was liable to be rendered fruitless by undercutting.[1]

Since the Millers Mutual Association was formed the two largest firms, Ranks and Spillers, have increased their share of the trade by buying up smaller concerns and, with the firms, the quotas which they are allowed to produce. They are now calculated to control more than half the trade which remains in the hands of members of the Association; and have been using their reserves to increase their trade and pay the necessary fines, so that if at any time the datum of each firm comes up for revision they will be able to claim

[1] After the MMA had been established in 1929 the Purchase Finance Co., Ltd., controlled by the most prominent firms in the industry, was set up as an instrument for reducing surplus capacity. See A. F. Lucas, *Industrial Reconstruction and the Control of Competition*. 'Funds to finance the liquidation of weak mills have been secured as in the shipbuilding industry by a levy on output. Although the amount of the levy has never been publicly divulged it has been sufficient to permit the acquisition of a large part of the equipment in the industry deemed by the officials of the company to be redundant, obsolete, inefficient or simply undesirable from a competitive point of view. . . . It is rather significant that there is a strong conviction among certain of the smaller firms that the Purchase Finance Co. still possesses a sufficiently capacious war chest to acquire any company that entertains grandiose ideas of its competitive position.'

a still larger share of production. Indeed so large is their share in the trade and so low must their costs be when compared with the smaller units that it is difficult to see why they should be willing to continue to work inside the Association.

Some 22% of the whole trade, however, is in the hands of the cooperatives, who are not members of the Association. The CWS owns eight flour mills employing in all 1,749 workers. The Scottish CWS has five flour and meal mills which employ 385 workers. The gross output of the thirteen mills was £11,320,000 in 1938. In addition ten retail societies mill flour, four of them on a large scale, and these produced in 1935 gross output valued at £627,730. The largest of these plants are comparable with the smaller ones run by the wholesale societies. The CWS surplus in grain milling was calculated to be between two and three times as great as the total rate of profit of competing organisations in grain milling.[1]

The flour which the CWS mills is all sold to cooperative societies. Whereas the private trade had tended to give more and more attention to sales organisation and to increase the number of travellers who periodically visit bakers, the cooperatives are able to a considerable extent to dispense with such services.

There are thus in reality two milling industries in the country, the one four times as large as the other. Representatives of the cooperatives and of the Millers Mutual Association sit together in the Flour Millers Corporation; but the organisations from which they come operate on altogether different principles, and may one day come into bitter conflict with one another.

This double system is not confined to grain milling; it extends to the baking of the bread itself. Cooperative baking is carried on by the United Cooperative Baking Society (of Scotland) and by local federal societies in England and Scotland. The total sales of local federal societies in

---

[1] Figures from A. M. Carr-Sanders, P. Sargant Florence, and R. Peers: *Consumers' Co-operation in Great Britain: an examination of the British Co-operative Movement*, 1938, and from the *People's Year Book, 1940*.

Great Britain is £442,000, while the UCBS has an annual trade of £1,237,000 which includes biscuits, pastry and confectionery and the supply of bread to Belfast. It has been calculated that the baking done by retail societies accounts for about half the aggregate net value created by retail societies—that is to say, it represents a value of more than £5 million.[1]

The amount of labour absorbed by the flour milling industry is comparatively small. It is difficult to speak with certainty because statistics given usually cover provender milling as well as flour milling; but it is probable that some 20,000 workers are at present engaged in the industry. Of these some 75% are operatives and the remainder managers and clerks. As mechanisation has progressed and smaller plants have been eliminated staffs have been cut down, and labour costs were reckoned in 1935 to account for less than 10% of the value of gross output.

The fact that labour costs are comparatively unimportant enabled the Joint Industrial Council, which represents employers and employed, to make special arrangements for the men displaced. Some were pensioned, some were placed in other industries, some were set up in small businesses or compensated with a lump sum.

Of the 15,000 or so operatives engaged in the milling industry about three-quarters are skilled men. Their wages vary according to locality from 62/6 to 73/-. Labourers' wages vary similarly from 48/6 to 57/-. The hours of work are 47 for day workers and 44 for shift workers. At the moment a three shift system is in force, but a proposal for a four shift system, which would reduce the hours of shift workers to 33 a week, has been canvassed.

The Supply of Wheat

The millers draw most of their stocks of millable wheat from abroad. The main peace-time sources are Canada, Australia and the United States, as is shown by the following table:—

---

[1] Registrar of Friendly Societies quoted in *Consumers' Cooperation*, p. 412.

BREAD

IMPORTS OF WHEAT IN 1938

	000 cwt	£000	% by weight
British India	4,329	1,606	4·30
Australia	31,006	11,936	31·00
Canada	28,853	11,212	28·78
Other British countries		negligible	
TOTAL BRITISH	64,188	25,754	64·10
Soviet Union	9,538	3,055	9·50
France	1,236	267	1·20
Rumania	3,607	735	3·60
U.S.A.	15,790	6,740	15·80
Argentina	5,810	2,507	5·80
TOTAL FOREIGN	35,981	13,304	35·90
TOTAL	101,650	38,018	100·00

Note.—As the figures for individual exporting countries are here given to the nearest thousand cwt and not in cwts, as in the Trade and Navigation Accounts on which this table is based, they do not quite add up to the totals shown.

The percentage of supplies from the Empire in 1938 was more than 64—a very marked increase since the Ottawa Agreements came into force. Under the Ottawa Agreements Act an import duty of 2/- per quarter was placed on imports of wheat from foreign countries. Wheat flour is subject to the general 10% ad valorem tax. From a comparison of the import figures for 1929–31, 1932 and 1933 it becomes clear that the big decline in foreign imports of wheat came in 1932—before the Ottawa Agreements Act, which was passed in the November of that year, came into full effect. The United States, the Soviet Union, France and the Argentine sent 54% of the wheat imports of the United Kingdom in 1929–31; but in 1932 they sent only 26%, and in point of fact shipments from the Soviet Union, France and the Argentine—but not from the United States—increased in 1933.

The principal agreement with a country outside the Empire affecting the import of wheat is with the Argentine. It should be noted, however, that the supply varies very much from year to year according to the harvest. In 1936 the Argentine sent practically no exports of wheat to Britain;

in the following year she sent nearly 15% of the U.K.'s imported supplies ; and in 1938 the percentage was between 5 and 6. Under the terms of the Anglo-Argentine Trade Agreement of 1933, in this respect confirmed by that of three years later, no quantitative regulation was to be applied to exports of wheat from the Argentine to the United Kingdom. The duty of 2/- per quarter had of course to be paid, but no quota restrictions were to be imposed on Argentine wheat coming to this country.

The competition between various exporting countries to fill the place in the world market vacated by Russia during the last war led to a considerable increase in the world output of wheat in the decade after 1928. Technical advances were taking place—fertilisers and machinery were more commonly used. This expansion of output, together with the world depression and the good harvests, particularly that of 1929, led to a collapse of wheat prices, and after the World Economic Conference of 1933 to a scheme for the restriction of export and the reduction of acreage. Acreage was to be reduced by 15% in 1934—but none of the nations participating in the agreement (with the exception of Australia) actually effected this reduction.

As a result of government policy over the past seven years the share of home grown wheat in the total supply has somewhat increased. It has, however, been increased at the price of a levy upon every sack of flour whether milled in the country or imported. The administration of this scheme has not been in the hands of a producers' board but of a commission nominated by the Minister of Agriculture from representatives of various interests. A minority of the members—five, to be precise—represent the farmers ; the remaining twelve (excluding the chairman and vice-chairman) represent the millers, dealers, importers, bakers, and other producers of flour.

The acreage under wheat, the total production and the market price, all fell considerably in the later 1920's ; and in an endeavour to reverse this tendency and to meet the discontent of the farmers the government introduced its Wheat Act in 1932. The vital provision of the scheme was the fixing of a standard price of 10/- a cwt (45/- a quarter) which was practically guaranteed to the producer. The gap between the average market price for millable wheat and this standard price was to be bridged by a subsidy, the funds for which were provided by a levy which has varied between 6d and 6/6, on every sack of flour home milled or imported. In the original scheme a limit of 27 million cwt of wheat was fixed with the object of preventing the uneconomic growing of wheat on unsuitable soil. If it was estimated that in any one year the millable wheat available for sale would be above 27 million cwt, the subsidy on each cwt was reduced in proportion.[1] In addition there were certain small administrative expenses to be met out of the fund, so the farmer could not rely on getting the whole of the ten shillings; but he came very near it, and as the market price of wheat had been no more than six shillings in 1931 and 1932 he had a real inducement to increase his acreage and production. And, as the Committee appointed to reconsider the standard price in 1935 observed, it would have been very strange if some such result had not been produced, since the total payments under the Wheat Act over three seasons amounted to £18 million or an average of 72/8 per wheat acre.[2]

PRODUCTION ACREAGE AND PRICE OF WHEAT 1931-2 TO 1938-9

Year	Produce (tons)	Acreage	Gazette price (per cwt)	Average quota payment (per sack of flour)
1931-2	1,010,000	1,246,721	6/1	-/3
1932-3	1,165,000	1,339,980	5/6	2/7
1933-4	1,660,000	1,738,746	4/9	4/3
1934-5	1,359,000	1,857,037	5/-	4/3
1935-6	1,743,000	1,873,028	5/11	3/6
1936-7	1,473,000	1,798,211	9/-	-/11 [3]
1937-8	1,510,000	1,832,100	8/7	1/-
1938-9	1,965,000	1,923,000	4/8	5/6

[1] This limit has since been raised to 36 million cwt—a figure not likely to be attained except in years of unusually good harvest. It means for practical purposes no limit at all.
[2] *The Report of the Committee on the Standard Price*, 1935.
[3] For five months during 1937 the quota payment was suspended altogether.

These figures, however, are rather unreal, since they are no more than calculations of the amount of wheat grown in a particular season. A more significant figure is the amount of wheat which is sold off the farm—for it is necessary to deduct from the figures of gross production the amount of wheat wasted, the amount fed to animals on the farm and the amount retained for seed. One effect of the Wheat Act was that farmers sold all the wheat they could to earn the largest possible subsidy, and then bought seed with which previously they would have provided themselves from their own crop. The report of the Wheat Commission drew attention to this, saying, 'wheat growers have generally sold and duly received certificates for the whole of their millable wheat, buying other wheat from merchants for seed.' A good deal, however, was still retained on the farms. Whereas in 1938-9 the total production of wheat was estimated at 1,965,000 tons, the certified sale of registered producers amounted to no more than 1,835,000 tons. Of that a certain amount was used for seed, and it is probable that the total production of flour from home grown wheat was not more than 1,150,000 tons—just over 25% of the total amount of flour used in that year.

An increase in the production of British wheat, however, does not necessarily make possible a ton for ton reduction in imports. Much British wheat is of a different type from the bulk of imports; it is what is termed ' soft '—that is, not able to absorb and hold such large quantities of water as the ' hard ' strains most favoured by the bakers of bread. The soft wheat is used either for mixing with the harder strains to give a satisfactory and palatable result, or for the manufacture of biscuits. It was calculated by the Ministry of Agriculture in 1928 that of the supplies of home grown wheat actually marketed some 30% was used for breadmaking flours, generally as a seasoning; while of the remainder one half was used in the manufacture of blending and scouring flours and the other half was used mainly for biscuits.

The intention and effect of the Wheat Act has been to give a subsidy to agriculture; but it has been a subsidy raised by adding surreptitiously a few shillings to the price of every sack of flour. Thus it has been in effect a tax upon the consumption of bread. On the other hand it weakened the position of the farmer selling his wheat to the dealer; although the farmer had some incentive to stand out for a good price (inasmuch as the basis of the subsidy was the difference between the average price and the standard price and a farmer selling above the average would benefit) the incentive was not a very great one. When a farmer is sure of getting four or five shillings subsidy for a cwt of wheat he is not going to bargain so long for an extra sixpence from the dealer.

Conclusions

There is not much reason for expecting a spectacular rise in the consumption of bread if the price is reduced; nor is there any particular reason for desiring it. The importance of bread from the point of view of nutrition and food policy is that it absorbs so large a part of the food budget of working class families. If the price of bread can be reduced, carefully husbanded money will be set free for buying other foodstuffs. There is in fact a strong case for making every effort to secure a reduction in the price of bread directly a Labour Government comes to power.

The trade is already very largely dominated by the millers; and it seems that that stage would be the best at which to apply government control. The milling industry is already highly organised in fairly large units; and there is available sufficient technical knowledge and experience among the personnel of the CWS for the industry to be carried on if the present directors of the private sector are unwilling to serve a socialised enterprise.

It is reckoned that the present profit being taken out of the industry prior to the war was at least 2/- per sack of 280 lb. If 6d were allowed for a compensation fund for shareholders that would still leave a reduction of 1/6 which could be effected in the price of every sack. Socialisation moreover would make it possible to close down some redundant factories and make other technical economies which have been estimated as likely to produce a further reduction of

1/6 per sack. Lastly, the competition in selling and advertising, which could be completely eliminated under socialisation, costs, it is calculated, 9d per sack. Against this must be set the claims of the workers for better conditions; but since the industry is so highly mechanised it should be possible to improve conditions and still reduce the price of flour by 3/6 per 280 lb.

Whatever steps the government might find it necessary to take to aid wheat farming by subsidy or any other device, there is an overwhelming case on nutritional grounds (and on grounds of equity) for avoiding a tax on bread, since such a tax falls so heavily upon the poorest. The socialised milling industry should buy its wheat as cheaply as possible, and should not be the collecting agency for any form of assistance for farmers. A levy upon flour used for industrial purposes might be imposed, but certainly there should be no imposition on the 50% of the flour which goes to be made into bread.

The socialised milling industry should not attempt to impose resale conditions upon bakers and should certainly refuse to be a party to preventing any baker from selling cheaper than his competitors. This, given the strong position which the Cooperative Movement already has in the retail baking trade, should produce a cutting of distributive costs and a lower price for bread. The Cooperative Societies might well take the lead in retailing bread cheaper over the counter than they deliver it on the doorsteps. There is little doubt that this would soon bring prices down in working class districts.

The attitude which should be taken to the wheat subsidy—apart altogether from the question of the way in which the money to provide it should be raised—depends upon general considerations of agricultural policy. Certainly it seems difficult to defend the subsidy on agricultural grounds or to understand what possessed the Government to advance it or the farmers to accept it as a substantial contribution to agricultural recovery. The Wheat Standard Price Committee in 1935 stated :—

Wheat on its own account and apart from its important place

in the farm economy as a whole,[1] is not of outstanding importance in the sum of the nation's agriculture. It represented 5·17% of the value of farm products sold off farms in the 1925 census and 1·77% only in the 1930–31 census. But these figures take no account of the considerable value of wheat retained on the farm. The next census will show a higher percentage due to the recent improvements in price, acreage and yield, and the higher proportion sold off farms since the Wheat Act in order to secure the benefit of the deficiency payments. But even making allowance for these factors wheat by itself cannot be compared in importance with any of the main livestock products and is not a leading farm crop compared with beet or potatoes. In conjunction with associated farm crops it assumes its true importance, and in the Eastern Counties in particular is of very real significance.

Wheat has a part to play in agriculture—and an important part. But in peacetime it is not such a part that the interests of agriculture are best served by subsidising the sale of wheat off the farms at such a heavy cost. Lord Addison has insisted [2] that the stabilisation of the price of wheat is absolutely essential as an ingredient in a plan of increased arable cultivation, but he suggests 37/6 per quarter instead of the pre-war 45/- as a figure which would cover the costs of efficient production. The essential point, however, is that whatever decision should be reached on agricultural grounds about wheat production no measures should be adopted which maintain the price of bread at its present level.

[1] Corn crops are important to farmers not only because of the return from marketing grain, but also because of the straw which is used for a number of purposes on the farm. Straw is expensive to transport; which is an inducement to a farmer to produce what he can on his own land.
[2] *A Policy for British Agriculture*, 1939, p. 227.

3 MILK AND MILK PRODUCTS

British milk is without exception the most expensive in the world. The retail prices determined for the season 1938-9 were as follows :—

RETAIL PRICES PER GALLON [1]

	London *	Towns of population over 25,000	Population 10,000–25,000	Rural and under 10,000 population
	s d	s d	s d	s d
October	2 4	2 4	2 4	2 0
November	2 4	2 4	2 4	2 4
December	2 4	2 4	2 4	2 4
January	2 4	2 4	2 4	2 4
February	2 4	2 4	2 4	2 0
March	2 4	2 4	2 4	2 0
April	2 4	2 4	2 0	2 0
May	2 4	2 0	2 0	2 0
June	2 4	2 0	2 0	2 0
July	2 4	2 4	2 0	2 0
August	2 4	2 4	2 0	2 0
September	2 4	2 4	2 4	2 0

* 'London' for this purpose includes urban districts of over 25,000 inhabitants in the counties of Hertfordshire, Essex, Surrey, Sussex, Kent, and Middlesex.

Thus consumers in London paid a regular 7d a quart throughout the year; those in the medium sized and large towns paid that for ten months a year while in May and June 1939 they paid a penny less; and it was only in the rural areas and small towns that 6d a quart was the usual price and 7d exceptional. The average price per gallon for the whole country over the year was thus about 2/2, compared with an average price of 14-15d per gallon in 1914, and of 18d in France and 13d in Sweden at the present time.

Medical opinion is unanimous about the valuable nutritional qualities of milk. The Advisory Committee on Nutrition stated that it was the only food which came near to containing all the materials essential for growth and

[1] Taken from the *Home Farmer*, September 1938.

maintenance of life in a form in which they could be easily assimilated; and recommended that pregnant and nursing mothers should take two pints a day, children up to 16 one pint a day and the remainder of the population half a pint a day. But because prices are high consumption is low. 1936 figures [1] showed Britain, France and Germany, all with approximately the same per caput consumption (3½ pints per week), far behind New Zealand, Denmark, the United States and Switzerland. Even the well-to-do in Britain scarcely reach the optimum standard of milk consumption, and Crawford's survey showed the following weekly consumption and expenditure in the case of working class and lower middle class families.

Family Income	Amount spent per head on milk (pence)	Quantity purchased per head (pints)
£125–£249	9·1	2·62
Under £125	5·7	1·57

These figures, however, do not show the whole truth. Consumption surveys in Cardiff and County Durham [2] have indicated that an appreciable percentage of working class families in those areas can afford no fresh milk at all and have to rely on tinned. In 'poor working class families' in Cardiff as many as one in four took no fresh milk, and the average consumption per head was 1·1 pints per week. According to the Merseyside Survey [3] one family in six in a group with incomes between 27/- and £2 a week did not buy any fresh milk at all; and average expenditure upon it rose from 5d per head per week in the case of families with incomes below between 27/- and £2 to 1/- in a group where family incomes ranged from 50/- to £5. The figures collected for this survey bear out the conclusion that within the working class the families which are better off are more

[1] Quoted in League of Nations Report, *The Problem of Nutrition*, volume iv.
[2] See C. M. Burns, 'A Study of Milk Consumption in Co. Durham' (*Journal of State Medicine*, 1933), and W. H. Jones and W. J. Cowie, 'The Consumption of Milk in Cardiff' (*Welsh Journal of Agriculture*, 1934).
[3] *Survey of Merseyside*, vol, i, p. 220.

likely to drink fresh milk and less likely to take condensed milk as a substitute.

The weekly consumption of butter declines just as sharply with falling income as does the consumption of fresh milk; while the consumption of cheese also falls.

Income	Weekly per caput butter consumption in ounces	Weekly per caput cheese consumption in ounces
Over £1,000	11·6	3·3
£500–£999	11·3	3·3
£250–£499	10·3	3·0
£125–£249	7·2	2·7
Under £125	4·5	2·1

Just as tinned milk is used as a substitute for fresh, margarine is used as a substitute for butter. Less evidence has been collected about consumption of butter and cheese than about milk; but Sir John Orr's figures and, as far as lower income groups are concerned, the Merseyside Survey, bear out the general conclusion of Crawford's figures—that consumption of dairy products rises as family incomes make their purchase possible.

Home Production

There is produced within the boundaries of the United Kingdom all the milk which its inhabitants consume in liquid form, and some of that which is used for butter and cheese, chocolate etc. The best starting point for an examination of the supply of dairy products is therefore the farm. Production is carried on by about 175,000 farmers, who maintain between them some 2½ million cows and heifers in milk. These produce every year something in the neighbourhood of 1,500 million gallons of milk, some of which is fed to calves or used on the farm in other ways; but the bulk of it—say 1,300 million gallons—is sold off the farm, usually through one of the Milk Marketing Schemes.

The lives of the cows responsible for this milk supply are short. They average four to five milking years as compared with nine or ten in the case of continental herds. Disease is prevalent and accounts for the short average life. As in the case of poultry, intensive production has weakened stamina; and moving of herds from one part of the country to another has helped disease to spread from herd to herd. The two main diseases which affect cows are tuberculosis and contagious abortion. From 1922 onwards the government made efforts to raise the general quality of milk by grading it, and the same objective has been pursued by the Marketing Board. Until 1937 sales of 'Certified' and 'Grade A' milk remained exempt from the operations of the Board. To stimulate the production of quality milk the Board decided to pay from its own funds a bonus of 1d a gallon to producers of milk whose buildings conformed to certain standards maintained by inspection, whose herds were certified after a veterinary examination and whose milk complied with certain bacteriological standards. These producers were described as 'Accredited' and by the 1937-38 season more than a third of the milk sold under the English scheme came from their herds.

Since their sales were conducted through the Marketing Scheme producers of Tuberculin Tested and Certified Milk have received a bonus of 2d a gallon also from the funds of the Board. In 1935 a third scheme was introduced for the improvement of the quality of milk—a bonus of 1d a gallon was to be paid for milk from all Attested herds. This was an endeavour to encourage tubercle free herds and the money for it was provided not by the Milk Marketing Board but by the Exchequer.

At present there are very wide variations in yield between different herds. The average yield per cow in the country is about 450 gallons per year, whereas the average yield in milk-recorded herds is 704 gallons per year.[1] Within limits the productivity of a cow depends upon the amount of cake which is fed to her. After a certain point, however, it is no longer economical to feed extra cake because the additional milk yielded after each additional unit of cake declines, and because intensive production harms the health of the animal. It seems to be true, however, that up to 1,000 gallons a year no serious harm is done.

[1] Professor Kay in *Scottish Journal of Agriculture*, January 1937.

It is not easy to give any reliable or significant figures upon the cost of milk production because of the very varying conditions under which milk is produced. It is, however, possible, as a result of the Milk Investigation Scheme which was begun in 1934 and on which three interim reports have so far been issued, to discuss the factors affecting the cost of production in peace time. The most recently published figures [1] refer to the period between October 1936 and September 1937; and are divided into three groups—those referring to milk sold wholesale, those referring to retail sales and those referring to tuberculin tested milk however sold. If the wholesale group, which includes in all 437 farms, is taken, it is possible to draw some conclusions about the relation between yield, size of herd and cost per gallon and to give some indication of the ways in which costs are made up.

The yield of milk per cow per day shows quite appreciable variations as between different parts of the country in winter; the variations are much less marked in summer. The average for all regions was 1·6 gallons in winter and 1·87 in summer. The average cost of production per gallon for all regions was a trifle over 9½d. That average was made up as follows:—

	Pence per gallon
Food	6·04
Labour	2·26
Miscellaneous expenses	1·29
Herd replacement	0·83
Gross farm cost	10·42
Less (credits)—	
Calves	·56
Manure	·31
Total credit	·87
Net farm cost	9·55

[1] Milk Investigation Scheme, *Cost of Milk Production of England and Wales*, Interim Report No. 3. Issued by the Agricultural Economics Research Institute, Oxford.

MILK AND MILK PRODUCTS

There was some general variation between summer and winter, especially in respect of food and labour.

AVERAGE COSTS IN PENCE PER GALLON

	Winter	Summer
Food	7·82	4·46
Purchased	4·20	2·39
Home grown	3·29	0·69
Grazing	0·33	1·38
Labour	2·52	2·02

There were also variations by region, of which the most notable is the low cost of herd replacement in Mid Western and West Midland regions, where the costs per gallon in respect of this were as low as ·22d and ·17d respectively.

But these averages do not mean a great deal; there were some farms where milk was produced at a net cost of less than 5d per gallon and one where the cost was more than 1/7. Costs varied with the yield per cow and with the size of the herd. Generally speaking costs per gallon fell with an increasing yield—from 12·25d per gallon in the case of cows yielding up to 1·25 gallons per day to 8·40d in the case of cows yielding over 2·5 gallons. But a point is reached at which the money value of the additional feeding stuffs plus the increased cost of herd replacement as a result of intensive production falls below the value of the additional milk produced; so that the farmer, whose interest is in maximum income and not, except in very special cases, in maximum yield will not always feed for the largest possible output in gallons.

The size of the herd does not, so far as can be seen, exercise a very great influence upon costs. The variation, if the herds surveyed are grouped according to size, was between an average cost per gallon of 9·27d and an average of 9·91d.

The Milk Marketing Scheme

The supply of fresh milk from the farm is controlled by the oldest and most firmly established of the schemes set up under government auspices to regulate the marketing of agricultural products. It came into existence in 1932 to save the dairy farmers from low prices; and since then it has been the subject of endless controversy and repeated official inquiry.[1] At the root of the trouble was the fact that less milk is produced in winter than in summer. The yield per cow is smaller; and the high price of feeding stuffs for the animals causes farmers to keep fewer cows during the winter. On the other hand consumption of milk is much the same in winter and summer, even when summer prices are rather lower; so that if there is to be enough milk during the winter there is likely to be more than enough during the summer. This surplus cannot be sold liquid unless milk prices are brought down; there is only one other use to which it can be put—it must be manufactured into butter, cream or cheese.[2] In that case it must meet the competition of milk products imported from abroad at very low prices; so milk for the manufacturing market fetches, and always has fetched, much less than milk for the liquid market. This was the case long before the Milk Marketing Scheme was conceived, and its effect was that in the years after the war farmers anxious to sell in the more profitable market competed eagerly with one another and cut prices drastically.

From 1922 onwards wholesale prices of liquid milk were supposed to be fixed by annual negotiation between the National Farmers' Union and the National Federation of Dairymen's Associations (who represented the distributors). Each farmer was paid at the liquid milk price for a basic

[1] The principal government inquiries dealing with milk have been: (1) The Reorganisation Commission for Milk, presided over by Sir Edward Grigg, 1933. This examined the general position before the scheme existed. (2) The Reorganisation Commission for Great Britain, presided over by A. E. Cutforth, 1936. This reviewed the working of the scheme and its effects and proposed certain changes. (3) The Committee of Investigation for England issued a *Report on Complaints made by the Milk Distributive Committee and the Parliamentary Committee of the Cooperative Congress as to the Operation of the Milk Marketing Scheme*, 1936. The complaint made was that the liquid wholesale price was too high. (4) The Food Council *Report on Costs and Profits in Retail Milk Distribution in Great Britain*, 1937.

[2] Some of the milk is actually used for industrial processes such as making artificial tortoiseshell; but the proportion used in this way is small.

MILK AND MILK PRODUCTS

quantity which was calculated on his production during the winter months and could dispose of any surplus at the lower 'manufacturing' price. In 1929 there was some change in this system and a 'declared quantity' instead of the basic quantity was adopted as the foundation of the scheme. Thus the farmer was able to give notice of the amount he would supply and was not bound by his production at any particular time of year.

During the post war period up to 1932 the gap between liquid and manufacturing prices was widening. Improved transport was making it possible to draw milk from all over the country to such large consuming centres as London; and consequently producers were the better able to use their supplies in the more remunerative liquid market. The increased import of cheap butter and cheese made the situation worse, and rendered some form of milk marketing organisation a necessity if the alternative of a heavy slump in producers' prices was to be avoided.

After the Grigg Commission had reported in 1933 elaborate machinery was established for the marketing of milk. Marketing schemes with the force of statutory authority and administered by boards elected by producers themselves were established for England, Wales and Scotland. The declared aim of the scheme was to strengthen the position of producers by combined as opposed to individual selling. In negotiating with buyers the representatives of the Board control substantially all the supplies of milk; the only transactions outside the Board are those of the producer retailers, who are allowed to sell direct but must pay a levy to the Board; and those of any producer who sells direct to his employees.[1]

The Board negotiates annually with the Central Milk Distributive Committee (a voluntary body representative of milk manufacturers and distributors) and fixes the wholesale price which the manufacturer or distributor shall pay. The farmer makes his individual contract on the terms which have been prescribed in these negotiations. From

---

[1] Before October 1937 the owner of less than four milch cows was exempt, but this is no longer the case.

the point of view of the producer the main feature of the scheme is the equalisation of returns by an elaborate pooling system. The country is divided into fourteen regions (11 in England and Wales and 3—each operated under a separate marketing board—in Scotland). Each region has a pool into which is paid (1) proceeds of sales of milk to retail distributors, (2) proceeds of milk sold for manufacture, (3) contributions from producer retailers, and (4) transport deductions from registered producers in respect of sales of manufactured milk.

All producers in a region receive monthly the same rate per gallon from the regional pool, irrespective of the use to which milk from their particular farm has been put and the price which has been paid for it by the distributor or the manufacturer. Naturally, however, the pool price varies from one region to another according to the proportions of supplies from that region sold for the less remunerative manufacturing milk purposes. To some extent these variations are offset by the interregional levy imposed on every gallon of milk sold in the liquid market and used to provide a fund by which the pool price can be raised in those regions where much of the milk is sold for manufacture.[1]

The effect of milk marketing organisation can be seen by examining the England and Wales scheme more carefully. Sales of milk off farms increased by nearly 25% between 1933-8.[2] This figure was not reached by a steady expansion; the quantity sold in any one year was affected by weather and other conditions. The increase in milk sold for liquid consumption was 17% in 1937-8, but had been very much smaller in previous years. In fact the bulk of the increased quantity of milk being sold off farms as a result of the marketing scheme was used not for liquid consumption but for manufacture. The figures for successive six month periods were as follows :—

[1] There is some feeling in favour of a *national* price for milk—to give the producer the same return no matter where his farm may be situated. The best defence of the regional system is that some encouragement should be given to the production of milk in those parts of the country which are most suitable and nearest to markets.

[2] 855 million gallons were sold off the farms in 1933-4 as compared with 1,063 million in 1937-8.

	Liquid wholesale price	Manufacturing price	Weighted pool price	Percentage manufactured
October 1933 – March 1934	15·5	5·27	13·5 }	24·9
April–September 1934	12·0	5·56	10·4 }	
October 1934 – March 1935	16·5	6·29	13·8 }	32·2
April–September 1935	13·7	5·26	10·6 }	
October 1935 – March 1936	17·0	6·03	13·6 }	35·2
April–September 1936	13·5	5·11	10·3 }	
October 1936 – March 1937	17·0	5·99	14·1 }	31·2
April–September 1937	13·5	5·69	10·9 }	
October 1937 – March 1938	17·7	7·50	15·0 }	29·2
April–September 1938	14·8	6·68	11·4 }	
October 1938 – March 1939	17·3	7·14	14·8 }	34·6
April–September 1939	15·1	6·41	11·6 }	

The greatest outcry against the Board on the part of consumers was in 1935–6. The pool price seemed to be in danger of falling, because so much milk was going into the manufacturing market. To prevent this fall the Board raised liquid wholesale prices (and retail prices too), but the consequence was that liquid consumption fell and the proportion of milk sold for manufacture went up. Thus the danger of a sagging pool price was made more acute than ever; the Board had got involved in a vicious circle, and as a result liquid prices were high in 1935–6 and during 1936 just 40% of the milk available was used for manufacture. The difficulty was to some extent solved and the amount of milk disposed of for manufacture reduced, not by any action of the Milk Marketing Board but by a rise in the price of feeding stuffs and an improvement in beef prices, which combined to reduce milk production. Retail prices, however, were maintained and consumption and prices since the scheme was initiated have been as shown in table on p. 42.

Thus the Milk Marketing Scheme, although administered by a Board representative only of producers, has, by the control over retail prices given to this Board and the existence of the two markets, strengthened the position of distributors and manufacturers rather than that of producers or consumers.

Year	Liquid Consumption[1] (in million gallons)	Average Retail Price[2]	Average Regional Wholesale Price of Liquid Milk[2]	Average Distributive Margin[2]
1933–4	642·8	24·83	14·01	10·82
1934–5	665·2	26·08	15·09	10·99
1935–6	663·8	26·21	15·26	10·95
1936–7	681·1	26·21	15·26	10·95
1937–8	752·4	27·48	16·26	11·22
1938–9	764·0	27·48	16·25	11·23

The Milk Scheme continued almost unaffected by the war. It maintained its independence of the Ministry of Food, although the Board's General Manager became Director-designate of milk supplies to the Ministry in an advisory capacity. Arrangements for milk distribution were upset by the partial evacuation of London: and in the first few weeks of war more than 9,000 gallons a day were being brought to London and handed over to the manufacturers of milk products because the demand for liquid milk had fallen.

The decision that it is not in the public interest to publish figures of milk production or milk utilisation makes it very difficult to see how the milk trade has developed. It is probable that the amount of milk going to manufacture is a higher proportion of the total even than in peacetime. First, there are the supplies of condensed milk to be provided for the troops; and then there has been since the war began the increased production of margarine of which milk is one of the constituents. There was until the beginning of November no increase in the sums paid for milk by the manufacturers, and the pool price which the farmers received showed a decline. Subsequently the manufacturing price which the farmers received was raised, but the Milk Marketing Board announced that at the end of the year the retail price would almost certainly have to go up.

This rise in the retail price has been avoided by a subsidy

[1] Includes cheap milk schemes.
[2] Figures in pence per gallon.

which according to Sir John Simon averaged early in 1940 £235,000 per week. The farmers, because of their increased costs, had pressed for a higher pool price, but now that this has been secured by the subsidy the distributors are asking for an increase in their margin. They plead for justification that evacuation has lowered the demand and that consequently their costs per gallon have risen. On the other hand, they have made some economies—for example, an order of the Ministry of Food at the beginning of the war cut down deliveries to one a day—and there seems little reason to believe that an increase in the pre-war distributive margin would be justified.

Retail Distribution

'We see in the proper organisation of the distributive trade,' said the Committee of Investigation in 1936, 'real hope of reducing prices to the consumer.' Costs of retail distribution of milk have gone up a good deal since the war and retail margins have been fixed at a high level under the marketing scheme.

There are four main ways by which milk may pass to the consumer. The first and most direct method of distribution is for the producer himself to sell milk in his shop or take it from house to house. About two-thirds of the distributors in the country trade in this way; but they handle between them only some 17% of the milk supply. In some districts, however, they dominate milk distribution—for example in the distressed areas and in some urban centres. Despite their comparatively small share of the trade these producer retailers had to be brought into the marketing scheme, because otherwise they could have wrecked it by undercutting. The second method of distribution—comparatively unimportant—is by the marketing boards themselves. It is found only in a few places in Scotland, where the North of Scotland Board has taken over the round formerly worked by producer retailers and has reduced the retail price per pint from 3d to 2½d. The third method is through the cooperatives, who have benefited by the fixed retail price for milk. The dividend paid on purchase applies to milk bought from a cooperative store just as much as to anything else; and they have been able to increase their share of the trade from 2½% in 1918 to some 25% by 1939. Their costs of distribution were estimated to range between 5·79d per gallon and 9·5d per gallon, while the range in the case of private firms is between 9·19d and 12·23d. The fourth method of distribution is through the private concerns, which vary in size from a small shop with a roundsman to United Dairies, which has a capital of £6 million and 23 subsidiary firms in canning, transport, wholesaling and condensing. More than half the total milk supply is handled by these private concerns, and, unlike the cooperative societies, it is the general practice for their roundsmen to sell groceries and other goods as well as milk.

The tendency after the introduction of the Marketing Scheme was for the larger private distributors to benefit at the expense of the smaller. For one thing, the Board has insisted upon prompt payment for supplies—this was said by the Cutforth Commission to have reduced the number of buyers from 20,000 in the first year to 16,500 in the third year. 'The buyers who have been eliminated,' commented the Commission—

> are mostly small purchasers with only one or two contracts. It does not of course follow that those who no longer buy through the Board have given up their businesses. It is probable that most of them are still in business, but now obtain their milk through wholesalers.[1]

A more direct source of profit to the large distributors was the system of transport deductions. Under the original scheme the producer was to bear the cost of transporting his share of the liquid milk from the local depot to the consuming centre. The distributor was accordingly allowed to deduct from the sum which he paid to the farmer the cost of sending the milk this distance by rail; but in fact the large distributors made a profit from the transaction, because they bulked the milk and so secured rebates from the railways. In fact the tendency was to draw liquid milk from the most distant districts and so make a large profit

---

[1] *Report of the Reorganisation Commission* (1936), p. 93.

upon it; a practice which meant a profit for the large distributor who made the arrangement and a better pool price for the district concerned, but which increased the burden of transport costs upon milk producers as a whole. The Cutforth Commission drew attention to this [1] and the 1937-8 contract made a change in the system; transport levies were imposed at a fixed rate on all producers in a region. The large buyers, however, remained at an advantage.

Again the big buyers have been able to increase their profits by the fact that they no longer suffer a loss on milk which they buy to retail for liquid consumption but which they find has to be disposed of at a loss in the manufacturing market. This is explained by the Cutforth Commission :—

> Before the scheme came into being, distributors were usually able to obtain a proportion of their requirements at manufacturing prices, but they had to bear any loss in disposing of milk bought at liquid prices which could not be sold in the liquid market Under the two main schemes, however, a large distributor only pays the liquid price for milk actually sold as such; for milk not so sold he obtains the rebate appropriate to the use made of the milk. This concession has not been extended to small buyers, largely, we understand, because of the difficulty and expense of checking their accounts. Those small buyers who were previously able to obtain a proportion of their milk at manufacturing prices must now pay liquid milk prices for all their requirements.[1]

Above all the large distributors have benefited from the fixing of retail prices. This meant in some years a limitation of consumption and the need for a small retailer to have a large margin if he was to keep in business. The margin which kept him in business yielded the large and more efficient distributor a handsome profit. The fixing of margins has meant that competition between firms has not been by price cutting but by expansion of special services, and here again the large firm is at an advantage.

The general tendency of the milk marketing scheme has been to increase the profits of the large distributing firms, whether wholesale or retail, and particularly to strengthen the position of a concern like United Dairies, which is in

[1] See Chapter 19 of the *Report* (1936).

both wholesaling and retailing. At the same time the expense of getting the milk from the farm to the doorstep has grown. The matter has been expressed as follows by the Committee of Investigation, whose views on this were endorsed by the Food Council when it inquired into the price of milk in 1937:—

> During the course of our inquiry we have been deeply impressed with the unnecessary elaboration and waste of effort in the present distributive organisation. We have had evidence for example of the overlapping of distributors, over twenty operating in one street, and this apparently is not an isolated or unusual occurrence. Moreover the evidence shows that a large amount of money is spent by some firms on canvassing, some of which from the standpoint of distribution as a whole must be regarded as wasteful expenditure. We are convinced that some rationalisation of distribution would make possible substantial savings in distribution costs. Again now that pasteurised milk is so widely distributed at least in London and the larger cities we cannot believe that two deliveries a day are essential . . . the average length of time taken by United Dairies roundsmen on the first round is $2\frac{1}{4}$ hours; on the second when goods are distributed it is approximately six hours. The elimination of the second round would also tend to reduce the need for the relatively expensive half-pint bottles of milk. . . .

The second delivery was a result of competition and was not an essential service, especially since the use of pasteurising plant became general. In one case the demand for a second daily delivery by 6% of the households served by one firm led to an increase of one-fifth of a penny per gallon in average delivery costs to all the households served.[1] In peace time the method of reduction in the number of half-pint bottles offered an economy—as was shown by the statistics of United Dairies quoted in the report of the Food Council. The costs of bottling (including bottles and cases) and transport to distributing depots was about $1\frac{1}{4}$d per gallon more for half-pint than for pint bottles. Competition between distributors not only involves wasteful advertising but leads to the multiplication of retailers serving a particular area. It is significant that the cooperative societies make a high rate of profit on turnover when compared with private

[1] John Cripps, *The Distribution of Milk*, Agricultural Economics Research Institute.

firms.[1] The lower costs of the Cooperative Society may be accounted for by the absence of shops 'for the dairy department'. Further, the cooperative societies' costs for distributing depots and rounds were smaller than United Dairies, although the latter bottled and pasteurised their milk and got it to the distributing centres more cheaply than the cooperatives.

The costs of house to house distribution vary according to the character of the area served and the number of milkmen competing for custom within it. Housing estates where the planning is more spacious and the milkman has to walk through the garden and down the side of the house to the back door are more expensive to supply than working class districts where the houses are crowded together. Again, when the milkman calls at every house in a street his costs are less than if he calls, say, at every fifth house. Where the milkman calls at 60 houses in every hundred he passes his costs may be as low as 3·35d or 1·97d per gallon instead of 3·51d or 2·11d, as would have been the case if he had called at no more than 45%. When these items are added together—waste on second delivery, waste on half-pint bottles, waste because twenty milkmen drive their carts in succession down one street—it is clear that the housewife is paying a very high price for the right to choose and change her milkman. The conclusion reached by John Cripps is that if there were one retailer in each district and one delivery a day, retail prices might go down by 4d a gallon; and when the figures given above of costs of delivery in congested areas where the milkman calls at a large percentage of the houses he passes are considered, it seems certain that so far as London is concerned a larger reduction could be effected by means of reorganisation.[2]

[1] The report of the Food Council showed the costs of the London Coop to be 9·43d per gallon as against 9·81d in the case of United Dairies operating in the same area *even after the liquid milk expenses had been credited with the whole of the profit on goods sold on the milk rounds*. Without such crediting the U.D. costs would have been just over 11·25d per gallon.

[2] It is particularly strange that the distributive margin on milk in London should regularly be 4d a gallon higher than in the rural areas—and that in fact the margin should vary inversely with the density of population in an area. It seems difficult to explain this except on the ground that the London milk trade is well organised enough to ensure that the distributive margin is sufficiently large for costs to be covered.

The experience of other countries and the handsome profits of large-scale British distributing firms confirm this view. Translate the distributive margins of some of the countries with cheap milk into hours of unskilled labour and compare with Great Britain:—

	Distributive margin per gallon in pence	Cost of hour of unskilled labour in pence	Margins in terms of hours of unskilled labour
Sweden	6·0	20·4	·29
Switzerland	9·4	29·5	·32
Great Britain	11·4	13·8	·82

Thus if the distribution of British milk were raised to the same level of efficiency as the Swedish or the Swiss the margin would be between 4½d and 5d instead of more than 11d. (It is worth noting that the Swedish milk is bottled and pasteurised and is cleaner than that which most English consumers get. The secret of the low costs is that the bulk of milk distribution is done by cooperatives.)[1] In the light of such figures John Cripps's conclusion that the retail margin could be reduced by 4d a gallon by re-organisation of distribution seems if anything too cautious.

Butter and Cheese

Nine-tenths of the butter and three-quarters of the cheese consumed in the United Kingdom before the war were imported. Supplies in 1938 were made up as follows:—

	Farm produced	Manufactured	Imported
Butter	530[2]	340	9,518
Cheese	266	601	2,927

Figures in thousands of cwt.

[1] These two paragraphs are based upon some unpublished material by Colin Clark.

[2] No reliable figure for farm produced butter is available. This is the figure given for the season 1936–7 in the *Agricultural Register, 1936–37*, published by the Agricultural Economics Research Institute, Oxford.

MILK AND MILK PRODUCTS

In 1937 New Zealand provided nearly a third of the total imports of butter and Australia provided 15%. These Empire countries were given an advantage by the duty of 15/- per cwt imposed on supplies from foreign sources; but despite this Denmark in 1937 accounted for nearly a quarter of the total butter imports. The special situation of Denmark and the other Scandinavian countries as sources of butter supply has been recognised in agreements which the United Kingdom has made with them wherein it is agreed that they shall be consulted if there is to be any limitation of imports of butter into this country.

The bulk of imported cheese comes from Empire sources. In 1938 New Zealand and Canada provided nearly 60% and 25% respectively.

The United Kingdom is the principal market for the dairy produce of the Dominions. In both New Zealand and Australia there are special export arrangements; and in the former country all dairy produce exported is handled by a state department—the Primary Products Marketing Organisation. The farmers get a guaranteed price and the price in the British market has been raised until in 1937 for the first time New Zealand butter commanded a premium over Danish. More regular deliveries through this organised marketing have given to New Zealand butter a goodwill among buyers which was previously enjoyed only by Danish. New Zealand butter was previously marketed in the United Kingdom under a variety of competing names; but the number of agents handling it has now been reduced to twenty and their margin limited to 2%.

The key points in the process of distribution of butter and cheese were the provision exchanges of London, Manchester and Glasgow. There the bulk of the imported supplies are disposed of; and some of the home supply was handled as well. Some big buyers, however, did not deal through the provision exchanges but fetched their supplies directly from the ships. The dealers on the provision exchanges were the importers—or the agents in the case of New Zealand produce—on the one hand, the large wholesalers on the other. The latter broke up the quantities which they purchased and distributed butter and cheese to the retailer, possibly through a second wholesaler. The deals took place on the exchange at prices which were fixed weekly.

Butter and cheese are handled by small independent grocers or by the large grocery chains. In either case the margin will tend to be low compared with that on other kinds of foodstuffs. It will vary from time to time and from shop to shop; but it may be taken that before the war it ranged around 16 to 17% of the selling price, and although it might rise over 20% in some cases, might fall in others below 15%.

The manufacture of butter and cheese on the farm from surplus milk was well established before the Milk Marketing Board was set up. Even at the best of times farm house butter making was not profitable in the winter months, because it took three gallons of milk to make one pound of butter. Indeed, according to the Linlithgow Committee butter made on the farm in the winter cost the farmer twice as much as if he bought the imported article in a shop.

When the farmer did make butter on the farm, and did further wish to dispose of it commercially, he sometimes supplied the consumer direct—often by post. But this was not the prevailing method of marketing. Usually the butter was sold to a blender who passed it on to the wholesale provision merchant or more usually the retailer, by whom it was sold alongside and in competition with imported supplies. Rather as in the case of eggs (see below) the wholesale market for the home produce seems to have been built up on the surpluses left in the hands of country dealers after local demands had been satisfied.

The farmer or his wife were accustomed too to make cheese from any surplus milk. The methods used varied from district to district, and the Linlithgow Committee was able to list no less than seventeen different kinds of cheese. All but two or three of these commanded—and still do command—only a small and special high class sale if they come on to the market at all outside the locality in which they were made.

Most of the cheese which was marketed was sold to a

factor at the local market from whom it passed to the retailer direct or occasionally through one intermediary; the factor's average cost of handling cheese, excluding rail charges, was according to the Linlithgow Committee about 4/- to 5/- a cwt. The factor, in addition to giving credit to his retail customer, also had to get the goods transported to him. The chain of distributors was sometimes lengthened; a factor did not usually wish to sell fewer than ten cheeses at a time, so a wholesaler would intervene to sell to the retailer in smaller quantities.

Before the introduction of the marketing schemes for milk more butter and cheese were manufactured on the farm than in the factory, and the tendency was for the amount of milk used for manufacture on the farm to increase rather than diminish. According to 1931 figures only 12% of the butter and 43% of the cheese produced in Britain was made in factories. Altogether just over 140 million gallons of milk were sold off farms for manufacturing purposes.[1]

The effect of the pooling system under the milk marketing scheme has been to encourage producers to sell as much milk off their farms as possible, whether it is used for liquid sale or for manufacturing purposes. Whereas the total quantity of manufacturing milk had been just over 80 million gallons before the marketing scheme was initiated, it had risen to 212 million gallons in 1933-4, and in 1935-6 reached its peak of 360 million gallons. It was stated in 1936 that it was probable that the greater part of the increase which had taken place was not due to the diversion of milk from the liquid market but 'to the transfer of manufacture from the farms to the creameries'.[2]

The milk destined for manufacture into cheese, butter or proprietary foods is disposed of by the Marketing Board to the firms concerned. Creameries existed, especially in Wales and the West of England, before 1932, but they were not highly developed. Such firms as Aplin and Barrett, and Cow and Gate, who marketed proprietary products of

---

[1] Appendix D of the *Report of the Reorganisation Commission for Milk*. The total includes milk used not only for the factory production of butter and cheese but also for cream, condensed milk, and other milk products.

[2] *Report of Reorganisation Commission*, 1936, p. 99.

one kind and another, had enjoyed remarkably high profits before the scheme was established. After 1932 they expanded their businesses and maintained their dividends at the same figures. Aplin and Barrett, for example, have paid dividends as follows : 1933, 30% ; 1934, 30% plus capitalised bonus of 20% ; 1935, 25% ; 1936, 17½% ; while Cow and Gate paid 16⅔% in 1934–5 and 1935–6, and 18% in 1936–7.[1]

The administration of the scheme has given the larger firms engaged in the industry considerable advantages over the smaller. In order to buy milk at the manufacturing price a firm must under the English scheme take an average of more than 500 gallons a day and manufacture not less than 300 gallons a day. Under the Scottish scheme not only was the minimum of 500 gallons per day imposed as under the English scheme but, in the words of the Reorganisation Commission [2]

> milk for butter manufacture continued to be charged at a higher price to small manufacturers than to large, apparently on the ground that most small manufacturers are able to realise better prices for the by-products.

There is not one price for all manufacturing milk, but a series of prices which are paid for it according to the exact purpose for which it is used. These prices are determined by the Board partly by means of complicated formulae based on the price of competing imported products, partly in the light of experience of the creameries which the Board itself has established.[3]

---

[1] Aplin and Barrett increased their capital from £450,000 to £1 million in 1936. Cow and Gate increased theirs from £550,000 to £700,000 in 1934 and to £1,400,000 in 1936.
The 1933 inquiry made by the Board of Trade under the Import Duties Act shows how profitable the milk products industry was even then. According to the report of this inquiry, the selling value of the products was about £20·5 million (of which butter accounted for £5,625,000 and margarine for £6,875,000), whereas the cost of materials and fuel was nearly £15 million and the wage bill about £1,650,000. The annual profit—to cover depreciation, advertising, and dividends—was thus £4 million.

[2] *Reorganisation Commission*, 1936 (Cutforth), p. 104.

[3] The recommendation of the Committee of Investigation on the price of milk for manufacture into butter provides a good example of the type of formula :—

> ' The price per gallon in any month of milk for manufacture into butter to be the weighted average, divided by 275 in the months from October to February and in the month of September, and by 295 in

MILK AND MILK PRODUCTS

In addition the Government has paid a small subsidy (varying between £1,100,000 in 1934-5 and £126,000 in 1936-7) on milk used for manufacture. The basis of the subsidy is the bridging of the gap between a 'standard price' (arbitrarily fixed at 5d a gallon in summer and 6d in winter) and the elaborately calculated prices actually paid for milk for the purposes of manufacture. As manufacturing prices have risen and the gap grown smaller, the amount of the subsidy payable has dwindled to nothing.

Quite soon after the initiation of the pooling scheme, with the encouragement which it gave to the farmer to sell his milk off the farm for manufacture, it appeared that the result would be a marked decline in the manufacture of butter and cheese on farms for consumption there or for sale in small quantities to higglers and dealers. In order to prevent this the English Milk Marketing Board, following the example of one of the Scottish Boards, introduced in 1934 a special scheme for paying bonuses to cheesemakers with eight cows or more (the figure was subsequently reduced to six) provided they kept all their milk on their farms. The rebate was at the rate of 1·9d a gallon to 2·4d for milk made into soft cheese and hard cheese respectively. This scheme was not applied to butter because it would have been more difficult to arrange inspection and supervision.[1]

The position in 1939 after five years of milk marketing was that English butter was marketed by the creameries at 1/3 to 1/4 per lb, and, to take one standard and popular cheese which does not command a particularly high price, English Cheddar was sold from the dairies at anything

---

the months from March to August, of the average prices per cwt in the previous month of New Zealand finest, Australian choicest, and Danish butter (excluding exceptional quotations) less 16/6, the prices to be weighted according to the imports into the United Kingdom of New Zealand, Australian, and Danish butter respectively in the said month: provided that the price of milk shall not be less than 3d per gallon in any month.'

[1] So difficult indeed is it to get reliable information about the making of butter on farms that it is not possible to say whether the quantity so produced is declining. The Reorganisation Commission in its report say that 'there is reason to believe that it has been declining rapidly. Unless the principles adopted for farm cheese are extended to butter, the higher returns from the sale of milk in liquid form seem bound to reduce butter making on most farms to very small proportions'.

from 92/- to 104/- per cwt (first quality and from the factories at 75/- or 76/-). Butter, however, requires three gallons of milk per lb and cheese only one gallon. Hence the realisation price for milk used for cheese has been since 1935 consistently higher than that used for butter. In 1938-9 the realisation price for butter (other than Cornish) was 5·5d per lb, for Cheddar cheese 5·11d, and 5·58d for hard cheese, other than Cheddar.

Just before the war, plans were complete for the establishment of a Milk Products Marketing Board (of which the Chairman was to be the Manager of United Dairies). This was represented as a reply to the large supplies of cheap imports on the one hand and the demands of the Milk Marketing Board on the other. A milk products scheme, it was urged, would enable the manufacturers to seek regulation of imports through the Market Supplies Committee; and the board set up by the industry would be able to meet the Milk Marketing Board on level ground. The looked-for result was an improvement in the prices secured for milk products. Since the war began, however, nothing more has been heard of the project.

Conclusions

To provide the whole population of the United Kingdom with liquid milk on the scale recommended by the Advisory Committee and to provide enough butter and cheese to bring the diet of all to the optimum would mean a total supply of these dimensions :—

	Supply required	Liquid equivalent	Peace-time supply
Liquid milk	1,400 mill. gallons	1,400 mill. gallons	780 mill. gallons
Butter	600,000 tons	4,032 ,, ,,	513,000 tons
Cheese	230,000 ,,	515 ,, ,,	230,000 ,,

In 1939 about 1,150 million gallons of milk was sold off farms in Scotland, England and Wales, 700-750 million gallons of this being for liquid consumption. The greater part of the remainder was used for manufacturing butter, cheese and cream.

Since manufacturing milk is sold at a lower price than milk for liquid consumption it would seem that the obvious course would be to close down the butter factories, import the requisite butter and cheese and sell all home produced milk for liquid consumption. Even then supply would fall short of that required by 250 million gallons. Since production during the summer is larger—it may be almost twice as great during a summer month as in the middle of the winter—there might have to be very drastic reductions in price to absorb all that was available.

Milk has a special importance in any positive policy of public health because of its unique nutritive qualities. By the outbreak of war nearly 30 million gallons annually were being distributed to school children through the Milk-in-Schools Schemes at the cut price of a third of a pint for a halfpenny. There is very little doubt that, if milk were available free, almost all the children would take it [1]; and to make a ration available would be very beneficial. To provide an average of two-thirds of a pint for children during term and an average of a half pint during the holidays (when probably a smaller number of children would attend to get it) would require about 140 million gallons. Some of this, it is true, would replace milk already drunk by children in their homes—but most of it would be going to children in families where consumption is now very small.

At present the milk costs 1/3½d wholesale and is distributed to schools for 7d a gallon. The local authority pays 1/- and the balance is made up by the Milk Marketing Board and the Government. If this financial arrangement were retained and if no charge at all were made for milk, the local authorities would pay about £7 million for the milk and the Government would make a contribution of between £2 million and £2¼ million. It should, however, be possible to make arrangements to get the milk cheaper than 1/3½d a gallon (in view of the large steady demand) and to lower costs of distribution. A figure of £8 million for the total cost to local authorities and the Exchequer does not seem excessive. In the early

---

[1] Evidence for this given by Marjorie Green, *School Feeding in England and Wales*, pp. 33-4.

stages of the scheme it might be desirable and possible to retain the income from those children who are already paying for the milk which they have (at the rate of a shilling a gallon) although it would obviously be necessary to avoid charging some children for milk which others in exactly the same economic circumstances were getting free ; and on the other hand to avoid making any distinction between those children who could afford milk and those who could not.

Shortly before the war began the Ministry of Health in a circular to local authorities outlined a new scheme for supplying liquid milk to expectant and nursing mothers and to children under five. The scheme, which has been preceded by some long continued experiments in especially distressed parts of the country, was permissive. Local authorities had to submit to the Ministry for approval the income scales which they proposed to apply to necessitous families ; and according to the results of this means test mothers and children might receive up to a pint of milk per head per day either free or at the rate of 1d or 2d per pint. The milk was to be delivered by approved distributors who got a margin of 8d per gallon—that is, 3d or 4d less than the normal.

By 20th February 1940 about 170 authorities had submitted schemes, but only 28 had been approved and no more than 12 were actually in operation. Difficulties arose in some cases over the scales which the local authorities put up ; what appears to have happened is that authorities in the more poverty stricken areas wished to have more generous scales than the Ministry would permit. Moreover, retailers were not disposed to look kindly on the scheme and finally refused to operate it on the original terms. Although it was intended to stimulate the consumption of liquid milk among those who were too poor to buy it on normal terms the retailers felt that they were losing some of their sales and were having their distributing margin cut very fine.

The scheme has grave weaknesses from a welfare point of view. If operated it will supersede the distribution of dried milk through clinics and welfare centres which brought those who benefited under medical supervision. The heaviest burden will be on the authorities in the poorest districts which need the free milk most. Moreover the scheme involves a great deal of clerical work and consequent administrative expense. It is, in fact, a poor substitute for a genuine attempt to reorganise the milk trade and bring retail prices down all round.

As far as liquid household consumption is concerned, the first obvious step which must be taken whether in peace or war is drastically to cut distributive costs. The conclusion of those who investigated retail distribution most carefully before the war began was that a reduction of 4d a gallon could be effected by zoning distribution and dropping the unnecessary services which competing dairymen had encouraged consumers to demand. The demand for milk is not very elastic, but if the price could be brought down in this way and the present advertising campaign intensified, there is little doubt that the consumption in working class districts would increase.

Precisely how this cut in distributive margins could be brought about is not so clear. The proposals embodied in the Milk Bill of Autumn 1938 (which were popularly—and incorrectly—believed to be likely to lead to cheaper milk) would have meant handing over control of the distribution to committees of those in the trade themselves, with little or no safeguarding of consumers' interests.[1] The Bill was withdrawn; but the proposals for rationalising distribution have not been forgotten by the Milk Board. It may well be that war conditions, with the danger of a rise in the price of milk because of increased agricultural costs, will revive the scheme.

The fixed distributive margin naturally gives a considerable advantage to the cooperatives, which offer a dividend upon

[1] Under the Bill a Milk Commission consisting of independent persons was to be set up with the power, among others, of making regulations about the number of deliveries and the types of containers used (Milk Industry Bill, Part VI, Clause 22). But a body or bodies substantially representative of distributors was to have power to establish distributors' schemes applying to the whole of Great Britain or part of it; the board administering the scheme (and elected by the distributors) might take over the functions of the independent Commission in respect of distribution.

purchase; this has been in part responsible for the recent growth of their trade in milk. A 'divi' of 1/8 in the £ means that the consumer is paying 2/1⅔d for milk instead of 2/4. Certainly the cooperative movement, if given a monopoly of milk distribution, could effect a reduction in price of at least 4d a gallon and possibly more. There are, however, towns where the coop still has only a small share of the trade, and where milk is supplied by one or two large firms and a number of small dairymen. In those cases there is a strong case for some municipal control. Examples from the Dominions show how this could be carried out. In Auckland, New Zealand, and in Sydney, milk supply has been reorganised under municipal control, and the costs of distribution in both cases reduced.

There remains the problem of the producer retailers, who still handle an appreciable percentage of the liquid milk in some parts of the country. Since they are generally working on a small scale with little capital, they cannot afford pasteurisation machinery and so constitute a solid and reliable body of opposition to any proposals for compulsory pasteurisation. Cooperative associations of these producer retailers, primarily for the purpose of establishing pasteurisation plants, seem to be the development most likely to solve the problem.

But what of the Milk Marketing Scheme itself? An independent Commission (with representatives of interested parties available if necessary to give advice) would be the best body to carry out a reorganisation which would realise the possible economies and the best body to fix retail prices if any fixing is to be done at all. This involves transferring to a new body one of the most important functions which the Milk Board has hitherto fulfilled; but it leaves to the Board —or Boards—those functions which more properly belong to an organisation elected by producers. The function of the Board should be to organise production, and to negotiate with the Commission the prices which producers are to receive. In the case of failure to reach a settlement the question should be referred to the Minister. The administrative machinery of the Board would remain as at present, and the milk would be sold by farmers to the distributors. It should, however, be possible to reduce the amount spent by the farmer on transport. At present it pays the large buyer to take his milk from a distance; a system of zoning under which the milk supplies of a town were drawn from within a certain radius would save unnecessary expense.

The milk once sold to the distributors, the producers' board should have no voice in how it is used. At present a large quantity of milk which might be consumed liquid is being used for manufacture, and it might seem that the obvious course to take after cutting distribution costs would be to close the creameries and import all our butter and cheese from abroad. A good deal of fuss has been made about the use of a very small quantity of milk for such industrial purposes as making imitation tortoiseshell, and far too little has been said about the large profits being made out of proprietary foods and cheeses for which milk has been bought at very low manufacturing prices. The consumer of liquid milk has in fact been subsidising manufacture to the tune of nearly $2\frac{1}{4}$d a gallon on liquid milk bought.[1]

The problem is, however, not a simple one. The defence put up for the manufacturing milk arrangement—that more milk is produced in summer than in winter and must be used for manufacture because the liquid market cannot absorb it—has got to be met. At present the farmer is receiving about 10d a gallon for his milk in summer and 1/3 in winter— those are the pool prices. Assuming an advance of ·75d a gallon in these prices, transport costs of 1·5d per gallon, ·75d for pasteurisation and 5d for retail distribution, it would be possible to put milk on the market at 1/6 a gallon in summer and 1/11 in winter. If the lower price during the summer did not dispose of the entire additional supply it might be permissible to raise the general retail price, say by a penny; and use the proceeds to make possible a still lower summer price. When milk bars were flourishing far more milk was sold in them in the summer than in the

---

[1] The exact figure is given as 2·22d per gallon in the Milk Marketing Board publication, *Five Years' Review*.

winter, which suggests that, provided the price is kept down and sufficiently attractive forms of milk drinks devised, the whole of the so called surplus could be absorbed by the liquid market to the benefit of farmer and consumer.

Although this should be the general policy of a Milk Commission charged with the supervision and distribution of supply, it is unlikely that this line of expanding liquid consumption rather than knocking down milk cheap for manufacture will be followed so drastically as to destroy the factory industry altogether. This country produces distinctive cheese and fresh butter which can in the long run be marketed most cheaply if they are available in large quantities. There is every reason for the producers' board regarding it as its duty to increase the supply of milk available and lower the price so that not only may the requirements of the country in respect of liquid consumption be met, but a butter and cheese industry maintained in competition with that of New Zealand. The realisation prices of manufacturing milk (1938–9) were 5·50d per gallon for use in butter making, 5·40d for cheese, 7·5d for condensed milk, 7·0d for milk powder and 8·34d for fresh cream. The Advisory Economists found costs on some exceptional farms as low as 7·5d per gallon—so that the gap between costs of production of milk and the price the manufacturer can afford to pay may not be so large as is sometimes thought.

There is another way in which the problem of the necessary surplus might be solved; so simple and obvious that it is very difficult to see why it has not already been adopted. The milk which was surplus to liquid requirements during the summer might be dried and used for distribution through clinics or through the ordinary retail channels during the winter. Already dried milk (primarily because of its cheapness and the ease with which it can be handled in bulk) has been used for distribution through maternity centres, and has proved popular and satisfactory. Dried milk, if properly stored, would keep for a year without any deterioration; and storage of this kind would have the additional merit of providing a wartime reserve.

At the root of the problem of milk supply lies the

unavoidable questions of milk yields and the health of the dairy herds. The annual average yield per cow must be in the neighbourhood of 580–600 gallons; whereas a number of cows on well run farms produce 1,000 gallons, and some yield as much as double that. To increase the total supply of fresh milk and to lower its cost calls for consideration of the number of additional dairy cows which could be pastured in the United Kingdom, the ways in which disease can be eradicated, and the extent to which the yield of the individual cow can be raised by a larger and better balanced ration of feeding stuff.

A study of the production side of the milk industry shows that costs per gallon in the case of cows yielding 450–500 gallons a year are far higher than of those yielding 900–1,000 gallons.[1]

Cost of Milk in Pence per Gallon according to Average Yield

	Yield per cow per day up to 1·25 gallons	Yield per cow per day more than 2·5 gallons
Food—		
Purchased	3·32	3·78
Home grown	2·47	1·03
Grazing	1·39	0·43
Total	7·18	5·24
Labour—		
Employees	2·01	1·86
Family	0·79	0·48
Total	2·80	2·34
Miscellaneous	1·69	1·30
Herd replacement	1·61	0·29
Gross farm cost	13·28	9·17
Credits	1·03	0·77
Net farm costs	12·25	8·40
Range of costs	7·12–16·40	4·58–10·17

These figures are founded upon a tiny sample so that not too much should be built upon them; but they appear

[1] Summarised from table in *Interim Report No. 3 of the Milk Investigation Scheme*, p. 21.

to establish fairly conclusively the point that to encourage higher yields by milk recording societies and by other methods is to cheapen milk as well as to increase the total supply. The large part of costs accounted for by feeding stuffs emphasises the need for examining closely the conditions under which these foods are supplied to farmers and the case for imposing public control. A beneficial consequence of nationalising the milling industry would be that it should make it possible to reduce the price of milling offals which farmers feed to livestock, and so should reduce the cost of milk production.

Higher yields up to 1,000 gallons do not necessarily weaken resistance and so lead to a high mortality; indeed the replacement rate was one of the main factors in making milk from low yield cows dearer. Thus there is no reason to fear that a well conceived policy for dealing with the prevalence of disease would be nullified by an increase in the average yield. Such a policy for the eradication of disease would have to be based upon a combination of the slaughter method—which cannot be applied forthwith to all herds affected because of the large number of animals concerned—with that already used of building up disease free herds; the fixing of a date, say seven years hence, when all herds should have been rid of disease by these methods, and the provision of £3½ million a year for compensation for slaughtered animals; and the expansion of the veterinary inspectorate, which at the moment consists of 22 officials to visit 170,000 producers. If the costs for herd replacement, which are already declining,[1] could be brought everywhere as low as in the West Midland and Mid Western regions, the average cost of milk production, quite apart from any other changes or economies, would come down by ½d per gallon.

To sum up, the farmer and the consumer need a three point programme: (1) Reduce the cost of milk production by cheaper feeding stuffs and wise expenditure on the eradication of disease. (2) Reduce the costs of distribution

---

[1] The figures for 1936–7 were markedly lower than those for the preceding season.

MILK AND MILK PRODUCTS

by cooperative and municipal control carried out under the direction of an independent Commission which takes advice from producers and distributors but is responsible only to the government. (3) Make every effort to distribute the bulk of the milk supplies for liquid consumption by reduced prices, special schemes and drying of surplus milk for winter distribution.

4 EGGS

Some 7,000 million eggs are consumed every year in the United Kingdom—an average of three a week for every man, woman and child. The average has fallen a little in recent years—it reached its peak in 1930–4—and international comparisons show that the average inhabitant of Canada or the United States eats half as many eggs again as this. Almost certainly war will reduce further the United Kingdom consumption. Feavearyear's calculation for 1936 was that £46 million were paid by the housewives of the country for eggs. For the same period the return to British agriculture in respect of eggs was £18,360,000, and the value of imported eggs £9,900,000.

It is not easy to give any more satisfactory detailed account of the consumption of eggs. Such information as Crawford, for example, gives, suggests that consumption af eggs falls low in working class families. Crawford's figures show an average weekly consumption per head of 3·8 and 2·6 eggs in the two lowest income groups respectively and a weekly expenditure of 5·8d and 3·6d on them.

Besides their use in the home, however, eggs are a raw material for the manufacturer of cakes, custard and other prepared foods. The needs of the manufacturer are of course partly met by the production and import of eggs in shell, but the main supplies of eggs used in this way are imported in a liquid state. These imports stood at about 45,000 tons in 1938, which may be reckoned as equivalent to about a fifth of the home production of eggs in shell over the same period. The bulk of these liquid eggs came from China and are produced very cheaply on small peasant holdings in the interior. They are bartered for needles, thread and similar articles with pedlars who come round to collect them at usually infrequent intervals. They make a slow journey, by water, to the coast, where they are bought for cash by representatives of foreign-owned packing stations; and from there they are shipped to Europe. Apart from their cheapness their advantage to the manufacturer and

EGGS

the catering trade is that since they have been taken out of their shells and consigned liquid, they save labour in preparation.

Retail Distribution

The levels of egg prices vary from month to month, and at any one time eggs will be offered for sale at a variety of prices. One random example will illustrate this. In one London working class shopping district in January, 1939, there were branches of large multiple provision stores such as David Greig, Pearks and Home and Colonial making large displays of eggs in their windows and occasionally even in flat boxes outside their shops. They were offering Danish eggs at 10 for 1/-, others at 1/3 a dozen, others again at 6 for 9d. 'Selected boiling eggs' were offered as low as 1/- a dozen, stamped merely 'Foreign'. Beside them were Dutch eggs at 1/8. 'English New Laid' were fetching a higher price generally than the imported. The multiple shop was offering them at 1/6 or 2/- a dozen; the dairy down the road was asking 2/- or 2/3 a dozen, while the small grocer round the corner advertised them at 2½d each. The housewife is willing to pay more for some eggs than for others because of their size, their freshness—one bad egg in a dozen makes them dearer than they seem—and their colour.

The small independent grocer does not generally make much display of his eggs. In contrast with the multiple shop, which pushes them out on the pavement in eagerness to draw the attention of possible customers to them, the small grocer will put only a few in his window, and probably put no price ticket on them. Often the coop makes as little display of its eggs as the small private grocer.

Most egg supplies go through the provision dealers, large or small, but even in the winter the housewife can often get them from the fishmonger or the cooked meat shop, while a number of small restaurants keep two or three dozen on the counter or among the flyblown cakes in the window. In the spring, when English eggs are plentiful, they are available in still more shops, especially in the country districts where the butcher and the fishmonger as well as the small grocer will display eggs which frequently they have had from their customers in exchange for other goods in which they normally deal. In the town cheap eggs are a good advertisement for the multiple grocer; and it is often worth while selling them on a small profit to attract other trade.

The retailers' margins on eggs, even apart from this complication, vary a good deal from time to time. The retailer when he gets his supplies wholesale (and does not derive them, as is so often the case in the country districts, from his own customers) buys by the long hundred (ten dozen). He can sell, however, in no larger units than the dozen; and that dozen must be priced at a certain number of pence. (He may resort occasionally to pricing his eggs at so many to the shilling; but usually he will name a price per dozen.) In the case of English eggs moreover the price will usually be based not on the dozen but on the individual egg; and the price will rise or fall in farthings per egg—that is, in steps of threepence per dozen.

Since the demand is sensitive to changes in price,[1] the retailer will be unwilling to raise prices until absolutely necessary; so that when wholesale prices rise the increase is not immediately passed on to the consumer. The retailer will carry on with a diminishing margin as long as possible before he raises his prices and receives a large margin on the new figures.

Thus it is not easy to generalise about the retail margins on eggs; but it may be taken that they vary between 6d and 2/6 per long hundred in the cheap season and between 1/- and 3/- when prices are at their highest. Over a period a retailer doing a large trade makes on the average 15–16%.

Home Production and Imports

1934 was the peak year of home produced supplies. Since the Great War the number of fowls and the output of eggs

[1] 'Several witnesses have assured us,' said the Reorganisation Commission in their report, 'that when the price comes down to 1d there is a big expansion in the demand, and when it rises to about 1½d each demand falls rapidly. The rise of prices in the autumn checks consumption for several weeks after more ample supplies are available.' This Commission, with Lord Addison as president, was appointed in 1934 to prepare a marketing scheme for eggs and poultry in England and Wales. It reported in 1935.

had steadily increased. After 1934 there was a substantial decline in home output from 4,817 million eggs to 4,320 million in 1937; but this was later checked. Despite the Ottawa Agreements Act, which altered the previous duties upon eggs to between 1/- and 1/9 per long hundred according to weight, imports from the Empire were in peace time slightly under 15% of the total; as home production declined imports increased.

Year	Production	Net Imports	Consumption
1934	4,817	2,244	7,061
1935	4,661	2,366	7,027
1936	4,525	2,939	7,464
1937	4,320	2,964	7,284
1938	4,220	3,324	7,544

(Figures in millions. They include a calculation of production on allotments and in back gardens.)

Between 1924 and 1934 the number of eggs produced in the United Kingdom practically doubled—partly as a result of an increase of 90% in the fowl population; and partly as the result of a rise of about 20% in the number of eggs produced by the average hen. To some extent the increase in fowl population and in productivity was due to the growth of specialist poultry farming. After the war a number of ex soldiers and others who wanted to live an open air life and to be their own masters took up poultry farming. Many of them failed fairly soon; others got into difficulties when the price of feeding stuffs rose very high two years ago. But some survived and by 1939 specialist farms accounted for about 20% of the total output of eggs. Since the war began these specialists have been passing through an extremely difficult time and had they accounted for the greater part of the egg supply of the country there would have been severe shortage.

A more important reason, however, for the increased supply has been the greater attention given to poultry by the ordinary non-specialist farmer and his wife. As other farming proved unprofitable they could not neglect the flock of chickens whose eggs might at least be bartered with the local shopkeeper. At the same time, fowls kept on holdings of less than an acre or in backyards are reckoned to account for between 20 and 25% of the fowl population; although only a very small percentage of the eggs from these flocks come on to the market. Altogether it is reckoned that about half a million families 'keep chickens' in one way or another.

The pace has been set in egg production by the specialist poultry farmer using battery methods, housing his fowls in cages with wire floors, keeping electric light on to lengthen the time during which they could eat and lay—and so on. Under such conditions hens can be expected to produce an average of 180 eggs per annum, which although a good deal lower than the freak results obtained in some laying trials (anything up to 300 eggs per annum) are a good deal higher than the figures which were reached under the old 'barn door' methods. But to get such egg production a good deal of money has to be spent. A pullet will cost 5/6 to 6/6, and at the end of a laying life of 18 months will have to be sold for what it will fetch. To erect and maintain a battery appears to cost up to 2/6 per fowl per annum.[1]

Labour costs are fairly high—2/3 to 3/- per fowl per annum. But the heaviest and most variable single item of expense is feeding stuffs. According to Beilby[2] feeding stuffs represent 60% of the total costs of commercial egg production; but he studied egg production at a time when a sharp rise in the price of feeding stuffs was causing particular difficulties for poultry farmers. According to another authority feeding stuffs, under conditions of battery production, cost 12/6 per fowl. That was in the period autumn 1937–autumn 1938, when prices had fallen once more.[3] Thus the costs of producing 180 eggs were approximately:—

Pullet	3/-
Housing and Maintenance .	2/6
Feeding stuff . . .	12/6
Labour	2/6
Total	20/6

[1] This includes capital depreciation, rates, electric light.
[2] *A Study of Egg Prices*. A.E.R.I. Oxford, 1937.
[3] Lancashire Institute of Agriculture: *Report on Management and Economics of a Laying Battery*. The estimate of labour costs comes from the same source.

Costs under the battery system, for labour, housing and feed, were a good deal higher than under less intensive methods of production.[1]

The increased production of eggs since 1918 has had the effect of weakening the stamina of fowls and lessening their resistance to disease. The Committee on Poultry Diseases points out how the mortality rate in all laying tests recognised by the National Poultry Council, in which naturally the most healthy birds are concerned, has risen from 6·6% in 1926–7 to 17·7% in 1936–7; such losses are naturally affecting the poultry farmers' costs very seriously.

But the birds which actually die are not the only ones which are lost because of disease. Constant supervision is necessary to weed out birds which go off laying. Anything between 25 and 75% of a flock will be culled in this way in the course of a year.[2]

The recent high prices and short supply of feeding stuffs have created special difficulties for the specialist egg farmers; uncertainty about the future has led them to kill off a large proportion of their flocks. Indeed, taking into account the different classes of poultry keepers, it is calculated that as much as 20 to 25% of the poultry of the country has been killed since the war began. The Government, moreover, so far as it has controlled the allocation of available supplies has given preference to cattle rather than to poultry or pigs.

England and Wales account for about four-fifths of the home production; and it is in England and Wales that the most noticeable increases have taken place in egg production and fowl population. The other fifth is divided fairly equally between Scotland and Northern Ireland. The main egg producing areas are now Lancashire and the West Riding of

---

[1] This analysis of costs based on the report of the Lancashire Institute of Agriculture, 1937–8, is confirmed by a Poultry Survey published by the Harper Adams Agricultural College. This survey, however, covering approximately the same period, shows an average annual production of less than 150 eggs per hen.

[2] See *British Agriculture*, p. 237. In the Report of the Lancashire Institute of Agriculture it is stated that at the end of 52 weeks' trial under conditions of battery production only 51% of the original birds were still in the laying flock.

Yorkshire, Kent, Devon and Cornwall, and Essex, Norfolk, Suffolk and Lincolnshire.

The value of home production varies very considerably from month to month. Home produced eggs are most plentiful in April and May—and then naturally prices are at their lowest. Supplies get shorter and prices higher as the summer goes on, and by November the prices may stand at as much as 150% higher than six months before.

The effect of the rise of prices in the early autumn is to diminish consumption.

> The high prices of the winter months make people lose the 'egg eating' habit. Instead of having an egg with a rasher at breakfast they go without; and they do not resume the habit until some weeks after the increased spring supply has begun to come on the market. There is a lag of about seven weeks. During that time this loss of the habit of consumption has the effect of exaggerating the stock of eggs on the market, and the spring fall in price is accordingly altogether out of proportion to the increase in supply.[1]

Imports might be expected to offset this trend; but much of the imported supply comes from European countries where the production cycle follows the same pattern.[2] In fact the volume of imports from month to month does not vary nearly as much as does home production. One peak comes in May and another in September and October; but the variations are only between 18 million dozen in January and 25 million dozen in May. Imports from European countries continue fairly high throughout the summer and autumn, while in October to January supplies from Australia and South Africa come on to the market. Storage is efficient in Denmark and eggs which have been stored there have not until recently had to be stamped with this fact as have eggs stored in this country. What happened therefore was that English dealers bought eggs in Denmark in the spring

---

[1] Lord Addison, *A Policy for British Agriculture*.

[2] The principal source of imports is Denmark, from which, despite the tariff, 40% of the total imported supplies came in 1937. Her position was recognised by the Anglo-Danish Commercial Agreement of 1933, which stipulated that there should be no quantitative regulation of the import of eggs from Denmark, and that if there were general quantitative regulation later on, the Danish allocation should not be less than 660 million, or in the event of a quota, not less than 38% of the total import.

and stored them through the summer to bring over and market when the price had risen.

The prices of home produced and imported eggs move in close sympathy with one another from month to month; despite the fact that, taking an annual average of wholesale prices, first quality ordinary English eggs may stand at about 16% above Irish, 25% above Dutch, and 85% above Polish eggs.

Wholesale Distribution

While the quantities of home produced eggs [1] brought on to the market in the United Kingdom practically doubled between 1924 and 1934, the organisation of the supply and the methods by which the goods passed from the poultry farmer to the consumer remained radically unchanged. The old established structure had been well adapted to handling the trade when it was largely a matter of direct transactions between farmers and shopkeepers in nearby towns; but it was not adapted to the larger scale of the trade in the early 1930's. The practice had been for a higgler to go from farmhouse to farmhouse buying the eggs which the farmer or his wife had to sell. Alternatively, the farmer might sell the eggs to a dealer in the local market. The higgler or the dealer would dispose of eggs to local retailers and any surplus supplies there were would be sent to a larger urban market—perhaps quite a long way off. Thus most of the eggs were disposed of to the retailer either directly or with only one intermediary.

As egg production increased, the surplus over local requirements grew larger and more regular; and by the late 1920's the packing stations—local assembly points to which the higglers brought the eggs for despatch to the more distant markets—had grown to a position of importance in the trade, especially in those parts of the country where consumption was small compared with production.

Sometimes the eggs are brought to the stations by the farmers themselves; sometimes they are collected at regular

[1] This refers primarily to England and Wales, which produce four-fifths of the United Kingdom total of eggs.

intervals by agents of the station. Where egg production is concentrated in a small area and the packing station handles a large proportion of the eggs produced, costs can be kept low. As little as 1/3 per long hundred—to cover costs of collection, packing and delivery to a local retailer—appears to be fairly common.[1]

Often these packing stations are not elaborate buildings; some of the more recent ones, however, have been specially built for the purpose and may pack as many as 2,000 eggs an hour.[2] They may be owned by companies or private individuals (who do not usually deal only in eggs but handle other produce or farmers' requisites as well) or be run on a cooperative basis.

Long before the last war the wholesale trade in imported eggs had become well established and a national market existed for them. It was in the sixties of last century that the four or so principal egg buyers began to meet on Monday mornings in the parlour of a public house in the Borough. From their operations arose the London Egg Exchange, now settled in a building of its own and with some two hundred subscribers who deal upon it. Sales are not by auction but by private treaty, and usually the eggs imported are sold before they land.

Eggs from Denmark, to take one important example, are exported by a cooperative organisation or by one of a dozen or so private exporting firms which have copied the cooperative method of collection at packing stations. They pass into the hands of a large importer either in the British port or in one of the large inland centres such as Leeds or Birmingham. Sometimes the importer will be a large provision retailer like David Greig or Sainsbury; sometimes a firm which deals in imported provisions—including bacon and butter as well as eggs—on a commission basis. Usually a firm of this sort will aim at a commission of between $2\frac{1}{2}$ and 5%.

The imports with which they grew up to deal still form

[1] The Ministry of Agriculture will shortly publish a short pamphlet on costs of packing stations.
[2] Clynderwen Packing Station. Ministry of Agriculture Marketing Leaflet 11.

the bulk of the trade of the central markets, although as home production has increased the proportion through these distributive channels has grown. The national market for English eggs has only become a reality since the last war.

In 1929 the National Mark Scheme was applied to eggs. A number of the larger packing stations voluntarily submitted themselves to national mark standards of quality and grading by weight—only large packing stations being permitted to enrol under the scheme.[1] They created for themselves a central agency—National Mark Egg Central, Ltd.—to market the eggs which passed through their hands. Only some 12% of the eggs passing through commercial channels are handled by National Mark packing stations; but the introduction of the scheme has, it was stated by the Commission, tended to improve standards all round.

Wholesale margins are difficult to estimate exactly; but it may be taken that the margin announced by the National Mark Egg Central is fairly representative. The margin varies according to the size of the retailer's order:

On 1–9 cartons [2] it will be 1/- per long hundred.
On 10–19 cartons it will be 9d per long hundred.
On 20 cartons and over it will be 6d per long hundred.

With still larger quantities the margin will be even lower—perhaps as little as 3d per long hundred.

The marketing machinery for home produced eggs has developed slowly and haphazardly to deal with surpluses, and it is still true to say that no wholesaler or retailer serving a large densely populated area knows of a central point to which he can go with the certainty of getting good quality English eggs. Despite the development of the national market, the local packing stations and local markets retain a very great importance in the trade. Their importance was recognised by the Reorganisation Commission, and the fact that they performed a vital service was emphasised by the proposal of the Commission to make local packing stations

---

[1] These packing stations are fairly evenly distributed over the country except in Wales and in Yorkshire, Northumberland, Westmorland and Cumberland.

[2] A 'carton' contains 15 dozen eggs.

under the control of a central board the key points in their scheme of reorganisation.

This marketing system has considerable drawbacks. The central markets, and to a less degree the local markets, are supplied most fully at times of surplus, when every producer tends to seek in them a remunerative outlet for whatever surplus he finds on his own hands. So any rise of production above the normal means a very much more than proportionate increase of supplies thrown upon the markets. This is particularly serious in view of the price changes which take place anyway as a result of the varying supplies of home produced eggs available at different times of the year.

The Reorganisation Commission found that there was a good deal of wasted effort involved in the system of assembling and distribution. But no class of distributor can be said to be profiteering or to be downright parasitic. The trouble seems to be that unnecessary trouble and loss is caused by the variations in supplies and prices and by the absence of assured supplies of good quality eggs. To quote the report:

> While we have not conducted any detailed inquiry into distributive margins it has to be recognised that until bulk supplies of home produced eggs of assured quality are made readily available, the distributive trades must be put to trouble, expense, and possible loss that should under other conditions be avoidable. When the position has been improved by the introduction of organised methods of assembly it should be possible for the distributive trades to work to lower margins for the benefit of the industry as a whole.

Conclusions

In peace time eggs probably yielded the home producer an average return of 16/- to 17/- a long hundred taking the year as a whole. (This did not allow a large margin of profit for the producer on the battery system; but he derived an advantage from the fact that his output fluctuated less from month to month, and he accordingly sold a higher proportion of the total output during the high price season than the general farmer.) Assuming a return of 16/- to the producer, a retailer buying through one intermediary paid

17/3 to 17/6, and buying from a wholesaler who had himself bought from a packing station would pay up to 18/6. The consumer then had to pay 21/6 or so per long hundred—which seems a reasonable weighted average of retail prices.

Imported eggs averaged about 8/9 per long hundred at the port.[1] The wholesaler's commission raised this to about 9/- and the retailer probably charged on the average 10/6 per long hundred. For Danish eggs alone the prices were probably a good deal higher—the price at the port averaged about 9/9 and the retail price 11/6 or so. Prices and margins, especially in the retail trade, varied and will still vary very greatly from one part of the year to another; but these estimates, based on averages, suggest that distribution charges did not account for quite that 35% of the retail prices which Feavearyear's figures seemed to indicate.

The rejection of the proposals based on the Reorganisation Commission's report made the Government rather chary of any proposals to deal with the poultry industry; the 1939 Poultry Bill was a timid document. Good as far as it went, it made proposals for the appointment by the Minister of Agriculture of a Poultry Commission which should keep the industry under review. This Commission was to have power to supervise the distribution of hatching eggs and day old chicks; so that the producer was protected to some extent at any rate against bad quality stock. Part of the improvement of stock was to be by a voluntary accreditation scheme for breeders; premiums costing up to £250,000 over seven years were to be paid by the Exchequer. On the marketing side an effort was to be made to secure that all eggs should be graded and that the grades should be uniform over the country as a whole. Loans and grants were to be made for the assistance of producer controlled packing stations. Finally, all imported eggs were to be marked as stored unless the exporting country could make it clear that stored eggs were clearly marked and that only fresh eggs were sent without mark; and the Board of Trade was to be given power to regulate the import of eggs and poultry by order to ensure stability.

[1] 1938 figures.

The main lines of a policy for the reform of egg marketing have already been sketched by the Reorganisation Commission; although the attempts to put the scheme into effect failed because of opposition from the farmers. The Commission recommended that the country should be covered by a system of packing stations, each serving an area with a radius of about ten miles. Subject to necessary adjustments to permit direct sales from producer to consumer, the packing stations were to be given a monopoly of collection within their respective areas. Although they were to remain under the same control as now, some in the hands of individuals or companies, some in the hands of cooperative associations, they were to be subject to the supervision of a Poultry Board elected by producers. The areas which the packing stations served were to be grouped in regions, each supervised by an official of the central marketing authority. This official was to be able to control all inter-area sales. The main purpose of marketing reform as seen by the Reorganisation Commission was that of ending what Lord Addison has called ' the unholy scramble to get rid of eggs anyhow ', which takes place in so many districts during the spring season. To this end the Poultry Board must have power to store eggs in the spring and release them during the autumn. To prevent conflict between the interests of different regions it would be necessary to fix a national price for eggs delivered from the packing station to the wholesaler, and to deduct extra costs of transport from the net price paid to the producer. It would be immaterial to the purchaser from what part of the country he took his supplies. It would seem desirable that the Board should itself set up stations where necessary and administer them with the aid of a committee of local producers.

The proposals do not cover the whole field of egg supply. A satisfactory policy must include proposals for lowering the average price of eggs as well as for lessening the differences between prices at different times of the year. Here the key is lower costs of production—for marketing reform, although it would be useful, could not be expected to lower the average price of eggs to any great extent. Disease would have to be tackled by a long term programme of research financed by a grant from the Exchequer, the Poultry Board (or some other organisation set up for the purpose and catering for all branches of agriculture) must be able to grant loans to farmers on easy terms to enable them to build suitable hen houses.

A total increase of some 25% in the total supply would be required to bring the peace time consumption nearer to the optimum. If the increase were to be provided without more imports it would mean expanding home production by about 40%, which could scarcely be done overnight. To bring the total annual production up to about 6,000 million eggs in the course of three or four years would be by no means impossible, especially in view of the fact that without a guaranteed price, without any control of feeding stuff prices, and without any specially favourable credit facilities, the number of eggs produced in this country practically doubled in ten years.

In the interim, however, the problem of imports, which has caused such difficulties in any attempt to organise the egg producers or to reform marketing, would continue to be a thorny one. Control should be handed over to a separate import board with instructions to buy wherever possible in the cheap season and to store for use throughout the ensuing months. There would be need for a coordinating Egg Supply Committee which would have representatives of the producers' boards and of the import board upon it, together with government nominees. This committee would have to be able to reach decisions binding upon both the boards.

Given some scheme whereby marketing was organised and costs kept down, the problem of imports would assume slighter proportions. Largely because of the high cost of feeding stuffs, it caused particular trouble when the Government tried to put the proposals of the Reorganisation Commission into effect. Given these lower costs and better marketing, the home poultry farmer would have little to fear from foreign competition, especially in view of the higher price which the consumer is willing to pay for English new laid eggs.

5 MEAT

By comparison with the peoples of continental countries the British are a nation of meat-eaters. The calculations of weekly meat consumption and expenditure in working class and middle class families given below show this [1]:

Family income	Consumption in ounces	Expenditure in pence
£250–£499	26·9	24·1
£125–£249	21·4	15·0
Under £125	17·7	9·95

The retail demand for meat is not level throughout the week. It rises as the days pass and reaches its climax on Saturday. As a result the middle of the week is the busiest time in the wholesale markets, and the joint which is served up to a suburban family on Sunday has probably come from an animal which passed through Smithfield on Wednesday or Thursday (or even as early as Monday) and, if home killed, was bought from the farmer some time in the previous week.

The demand for different kinds of meat is subject to variations according to season. More mutton and lamb is eaten during the warm months of the year than during the winter. In the spring the lamb which is bought is mostly imported; but home killed is in demand in the summer months until in the autumn its place is gradually taken by mutton. The demand varies too according to districts. Although in general smaller joints are demanded now that families are smaller, different parts of the country favour different carcase weights. In the case of mutton, for example, the South Wales and South Coast demand is for a much lighter carcase than is favoured in London. Lancashire wants lean rather than well finished carcases—and so on.[2]

[1] Crawford, *The People's Food*, p. 178 onward.
[2] Report on *Marketing of Sheep Mutton and Lamb*. Ministry of Agriculture Economic Series, No. 29.

MEAT

Rather more than half the peace time meat supply came from overseas. The figures for the supply of livestock products in 1936–7 were as follows :

	Home Production	Imports	Total	% Home Produced
Beef and veal	12,523	13,857	26,380	47
Mutton and lamb	4,642	7,009	11,651	40
Pig meat	8,018	9,754	17,772	45

Figures in 000 cwt.

Imports of live cattle, sheep and pigs were comparatively small ; the main source was Eire.

Home Production

The home production of meat for the market is not easy to describe briefly. The raising of cattle is in some respects similar to the raising of sheep and pigs ; but there are problems peculiar to each kind of meat which make it impossible to generalise readily. For example, 40% of the total supplies of beef are derived from animals which have been raised and maintained for milk, and so are sold at low prices to the disadvantage of fat cattle ; this situation does not arise with mutton. Again pigs, despite the attempts at organisation, may be sold for either bacon or pork, and the market for pig meat is complicated accordingly.

Broadly speaking the production side of the home killed meat industry is divisible into two stages—rearing and feeding—carried on by different farmers often in different parts of the country. The division is particularly marked in the case of fat cattle, which remain in the hands of the breeder for anything from eighteen to thirty months and then pass to the feeder for four to six months to be fattened before marketing. During the latter period the weight is usually increased by about 2 cwt. Generally they are raised on the hills and the store cattle—that is to say the unfattened animals—are moved to the plains to be fed. Sometimes this movement is merely local—say from the Quantock Hills to the adjoining lowlands, or from the Pennines to the plains of Yorkshire—but sometimes the cattle are moved a long distance for fattening—from Devon to Sussex, Essex or Northants, from Wales to the Midlands, or from Ireland across the Irish sea to almost any of the fattening counties of England. The movement of store sheep, on the other hand, is usually local. Again the animals are bred on the hills and fattened on the plains, but in the past there was a good deal of specialisation in breeding to meet the needs of particular districts. The proportion of sheep marketed and slaughtered young is a good deal larger than is the case with cattle—and the popularity of 'lamb' as opposed to 'mutton' has increased in the last few years. (Meat produced by a sheep when it is over a year old is classed as mutton.)

Sometimes the same farmers will rent land in two different places and will rear cattle or sheep as well as fattening them; but more frequently the animals are sold by the breeder to the feeder. Sometimes the sale will be direct, but more often it will be through an intermediary. The trade in store cattle is more highly developed than the trade in store sheep; store fairs take place at different times of the year in the breeding areas and at them the dealers have an opportunity of buying cattle for despatch to the feeding areas. In addition they buy animals at the smaller and more frequent local markets and so make up consignments for despatch. In these markets the dealer will in many cases find himself bidding against the local farmers who wish to buy their neighbours' stock for fattening; but these farmers are likely to be more anxious than the dealer to get an animal of a particular type and to take none at all if they cannot get it.

The small scale dealer may do merely a local trade between farmer and farmer, or may in addition act as the agent of a larger dealer operating over a distance. The small dealer's buying tends, it seems, to be speculative, while the large dealer concerned with moving cattle from, say, Wales or Ireland to East Anglia will prefer to work on commission—and can usually rely on a fairly steady sale. It may be reckoned that the cost of marketing store cattle is between £2 and £3 per head.

The total stock of cows and heifers in Great Britain is about

3½ million, and of ewes 10 million. About 3 million calves are born yearly, of which perhaps a third are sold for veal. To the two million remaining must be added about half a million store cattle imported mostly from Ireland. Of the total about a million replace the foundation herd (since the average life of the cow is between three and four years), and the remainder are slaughtered as fat stock. The foundation stock itself is ultimately sold for meat—but a cow which has produced two or more calves produces meat of poor quality. Of the 11 million lambs produced by the ewe flock in any one year about 6 million are slaughtered before they are a year old, 2¼ million are slaughtered in the following year as mutton, and the remainder replace the foundation stock, to be sold in the end at a lower price.

Cattle and sheep rely mainly for food upon grass in the summer and upon arable crops in the winter. Again there is some regional specialisation—grass feeding tends to predominate in the East Midlands and yard feeding on arable crops in the Eastern Counties and especially in Norfolk. Most of the grass-fed cattle are sold between June and the end of the year, whereas the winter fed cattle come on to the market between January and May. These two branches of the industry, dividing the total output almost equally, are carried on independently of one another in different parts of the country by different people.

Livestock has an important place in the general system of agriculture. Sheep and cattle are suited to both arable and grassland farming and return a large quantity of fertilising material to the soil. This factor must be borne in mind when assessing the profitability of livestock.

There is not so sharp a division between breeding and feeding in the case of pigs; nor does pig-raising demand such particular natural conditions. They can be kept almost anywhere, irrespective of soil or climate. There are, however, two or three types of country where pig production is specially important. These are areas near centres of population (such as Middlesex and Surrey) where large quantities of scraps and waste are easily available; the arable counties of East Anglia where poor quality grain and surplus potatoes can be fed to pigs; and the dairying regions of the West where skimmed milk or whey is available as a by-product.[1] In addition to cheap waste of various kinds, imported feedingstuffs are used for pigs; and the variations in their price affect the production of pork and bacon.[2]

Prices of fat stock fluctuate according to season. Generally speaking prices of fat cattle and sheep tend to fall in the summer and autumn. The feeder's margin—the amount he receives for his animals less what he has paid for them as store—is also subject to fairly regular seasonal fluctuation. It is highest in May and June and lowest in October and November—a reflection of the higher costs of winter feeding. Take for purposes of illustration a mont when prices are neither particularly high nor particularly low—February. In 1939 cattle (first quality) fetched 42/- a cwt at Bridgwater, 41/- at Cambridge, 39/6 at Carlisle, 42/6 at Exeter, 41/- at Hereford, 47/- at Ipswich, 43/- at Manchester and 42/- at Preston. Assuming an average weight of 10 cwt and omitting the subsidy, the feeders' margins were as follows:

	Selling prices February, 1939	Store prices September, 1938	Feeders' margins
Bridgwater	412/-	230/-	182/-
Cambridge	405/-	222/6	182/6
Crewe	437/-	261/-	176/-
Gloucester	397/-	230/-	133/-
Norwich	415/-	248/-	167/-
Preston	426/-	230/-	194/-
Truro	396/-	220/-	176/-

The figures are averages of the weekly quotations in the *Agricultural Market Report*.

An examination of pre-war costs in the North of England, where the farmers had to depend on their purchases of feedingstuffs, illustrates the high cost of winter feeding and emphasises the interdependence of cattle farming and the other branches. The Department of Agriculture at Leeds University made a study relating to 461 cattle during the winter and spring of 1937-8. The animals were fattened for

[1] See *Regional Types of British Agriculture*, edited J. Maxton, Chapter 1.
[2] See below, p. 115.

four months and the farmers were rewarded at the end by an average loss of 2/1 per beast.

The costs per animal per day were between 1/5 and 1/6—of which feeding accounted for 1/3—whereas the increase in value per day was only 10d. The cattle subsidy averaged $4\frac{3}{4}$d a day, and the loss was thus reduced to $2\frac{1}{2}$d to $2\frac{3}{4}$d a day. Only if the farmer was prepared to value the manure which the cattle provided as highly as that could he be said to have avoided a loss.

With these margins may be compared the figures for animals sold in September, 1938—bought as store in the previous spring and grass fed during the summer months.[1] Feeders complain of narrow margins in these grass fed animals.

	Selling price September, 1938	Store price April, 1938	Feeders' margins
Bridgwater	405/-	220/-	179/-
Cambridge	430/-	273/-	157/-
Carlisle	380/-	285/-	95/-
Chelmsford	430/-	285/-	145/-
Hereford	400/-	283/-	117/-
Shrewsbury	390/-	300/-	90/-

Or take for comparison the feeder's margin in the case of sheep. Taking the dressed carcase weight of a sheep as 55 lb the margins run as follows:

	Selling price	Store price five months before	Feeders' margins
Doncaster	48/4	37/-	11/4
Exeter	50/5	32/-	18/5
Gloucester	48/1	30/-	18/1
Ipswich	50/5	35/-	15/5
Shrewsbury	47/-	31/-	16/-
York	48/1	34/-	14/1

The Marketing of Livestock

When the farmer had fattened his cattle or sheep and wished to dispose of them there were before the war several alternatives open to him. He might sell an animal on the farm to a local butcher or a dealer, he might take it to market

[1] Taken from *Agricultural Market Report*.

where again the local butchers and dealers would be the buyers, or he might retain an interest in the meat much longer and send his animals to the wholesale market for sale to a carcase butcher or to be disposed of when slaughtered to a wholesaler.

Of these methods of sale the most common was by auction in a local market. These markets were some 1,300 in number [1] and were particularly numerous in the South West. Most of them grew up when transport facilities were very poor; and, although there has been some tendency since the last war to collect cattle from over a larger area together in one market (as, for example, in that run by Midland Marts, Ltd, at Banbury, which draws livestock from a number of counties) the scale of marketing was still generally small. In many cases the principal buyers would be men doing a local trade, either as butchers slaughtering cattle for the retail trade in the district or as dealers catering indirectly for that trade. Since their requirements were fairly regular and did not vary much with the price they had to pay the farmer found himself in a weak position if rather more than the usual amount of livestock was being offered on a particular day. Then he must either dispose of his livestock at a lower price than he had anticipated to a dealer who proposed to resell either alive or dead in a larger market at a distance, or he must refuse to sell and go to the trouble and expense of carting his animals away to try again at another market or on another day. Moreover there were constant complaints that the dealers in those markets where they predominated formed agreements among themselves not to buy at more than a certain price. Certainly it seems true to say that in view of the size of the local markets and of the expenses of 'repitching' their livestock—that is, taking it to one market after another to get a satisfactory price—farmers were in a weak position.

Since the autumn of 1934 the producer received a direct subsidy from the government for all fat cattle sold. The rates were modified in the middle of 1937 and until the outbreak of war stood as follows :

[1] *Linlithgow Report*, 1923.

	Subsidy per cwt live weight	
	Quality standard	Ordinary standard
Home bred	7/6	5/-
Imported	5/-	2/6

Among the qualifications for subsidy at the lower rate was a killing out percentage of 54%; and for the higher rate a percentage of 57%. In all 34% of home bred and 52% of imported cattle received the quality payment.[1]

The whole of the subsidy, however, did not go to benefit the farmer. The introduction of it was followed by a sharp fall in prices (although not to the full extent of the government payment). Addison, drawing attention to this, calculates that between autumn 1934 and summer 1937 the farmers received the benefit of no more than £4 million of the £10½ million spent by the government, while the rest had gone to ' other participants in the existing distribution system ',[2] who received auction charges, dealers' commissions and other payments which amounted in the aggregate to a substantial part of the distributive cost.

Parts IV, V, and VI of the 1937 Livestock Act dealt with the situation in the local markets. This Act established an independent Commission appointed by the Minister of Agriculture which was to keep the production, marketing and sale of livestock under review. No new markets might be opened without the Commission's approval and no premises not used as a livestock market during the year ended 30th November, 1936, might henceforth be used for that purpose unless approved by the Commission. Further, the Minister might on the advice of the Commission specify the markets which may be held in a particular area, and so close any which were redundant (the markets which benefited by such an order must contribute to a fund to compensate those who had businesses in the markets which were closed). Finally, the Commission might make bylaws to regulate the conduct of livestock auctions, applying to all auctions or to any specifically designated.

[1] See *Agricultural Register*, 1937–8, pp. 60–2.
[2] See Addison, *A Policy for British Agriculture*, pp. 127–8.

Since local markets had such disadvantages it is strange that more farmers did not seek to dispose of their cattle direct to the wholesale market. Especially was this surprising since there existed an arrangement at a number of large markets (including those at Smithfield, Birmingham, Liverpool, Leeds, Sheffield and Manchester) whereby a farmer could get into touch with a government official and receive through him a quotation from the wholesale buyers for the livestock which he had to sell. This inquiry carried no obligation with it; if the farmer did not think the price good enough he kept the animals and did not waste time or money by his negotiations. If, however, he decided to sell, the stock was despatched direct, was graded by the official after slaughter and the farmer received the cheque without having to make any payments except on account of transport. Prior to the war only some 3% of the livestock in the country was sold in this way. More frequently the farmer who retained his interest in the animals until they were sold, alive or dead, to a wholesale butcher, dealt through a commission agent in the larger market. In that case the farmer must pay transport and commission as well as bear the risk of getting a bad price.

These charges per head varied as follows [1]:

	Cattle	Sheep	Pigs
Transport	3/- for 20 miles, then 1/3 for 10 miles, gradually decreasing to less than 1/-.	8d for 20 miles, then 4d for 10 miles, gradually decreasing to less than 2d.	10d for 20 miles, then 5d for 10 miles, gradually decreasing to just over 1d.
Dealer's Commission	7/6	1/-	—

There were, it is clear, a variety of ways of marketing and distributing livestock; but one stage all animals passing from the farmer to the consumer must go through—they must all be slaughtered. Slaughtering is important from the economic point of view because it involves getting the animals to a particular place equipped for slaughtering and the use of the special skill of the slaughterman. Moreover,

[1] Based on information in the *Linlithgow Report*.

it is at this stage that the offals which account for an appreciable part of the total value of the animal are made available. The facilities for slaughtering in an economical and hygienic manner and for collecting and utilising the by-products are therefore of very considerable importance in the distribution of meat.

The dressed carcase weight of cattle averages about 52% of the live weight and that of sheep about 55%. There are, however, very considerable variations in the percentages in the case of different carcases according to the build and feeding of the animal. Thus sheep may kill out at anything from 42 to 64% of the live weight; and in the case of lambs the killing out percentage is occasionally higher still.

Until the Government took control at the beginning of 1940 some slaughtering was still done by retail butchers who killed in their own slaughterhouses animals which they had bought in the local market; in other cases it was done at or near the wholesale market, and in the case of bacon pigs, at the factory. There were some 16,000 slaughterhouses in England and Wales. Of these only just over 100 were under public control—owned by local authorities—but more than a quarter of the slaughtering was done in them. The private slaughterhouses, mostly in the hands of dealer slaughtermen or small retail butchers, had an average throughput of not more than ten animals a week (although the private abattoirs operated, for example, by cooperative societies were very large).[1] The public slaughterhouses were on the average far larger, and served the populations of the larger towns. Twelve of them had a throughput of more than 1,000 head a week.

The slaughtering of livestock in thousands of small and mostly unregulated slaughterhouses—subject only to inspection in the interests of public health—contrasted with the carefully organised and large scale packing houses abroad, particularly in those countries which do a large export trade in meat. The United States packing houses, for example, usually

[1] This account of slaughtering facilities is based upon the *Report of the Committee on the Slaughtering of Livestock* (*Economic Advisory Council*), 1933. According to the Livestock Commission the situation has not materially altered since then.

handle each day 1,000 head of cattle together with large numbers of sheep; and particular attention is given to the utilisation of by-products. Most of the meat supply naturally passes through Chicago, situated between the grazing lands of the West and the consuming areas of the East; the methods used there cannot be carried over without modification to England where the supply is smaller and the geographical layout different. But nevertheless the Committee on the Slaughtering of Livestock drew attention to the waste which resulted from the large number of small slaughterhouses. Not only were the overheads and operating expenses heavy, but the small scale of British arrangements prevented full use being made of offals.

The cost per beast in a small private slaughterhouse was reckoned by the Committee to be 15/-, whereas the cost in a municipal slaughterhouse was 13/-. These costs were made up roughly as follows [1]:

	s	d
Lairage (one day)		8
Use of slaughterhouse	3	10
Killing and dressing	4	6
Use of chill room (one day)	4	0
Total	13	0

The Committee calculated that the loss by failure to utilise offals was between 10/6 and 12/- a beast. 40% of the hides, for example, were classed as 'seconds' and so fetched 5/- less because of inadequate treatment in the slaughterhouse; at the same time the extra cost of their collection from small slaughterhouses amounted to about 1/- or 1/6 each. Cost of collection again meant that the small butcher got ½d per lb less for the fat from the beasts than did the man who used a municipal slaughterhouse; this would mean an appreciable difference in total return, since the fat on the beast is probably between 50 and 70 lb.

[1] Municipal abattoirs are frequently subsidised from the rates, so that the charges made for the various services may well be below cost. The Committee after examination of various public slaughterhouses estimated the total charges actually made to amount to 10/3¼ per beast.

Lastly, the small butcher may get very little for rops and blood, although their value together is between 2/6 and 3/- per animal.

Although the abattoirs maintained by the local authorities were on a larger scale and more economical than the private slaughterhouses, they were more expensive than the American packing houses. For they were only public enterprises in the sense that the municipality erected them. Apart from inspection in the interests of public health it does not control the slaughtering or the disposal of offals. The farmer or butcher used the slaughterhouse when he pleased within the hours of opening—so that the throughput was irregular, more capacity had to be maintained than would be necessary if the killing were regulated, and many of the disadvantages of the private slaughterhouses continued—it quite frequently happened that 70% of the stock was killed on two days of the week because of the needs of retailers. This concentration of killing was uneconomic and wasted both space and labour.[1]

The Livestock Industry Act, in addition to providing for the payment of the cattle subsidy and for making markets orders, gave to the Livestock Commission power to encourage by grant and loan the establishment of three large experimental slaughterhouses.

The purpose of these was stated by the Minister to be to find out how far the technique of the meat packing houses of America is applicable to British conditions. All existing slaughterhouses within a specified radius might be either closed or controlled as soon as the experimental period began—so that an economic throughput for the central slaughterhouse was ensured. The essential difference between the slaughterhouses proposed and the ones which already existed was that

> All the operations at the slaughterhouse, from the time of the reception of the stock at the entrance to the lairages until the finished products are delivered from the slaughterhouse premises, should be under the *sole control* of the slaughterhouse authority. It follows that the owners of stock or their employees would not

[1] Livestock Commission, *Advisory Leaflet No. 2*, Memo (2), para. 15.

be allowed to take part in the actual operations inside the slaughter-house.[1]

Large wholesale butchers were already able to slaughter comparatively cheaply because they took more care with offals and because they had a sufficiently large throughput to employ a gang of men who divide the operations of slaughtering between them. This is a skilled job, and it is a considerable advantage to be able to divide it up among four or five men, each of whom specialises in the particular operations allotted to him. Even the scale on which these wholesalers worked was, however, scarcely large enough for all by-products to be economically utilised.

Imported Supplies

More than half the supplies of meat absorbed by the United Kingdom market was brought from overseas. In 1938 the sources of supply of the principal classes of imported meat were as follows:

Beef	Chilled	Frozen	Boned
Australia	534	1,191	467
New Zealand	361	207	336
Other British countries	110	1	24
Brazil	517	4	33
Uruguay	558	72	14
Argentina	6,881	158	38
Other foreign countries	—	—	—
Total	8,962	1,634	913

Chilled Mutton and Lamb	Mutton	Lamb
Australia	367	1,532
New Zealand	1,015	2,661
Other British countries	3	7
Chile	97	99
Uruguay	24	148
Argentina	99	795
Other foreign countries	1	43
Total	1,605	5,284

[1] Livestock Commission, *Advisory Leaflet No.* 2, Memo (2), paras. 3 and 4.

Pork	Fresh	Frozen
Eire	37	—
Australia	—	284
New Zealand	—	577
Other British countries	—	8
United States	—	62
Argentine	—	239
Other foreign countries	—	10
Total	37	1,181

Figures in 000 cwt—adjusted to the nearest thousand. From this adjustment arise certain small discrepancies in totals.

Meat imports were subject before the present war to careful quantitative control. They were on the 'free list' in the Import Duties Act of 1932; but the Ottawa Agreements Act of the following year gave power to the Board of Trade to regulate the imports of meat (and of other commodities) by order—subject to certain conditions laid down at the Ottawa Conference. These conditions were intended to reduce foreign supplies and to limit the expansion of Empire shipments to the United Kingdom. To quote the Agricultural Register 'they contain the nucleus of the Government policy of raising prices by supply restriction'. Chilled beef supplies from foreign countries were to be stabilised at the quantity which came in during 1931-2 ('the Ottawa year') while imports of frozen beef and mutton in successive periods of three months were to be limited to a decreasing percentage of the imports during the corresponding quarter of the same year. By the second quarter of 1934 the supply of foreign frozen meat brought in was to be no more than 65% of supplies in the corresponding quarter of 1932.

At the same time that foreign supplies were being cut down so drastically the Dominions undertook to impose a voluntary limit on their shipments to the United Kingdom. As a result, imports of chilled meat fell off as compared with 1929-1931, but on the other hand imports of frozen meat grew appreciably greater by the beginning of the war.

In 1937 the form of quantitative regulation of beef imports which had existed until then—that is to say, regulation by order of the Board of Trade after consultation with the Ministry of Agriculture—was replaced as far as beef was concerned by control through an International Beef Conference. This Conference consists of members nominated by the governments participating—Argentina, Brazil, Eire, New Zealand and Uruguay. The interests of the producers in Canada, South Africa, Southern Rhodesia and Bechuanaland are watched by the United Kingdom Government. The Conference is supposed to adjust supply to demand and can make recommendations about the total quantities of beef to be exported to the United Kingdom and the share to be provided by different countries. The Conference must take into account the complicated trade agreements between the United Kingdom and the beef producing countries—thus for example it may limit the imports of frozen beef from the Dominions but must not check the growing trade in chilled beef from Australia and New Zealand. Moreover, its decisions must be unanimous; otherwise the United Kingdom may resume the right to regulate beef imports. As a result of the conference activities wholesale prices of imported meat were definitely higher in 1937 than in 1936; and prices the following year showed on the whole a further rise.[1]

Meanwhile imports of mutton and lamb from foreign countries continued to be limited under the Ottawa Agreements Act and from Empire sources in accordance with agreements made from time to time with Dominion governments.

South America

The most important source of supply of meat apart from the Dominions is Argentina—which sent three-quarters of the United Kingdom's supplies of chilled beef in 1938. The Anglo Argentine Trade Agreement in 1936 guaranteed to Argentina a minimum quantity based on imports in 1935. These could be reduced by 2% in any of the three years 1937-9 and by up to 5% in 1939. The trade in imported meat is, however, not regulated only by legislation. It is

[1] See Average Quarterly Prices quoted in the Reports of the Superintendent of Central Markets for 1937 and 1938.

a highly organised trade concentrated in the hands of a comparatively few firms which are accustomed to act together a great deal.

The trade arose after the development of refrigeration, which made available livestock from the plains of America and Australia to the consumer in the United Kingdom. The first consignment of refrigerated meat came from the United States in 1874. South America began to send supplies in 1878 and Australia in the following year. The big American packing companies, which had already established Chicago as a packing centre and built up a sales organisation in their own country, were not satisfied with the service which they got from agents in Britain and set about establishing machinery for getting their product direct to the British consumer. As a result there has grown up in the course of half a century the enormous Union Cold Storage group. Associated with this, linked in one way or another to Vestey Bros and Union Cold Storage Co, are dozens of firms in all branches of the trade. Wholesalers' companies, packing companies, transport contractors, margarine firms, ice and ice cream firms, and proprietary food concerns are all included in the group; and so are retailing firms which control at least 2,000 shops.[1] The group has a very large share of the trade between Britain and Argentina and is also interested in the trade with Australia.

The Anglo Argentine trade differs in a number of respects from that between Britain and Australia or New Zealand. It is more highly organised—six companies have the lion's share.[2] These importing companies—Union Cold Storage, Armours, Sansenina, Smithfield and Argentine Meat Co, Swifts and Wilson Meats Ltd—handle 85% of the trade directly; and each of these companies is closely linked with the exporting agency in Argentina whose meat it handles. Thus, to take one example, the Union Cold Storage

---

[1] Among the firms in the Vestey group are Weddel Beef Co Ltd, Pure Ice Co Ltd, Eldorado Ice Cream Co Ltd, Union Cold Storage Co Ltd, Union Cartage Co Ltd, B. and A. Meat Co Ltd, British Beef Co Ltd, Eastmans Ltd.

[2] The trade was investigated by a Committee of Inquiry on whose report this account is based (Joint Committee of Inquiry into the Anglo Argentine Meat Trade, 1938).

Co (who import to Britain through their subsidiary the British and Argentine Meat Co) actually control the packing house—Frigorifico Anglo—from which the British and Argentine draws its supplies.

The packing companies have an aggregate capacity far in excess of the annual export of Argentina, and the six importing companies cooperate to regulate the supply of meat which they will bring on to the British market. They combine in the South American Meat Importers Freight Committee to reserve shipping space and divide up this reserved space among themselves in agreed proportions. U.C.S., Armours and Swifts have about a quarter of this space each.

This position has been made permanent by the policy of the British Government. Under the Ottawa legislation those engaged in importing meat from foreign countries were licensed and asked to limit the total imports to the quantities fixed by the Board of Trade. This confined the Anglo Argentine trade to those who were already in it; but the arrangement was modified by a clause to the effect that if the Argentine Government or the Argentine producers sought to export meat for the purpose of regulating the trade, the Government of the United Kingdom would be prepared to license importers to deal with such meat up to 15% of the total imports from Argentina. Already there were two small importing firms drawing supplies from two small packing works which were reckoned to account for part of this 15%; in the following year a cooperative Corporacion Argentina de Productores de Carnes was set up by the Argentine producers, who saw how well maintained the profits of the packing and exporting companies were, and did not feel that they were getting a square deal. This Corporacion dealt with three companies importing meat into the United Kingdom. One of them was the CWS; the others were two of the six big importing companies— the Sansenina and the Smithfield and Argentine.[1]

---

[1] Thus these two companies handle 5% of the trade in addition to that which they and the four other large firms control directly.

The six companies, which have an aggregate of 90% of the trade, are clearly in a very strong position. They buy meat from the producer and distribute it in Britain by rail and van to their own depots in the provinces or on the wholesale markets. Some of the meat passes through the hands of wholesalers, but most of it is sold by the company direct to the retailer or—in the case of the U.C.S. organisation —to the housewife. Having acquired the habit of cooperation as far as freights were concerned, the companies showed an unwillingness to compete with one another in buying meat in the Argentine. In the words of the Committee of Inquiry :

> It seems to be fairly clear from this evidence that whether or not there is a formal agreement among the Frigorificos that they will not compete against each other, such competition does not normally exist in practice.

At the same time they were very unwilling to allow the representatives of the Joint Committee to examine their books—which led the Committee to comment upon the fact that a trade so important to two countries should be

> in the power of half a dozen private concerns which are so jealous of their rights to conduct their operations with freedom and secrecy that they have refused to cooperate in this inquiry which was set up for public purposes by the two Governments....
> The whole of the operations have now been brought to a high degree of standardisation and efficiency, so that the scope and need for inventive improvement is greatly reduced. Working arrangements as between the various companies have in practice lessened the element of competition, while for independent reasons of public policy, a system of government regulation has, as already explained, been imposed upon the trade and thereby incidentally conferred an additional measure of security on those who are licensed to conduct it.

Such information as the Committee was able to get about the costs and margins of the trade may be summarised as follows :

	Pence per lb
Purchase cost of chilled steers	2·9111
Allowance for killing floor transfers	·0375
	2·9486
Less sales of by-products	0·6516
	2·2970

Allowance for loss—condemned meat	·0108
Packing costs (including overheads)	·3786
Allowance for shrinkage	·0644
	0·4538
F.o.b. cost therefore	2·7508
Marine freight and insurance	·6307
Bank charges	·0091
Dock and landing charges	·0653
Distribution	·1628
Storage	·0161
Selling expenses	·1382
Post f.o.b.	1·0222
Total costs in pence per lb	3·7730

Pence per lb

On the other hand the realisation value per lb sold was reckoned to be 4·5404d and, making allowance for freezing down of chilled beef and for the loss of a small quantity through condemnation, 4·5373d. Thus the profit margin per lb landed was ·7643d or, on the trade as a whole, on the basis of 1934 figures, £2,476,000.

Australia and New Zealand

The frozen meat from Australia and New Zealand is not in peace time unloaded on to the market in quite the same regular way as the supplies from South America. The South American companies, having booked certain space for which they must pay whether they use it or not, continue to send supplies regularly even at a temporary loss. Meat sent from Australia and New Zealand, however, is forwarded only after inquiries have been made in London and a price actually agreed between the agent of the packing company and the wholesaler. Indeed the meat is often not bought by the packing house from the farmer until a satisfactory price is assured for it on arrival in London. There are clearly considerable risks involved in business done in this way; the meat which is ordered at a certain price in September will not arrive in London until November and by then the price may have slumped.

Supplies from New Zealand are regulated by the New Zealand Meat Producers Board set up in 1922, which not only seeks by means of prizes and competitions to improve the quality of meat produced, but also regulates the shipments

MEAT

to the principal market—the United Kingdom—and advertises New Zealand products there. The Board is a cooperative organisation controlled by representatives of the farmers and of the freezing works (some of which are themselves under cooperative control). The year ending June 1938 was marked by a rush of stock into the killing works in the early months, and the Board had a difficult time gauging the amount which the United Kingdom market could take. The Annual Report gives an indication of the factors which have to be taken into account:

> A season such as the one just experienced severely tests out the refrigerated store capacity of freezing works. It also tests out the Board's machinery in its work of spreading shipments to feed the market. That it can claim success in this work is shown by the fact that at no time during the year has there been an excess of New Zealand lamb supplies in store in the United Kingdom, and the course of market prices has remained very steady.... In arranging shipping tonnage, the distribution of supplies over as wide a geographical area as possible in Great Britain has to be given careful consideration. Whilst London remains the greatest consuming area great care must be exercised to avoid overloading this market and to cater for other centres having regard to their capacity.[1]

The prices which producers receive generally tend to fall as the season progresses. Thus lamb may stand at 8d–8·5d per lb in November and 6d–6·75d the following March.[2] For cattle the price is probably between 3·9 and 4·8d per lb.[2] The producer is paid on the frozen weights and the buyer takes the skin and offals as a matter of course. Figures are not available of the realisation value of the offals, but 3/– to 7/– will be paid for the skin according to market conditions.

	Killing, freezing, or chilling and putting on board (pence per lb)	Freight to U.K. (pence per lb)
Lamb	0·600	·929
Mutton	0·500	·793
Chilled beef	0·675	·750 (approx.)
Frozen beef	0·650	·645
Frozen beef (boned)	1·075	·645

[1] New Zealand Meat Producers' Board, Annual Report for year ended 30th June 1938.   [2] 1938–9 season prices.

Thus in normal times the price paid to the farmer, the costs of slaughter and freezing and the freight charges are all larger than is the case with South American meat; but the acknowledged quality of New Zealand mutton and lamb enables it to command a higher price in the United Kingdom market.

The marketing of Australian meat is regulated in a similar way by an organisation of producers—although, as in the case of New Zealand, the actual export is controlled by packing companies. The packing companies, however, clearly do not dominate the trade between Britain and New Zealand or Australia as they do that between Britain and South America.

The Wholesale and Retail Trade

Before the war a great deal of the wholesaling of meat in the United Kingdom took place in London. Smithfield fulfilled the function of a meat exchange of international importance; and in addition was the most highly developed wholesale meat market in the country. It grew up, however, to deal with imported supplies of dead meat, and the percentage of the home killed trade which passes through it is still comparatively small. In 1937 less than 7% of the beef and veal produced in Great Britain passed through Smithfield; and this home-produced meat accounted for only 15% of the total amount of beef and veal handled in the market.

Wholesaling is carried on in a number of provincial centres as well. It has been suggested that a wholesale market must serve a population of half a million to be successful; Smithfield served directly retailers providing meat for some ten million people and in addition it had national functions. Run in conjunction with the market was the abattoir in Islington—the only public abattoir in the Metropolitan area and associated with it Islington Market—almost exclusively confined to livestock.

Smithfield was a field of operations for merchants of several types. Some used to buy and sell meat on commission —the usual charge was 4d per 8 lb. Others acted as principals, buying from the farmer or the dealer and selling to the retailer. Others again—the jobbers—bought whole carcases and cut them up for resale to retailers doing a particular specialised trade and hence unable to use entire carcases economically. In addition the large firms importing refrigerated meat from South America had their depots in Smithfield and in the main provincial markets.

Smithfield itself is well planned and adequate in size—particularly by contrast with the London wholesale markets for other foodstuffs. It is calculated that the cost of market facilities to salesmen was about 8/7 per ton of produce handled. In addition the charge for porterage on arrival at the market was about 3/7 per ton.

The strike of Smithfield porters early in 1936 led to the use of an emergency organisation for distribution of supplies through suburban depots; and so inevitably gave rise to discussion of the possibility of eliminating the central market altogether. It seemed that many of the functions now performed by Smithfield could be performed as well by the proposed smaller centres situated in the suburbs. ' To ask whether Smithfield *can* be bypassed is a futile question; it *was* in the recent crisis bypassed with only slight inconvenience to the retail trade '—that was the verdict of a contributor to one trade paper.[1] It was the general feeling in the trade, he went on, that nevertheless Smithfield had an essential function to perform—particularly as the field of operations of the jobbers upon whom the smaller retailers have come to rely.[2] These jobbers could not set up suburban depots—they would not be able to dispose of all the various parts into which they cut the carcases unless they catered for a large population among which the demand was varied and not exclusively for either high or low priced cuts.

These arguments are scarcely conclusive; if it were a question of replacing Smithfield by eight or ten suburban

---

[1] *Modern Meat Marketing*, 1936.
[2] ' Every small butcher to-day is a specialist,' said one jobber; that is where he is able to hold his own against the Cooperative Society and the multiple shops. . . . He finds that the jobbers at Smithfield are best able to satisfy his requirements; he can go from stand to stand and skewer or reject at will. If he requires 50 legs of lamb he does not have to buy 25 carcases to get them.'

depots each would serve a population of at least a million sufficiently varied in its social composition, and so in its demand for meat, to enable any jobber to carry on economically. On the other hand, the economies which it should be possible to make by lower market rents and more direct consignment (in the strike one importing firm found that meat sold from a suburban depot returned a saving of 10/- a ton compared with Smithfield returns)[1] suggest a strong case for some decentralisation of meat wholesaling.

Both home produced and imported meat are handled in the wholesale market. Despite freights the prices of the imported supplies were in peace time lower, as is illustrated by these average figures at Smithfield for the four quarters of 1938:

	March quarter		June quarter		September quarter		December quarter	
	s	d	s	d	s	d	s	d
Beef								
Scotch long sides	5	6	5	7	5	5	5	1
English long sides	5	2	5	1	4	9	4	5
Argentine chilled hind-quarters	4	5	4	4	4	5	4	6
Australian chilled hind-quarters	3	10	3	4	3	7	4	1
New Zealand chilled hind-quarters	3	10	3	7	3	10	4	1
Australian frozen hind-quarters	3	0	3	1	2	11	3	0
Mutton								
English	5	3	5	2	4	9	4	6
New Zealand wethers	3	6	3	5	3	5	3	3
Australian	2	11	2	11	2	8	2	7
Lamb								
English	8	9	7	5	5	9	—	
New Zealand	5	0	5	2	5	1	5	2
Australian	4	9	4	9	4	9	5	0
Argentine	4	9	—		4	9	4	9

Prices per stone of 8 lb. Taken from the Report of the Central Markets Committee, 1938.

It is calculated that there are about 45–50,000 butchers' shops in Great Britain. Some 2,500 are connected with the Vestey interests; but most of the shops are independent concerns or branches of small businesses. If this estimate

[1] *Modern Meat Marketing*, 1936.

is approximately correct the average turnover must be about £85 per week.

Like other distributors of foodstuffs the butcher has changed his function. Originally, as his name suggests, he slaughtered the animals he sold to his customers; but as the supplies of imported meat increased in importance and the trade in home killed became more developed, the butcher became more and more a purveyor of carcases which he bought from the slaughterer or the wholesaler. Not more than 25% of the present day butchers, it has been authoritatively estimated, have the experience necessary to buy the animals they require on the hoof or to feed them themselves.[1] The butcher's skill now consists in cutting up in the most economical manner the sides which he buys and in displaying them effectively to get the best price.

The different parts of a side of beef or a carcase of mutton will sell at a wide range of prices per lb. This has always been the case; but in recent years the tendency has been for the gap between the highest and lowest priced cuts to widen. The butcher's profit depends upon charging sufficient for the cuts which are in greater demand to cover the lower cuts which are likely to be selling below the average price he paid for the whole carcase. Thus to allow a gross profit of $33\frac{1}{3}$% on a carcase of New Zealand lamb bought at 8d a lb the butcher will charge probably 1/3 per lb for legs, 1/2 for shoulder, 1/2 for loins, 1/1 for best end, 7d for neck and 4d for breast.[2] The exact proportions in which the carcase will be divided by an experienced butcher vary according to the total weight. A 32 lb lamb, for example, will probably be divided as follows [3]:

	lb	oz
Legs	9	0
Shoulders	7	0
Saddle	6	8
Neck	6	5
Breast	3	3

[1] Introduction to *Butchers' Selling Price Guide* published by *Modern Meat Marketing*.
[2] Based on *Butchers' Selling Price Guide*, published 1936.
[3] Ministry of Agriculture Economic Series, *Report on Marketing of Sheep, Mutton and Lamb*.

At the prices quoted above such a division would mean that some 30% of the carcase was sold below cost.

The retail meat trade has been the subject of two inquiries by the Food Council.[1] The results of these inquiries suggest that the profits of retail butchers rose sharply after the last war and have varied a good deal from time to time. The Royal Commission on Food Prices stated in 1925 that 'London butchers, judging by the accounts submitted... had doubled their money incomes since before the war'. The control of prices during the last war had benefited meat retailers and the favourable position had been maintained after 1918; moreover, there was less competition between butchers since the number of their shops, at any rate in England and Wales, barely kept pace with growth of population. After 1925 conditions were still better; wholesale prices were falling and the retail margin increasing. 1927 seems to have been the butchers' best year; but after that wholesale prices again rose. Over the period 1925–9, moreover, the number of butchers' shops was increasing fast, and the general consequences of these changes are shown by these figures:

Year	Chilled or Frozen Beef			Home grown Beef			Home grown Mutton			Frozen Mutton		
	(a)	(b)	(c)	(a)	(b)	(c)	(a)	(b)	(c)	(a)	(b)	(c)
1924	5·5	7·9	2·4	9·8	13·8	4·0	13·4	15·6	2·2	7·7	8·8	1·1
1927	5·1	7·5	2·4	8·2	12·9	4·7	10·1	13·9	3·8	6·1	8·2	2·1
1929	6·3	8·1	1·8	9·1	13·0	3·9	11·0	14·1	3·1	6·4	8·5	2·1

(a) Wholesale price derived from Ministry of Agriculture average of prices in England.
(b) Retail price, derived from Ministry of Labour average.
(c) Excess of (b) over (a).
Figures in pence per lb.
Obviously these figures are of limited use in view of the seasonal variations in wholesale prices and in sales; but nevertheless they give a valuable general indication of the profitability of different lines at different times.

In 1926–7, when the retail meat business was good, the

---

[1] The Report of the first (Report 13) dated July, 1929, and that of the second (Report 33) dated February, 1939. Quotations in this and following paragraphs from the Report of the Linlithgow Commission and of the Royal Commission on Food Prices are taken from these reports of the Food Council.

Food Council made inquiries into profits which it summarised as follows:

Net profits after charging management costs or where necessary proprietors' allowance for management were earned at the following rates:

Private traders (less than 8 shops) . .	4·5% on sales
Limited companies (less than 8 shops) .	4·7% ,, ,,
Multiple shop firm (8 shops or more) . .	3·6% ,, ,,
Cooperative societies	11·7% ,, ,,

The gross margin was between 18 and 20% of sales, and the profit on capital in the case of the private traders whose capital was known was 51·1% (it was a good deal less—27 to 28% on capital—in the case of the limited companies and multiple shops) and on this evidence the Food Council concluded that in 1929, taking into account changes in price and in the number of shops since the figures were collected, 'the financial position of retail butchers has not only improved since before the (last) war but has improved out of proportion with the increase in the general cost of living.'

After that, it appears, butchers' net profits fell, partly because their expenses rose in common with the expenses of other retailers, while gross margins which rose in 1930–1932 were in 1939 not above the 1929 level. The Food Council in its report on the *Retail Meat Trade* published in 1939 points out that the number of butchers' bankruptcies had increased in the last four years when total bankruptcies were falling.

> There seems to be a general agreement that the demand for meat is concentrated to an ever increasing degree on the best joints and cuts,[1] while the cheaper cuts are frequently saleable only for manufacturing purposes at very low prices.

Wholesale prices of meat constantly fluctuate, but the tendency of the butcher is to keep retail prices as steady as possible in order to avoid disturbing consumption habits. Thus, as 1937 seems to have been generally regarded as

---

[1] Despite the fact that the cheaper cuts are often very good value for money and that the Ministry of Agriculture arranges for lectures to Women's Institutes etc., on the use which can be made of them.

a bad year for butchers, they felt justified in keeping up the retail margin in the early part of 1938 to such an extent that farmers' complaints forced an investigation by the Food Council. Gross retail margins in 1936–8 comparable with those already quoted for earlier years were as follows:

Year	Chilled or Frozen Beef			Home grown Beef			Home grown Mutton			Frozen Mutton		
	(a)	(b)	(c)	(a)	(b)	(c)	(a)	(b)	(c)	(a)	(b)	(c)
1936	4·6	6·5	1·9	6·7	10·2	3·5	8·7	11·2	2·5	5·0	6·8	1·8
1937	5·2	7·0	1·8	7·4	10·8	3·4	9·7	11·9	2·2	5·2	7·1	1·9
1938	5·5	7·3	1·8	7·7	11·2	3·5	7·8	11·8	4·0	5·0	7·3	2·3

(a) Average wholesale price. (b) Average retail price. (c) Excess of (b) over (a). The figures are in pence per lb.

The Food Council, after an examination of monthly figures, concluded that 'retail butchers appear to have taken advantage of the fall in sheep and lamb prices (i.e. wholesale prices) in the first half of 1938 to recoup themselves for any lack of profits in 1937'. On the whole, then, it seems that butchers' shops, whether they are independent undertakings or controlled by large importing interests, were fairly profitable, despite the increase in numbers. Butchers themselves point to increased overheads since 1914—the increase has been estimated at anything from 50 to 100%. Such figures as are available indicate that the amount of meat handled in a day by an assistant was not more than 75% of what it was before the last war. To some extent this is due to shorter hours; but to a far greater extent it is due to the expansion of delivery services. Examples can be quoted—and are apparently regarded as not out of the way—of delivery vans going on a 30 mile round (at a cost of 3d a mile) carrying £5 worth of meat. In such a case 7·5% of the retail price would be accounted for by the passage from the shop to the home. But at the same time that costs have increased profits have been on the whole well maintained—so that to get a pound of meat from the wholesale market to the housewife costs a great deal more than it did in 1914.

War Time Controls

After war broke out the Ministry of Food became the sole importer of meat. The Director of Imported Meats Supplies was the former London manager of the New Zealand Meat Board and his Assistant was a Director of the Weddel Beef Company.[1] The Ministry passed the supplies which it acquired to the consumer through the normal trade channels by an agency planned beforehand. This agency, which began operations in December 1939, was the Meat Importers National Defence Association, Ltd., formed by those who had previously been in the import trade. Total supplies were expected to be smaller than in peace and were to be allocated to traders on the basis of a datum period, which in this case was 1938. Each importer put up a nominal amount of capital for the company—based on his datum period quantity—and this determined the dividend payable even if the allocation of meat supplies was not always strictly proportionate to the division as between importers during the datum period.

The allocation of supplies to retailers even in the early months of the war did not always give satisfaction. For example, on 22 November a mass meeting of London butchers (called by the London Retail Meat Trade Association) showed itself in an indignant mood. On the outbreak of war Smithfield Market was decentralised to a number of depots in different parts of London; and through these the imported meat which sells to working class households was distributed to retailers. The Chairman of the protest meeting declared that

> the Association had been surprised to see how imported meat had found its way into multiple shops when the small retail butcher had had practically nothing.

The Ministry of Food had declared themselves satisfied that the multiples were drawing supplies from the same sources as the small man and on the same percentage basis—but the butchers' meeting greeted the report of this reply with incredulous jeers.

At the same time the Ministry of Food was seeking to

[1] Mr. H. Jones, a Director of W. Weddel, one of the Union Cold Storage Group.

regulate retail prices of meat. The formula adopted was that prices should not exceed the average of those ruling for various cuts during the week ending 25 August—despite rises in wholesale prices. A. V. Alexander, speaking in the House of Commons on 8 November, quoted a comparison between August and October prices.

> It shows that for English bullocks and heifers the wholesale price has been up by 8·6% to the butcher, for sheep and lambs 11·9%, for bacon pigs 7·5%, for Argentine chilled forequarters 5·9%, for Argentine chilled hinds 15·5%, for Australian lamb 5·3%, and for New Zealand lamb 25%.

He went on to reveal that whereas the Cooperative Wholesale Society normally made a profit of 10/- in handling a beast for the retail societies, recent transactions of which he had records showed average profits of £2/7/10 to £4/4/11 per animal.

As part of the government's agricultural programme a guaranteed price was promised; this was to be such as to ensure an average over the year of 1/- per lb for fat sheep, and was to come into effect when the Ministry of Food took control of the home market and purchased all livestock. Similar guaranteed prices for cattle, to vary with the killing out percentage and modified according to season, would be announced later. Pending the establishment of full control an order of the Ministry directed that as from 13 September all sales of fat cattle, calves, and sheep must be through livestock markets and not on farms. Maximum prices—10d per lb for sheep and 37/- to 48/- per cwt for cattle (according to killing out percentage) must be observed.

Almost at once, however, there were widespread complaints that the maximum price arrangement led to agreements between buyers to share the available supplies among themselves. From such agreements it was but a step to collective refusal to bid up to the maximum price; and there were complaints from various parts of the country that farmers were not even getting a price as high as the Government scale permitted. The withdrawal of these maximum prices was followed about the beginning of December by a general increase in prices paid to farmers.

So the position remained until in February, 1940, the Ministry of Food took over the control of home killed meat. The number of slaughter-houses used was reduced from 16,000 to 801, and the Ministry bought, at fixed published prices, all the livestock offered at the collecting centres. Farmers had to give twelve days' notice to the appropriate collecting centre of stock which they desired to sell. At the centre the animals were graded by a District Chairman of Auctioneers and a certifying authority consisting of an auctioneer, a farmer, and a butcher. The farmer and the butcher member of this authority were paid fees for each animal graded—3d per head for cattle, ¾d for sheep, and 1d for calves. All the tolls, weighing charges, and other expenses incurred in connection with marketing, collection, purchase, and dispatch of stock were covered by flat rate payments to an Auctioneers' Pool in each market. These were 6/- per head for cattle, 1/- for calves, 9d for sheep, and 1/6 for pigs.

The slaughtering in the restricted number of slaughter-houses through which the Ministry worked was done by contractors again at headage rates. These were normally to be as follows:—

Cattle	10/-
Calves (flayed and dressed)	3/-
Calves (gutted only)	1/-
Sheep and lambs	1/9
Pigs (up to 120 lb)	3/3
Pigs (over 120 lb)	4/-
Boars and sows	6/-

Further, the Ministry was responsible for getting the meat to the wholesale depots from the slaughter-house in the case of home killed and from the port in the case of imported meat. At this depot the meat is allocated by officials of the Ministry and the prices charged to retail butchers include delivery to their shops. Retailers have the option of performing this service themselves and so securing a rebate of ½d per lb on the price of meat.

Conclusions

The aggregate retail value of meat sold in 1936 was calculated as £118 million for beef and veal, £57 million for mutton and lamb and £116 million for pig meat including bacon.[1] If the gross return to British agriculture in respect of livestock is added to the value of imported meat at the time of its entry into the country the figures for the three classes of butchers meat listed above were over the same period £56 million, £41 million and £57 million respectively.[2] Thus by these very rough calculations distribution costs appear to account for some 50% of the retail cost in the case of beef, veal and pig meat, and more than 25% in the case of mutton and lamb.

It is not easy to sum up in a few words the peace time organisation of meat distribution, which is apparently to operate again when war conditions are at an end. There are several channels by which home produced meat may pass from the farm to the consumer, and the margins and profits of intermediaries vary from year to year. To take figures for the autumn of 1938, first quality cattle sold at about 38/- a cwt. Assuming an average weight of 10 cwt the buyer in the wholesale market would be paying just under 9d a lb.[3] The wholesale marketing costs amounted to about ¼d a lb. Average wholesale prices of English long sides at Smithfield in autumn 1938 were about 4/5 per stone of 8 lb. Not all the meat going to make up this average was first quality, so that probably 9d–9½d per lb represents the average that best quality beef was fetching. Sold to the butcher at that price the meat was retailed at an average of 11d to 1/1 per lb, although the prices of different cuts varied a good deal.

During the same period New Zealand producers were receiving 3½d–4d per lb (dressed carcase weight) for their sheep. The killing and freezing cost ½d per lb, and the freight to Britain just over ⅜d. New Zealand mutton was selling in Smithfield at about 5d per lb and so was retailed to the consumer at an average of 6d to 6¼d per lb. Again,

---

[1] Feavearyear's calculations.
[2] The calculated return to British agriculture does not include the livestock subsidy.
[3] Assuming a killing out percentage of 56 and costs of 15/- for slaughtering, 15–20/- for miscellaneous auction fees and commissions and 8–9/- for transport with a deduction for offals, the farmer has received about 7½d per lb dead weight.

of course, the prices charged for different cuts rose above or fell below the average.

The figures of consumption do not suggest that so large an increase in supply is required in the case of meat as of other foodstuffs. To make available to everyone an optimum diet would only require an increase of 12% or so in the supply of meat. There are no technical reasons why this increase—and a good deal more—should not in the course of time be met by maintaining larger herds on British pastures. Sir Frederick Keeble has calculated [1] that with full utilisation of nitrogen fertilisers British pastures could carry 67% more cattle during the summer than they can at present. Further, he pointed out that the land is not at present stocked to full capacity. The number of cattle on present pasture could be increased by 33% without any further fertilisation. Thus—if technical factors alone are taken into consideration—the cattle-carrying capacity of the present pastures could be increased by over 100%. Sir Frederick calculated that the cattle in the country could be increased to a corresponding extent within ten years. The increase in the sheep-carrying capacity would be rather less—a number of flocks are already pastured on the rough grazing land which it is proposed should be improved.

The tendency between the last war and the present one was for more grass fed cattle to be sold in comparison with yard fed sales; but nevertheless a substantial increase in the home produced meat supply would involve some additional winter feeding. Lord Addison quotes Sir Daniel Hall as saying that an acre of land under arable cultivation produces 256 lb of meat. Assuming that arable feedingstuffs would be required to produce the equivalent of half the increase in the supply of meat required, $2\frac{1}{2}$ million acres would have to come under the plough.

At the same time there should be no difficulty in improving the position of the home farmer and reducing the price of meat by marketing reform and economy in slaughtering. First there is room for economy in the trade in stores. It has been calculated that marketing by farmers' cooperative

---

[1] *Fertilisers and Food Production*, 1932.

associations which had arrangements with the railways would save £1–£2 per head on the transaction between breeder and feeder.[1] This would reduce the cost to about £1 per head. The main defect of the system—

> is that a proportion of the stock is repitched at half-way markets or at several terminal markets and that repitching must add to selling expenses and check the physical development of the stock even if it does not cause actual deterioration.[2]

In peace time conditions there are a variety of ways in which the livestock gets from the farmer to the consumer; and it might be unwise to attempt to impose upon the industry too rigid a uniformity of marketing and slaughtering. Meat for local requirements passes fairly directly to the consumer, and there is no reason why that trade should be altered to any great extent. What does require more examination is the case of the meat passing from the farm to the large consuming centres. At present this distributive process is costly—livestock are as often as not offered at one market after another, then taken by rail or road to the consuming centre, and have to bear the cost of slaughtering as well as agent's commission or dealer's profits. It should be possible to devise a more direct and economical method of marketing.

As described above, about 3% of the livestock was sent before the war direct from the farmer to the wholesaler on quotations offered via a government official.

> The Council of Agriculture in 1935 proposed the extension of this scheme and the formation of associations or groups of farmers as had already been done in Yorkshire and Wales so that they may appoint agents for the purpose of obtaining quotations from wholesalers through the official grader's office, and of subsequently arranging for the transport of the stock according as they are sold.

The costs incurred in marketing in this way are no more than the charge for transport of the animals to the market

---

[1] This is proposed in T. B. Wood and L. F. Newman, *Beef Production in Great Britain*, quoted in the Ministry of Agriculture Economic Series, No. 20.

[2] According to Ministry of Agriculture Economic Series, No. 20, *The Marketing of Cattle and Beef*.

plus slaughtering charges and a negligible contribution towards the salary of the official.

The Committee on the Slaughtering of Livestock in 1933 made out an effective case for centralised slaughtering. Economies, which have been reckoned by Lord Addison to amount to £2.3.4 per beast,[1] could be effected by the establishment of large scale abattoirs preferably under the control of farmers' cooperatives.[2] Before the war the provision was included in the Livestock Industry Act that three large experimental slaughterhouses with a monopoly within a given radius should be set up. Each of these was to be controlled by one authority and so was to be more than mere aggregation of private slaughter pens used when the owners pleased. Thus the fullest economies could be effected by regularity of working and utilisation of offals.

The Committee on the Slaughtering of Livestock opened its discussion of the problem of where to put the abattoirs as follows:

> In packing houses the net operating costs per head decrease as the scale of operation increases. But, as the size of the area served increases the cost of transport per head increases. The interaction of these two tendencies defines the area which may best be served by any slaughtering area.

What is more, it has to be decided whether generally speaking the centralised abattoirs should be put in the consuming or the producing areas. Surprisingly enough it is not easy to say whether it is cheaper to send livestock by road or rail than to send dead meat; there are a number of factors to be taken into consideration, and the Committee on Slaughtering regarded it as reasonable to assume that the costs were the same. If this assumption is made the Committee concluded that the slaughterhouses should be put up in the centres of consumption. The area which it

---

[1] Lord Addison, *A Policy for British Agriculture*. The saving could be effected by reduction of auction charges and commissions, avoidance of repitching and unnecessary movement of cattle and more efficient sale of by-products.

[2] As long ago as 1931 a Ministry of Agriculture Report (on the Marketing of Sheep Mutton and Lamb in England and Wales) concluded that 'it is certain that the marketing problems of the livestock industry cannot be completely solved until livestock producers as such are organised for marketing purposes'.

would be necessary to serve to secure an economic throughput would be smaller (since the consumption per square mile in a town would be likely to be larger than the production per square mile in the country) and so the costs of short distance transport for livestock and dead meat probably less. Moreover, since areas of winter feeding and summer feeding in this country do not generally coincide, whereas meat is eaten the whole year round, slaughterhouses set up in the consuming centres would have a more level monthly throughput than if they were in the areas of production.

A good deal of home killed meat is consumed, however, actually in the producing areas; only 5% of the British output of beef and veal in peace time went through Smithfield, and this suggests that the amount going to the wholesale markets serving the other large centres of population is not large.[1] Nevertheless the greater concentration of population in the consuming areas and the seasonal production of meat suggest that it would be better as a long term policy to locate the abattoirs in the larger towns and perhaps leave a large part of the slaughtering in the country areas in the hands of those who already undertake it.

The supply from New Zealand and Australia appears to be provided economically—at any rate in peace time; but the trade with South America is dominated by large importing companies whose operations are veiled in secrecy. There is no doubt that substantial profits are being made in this trade at the expense of the consumer and the overseas producer. The importing concerns could without much difficulty be taken over by the government; and pending that, strict regulation or taxation of profits should be imposed.

There remains the exceedingly difficult problem of the retail trade, where it should be possible to reduce costs. Control over slaughtering would probably steady the market and so prevent the short term fluctuations which, since they involve an element of risk for the retailer, have been held to

---

[1] Ministry of Agriculture Economic Series No. 19 states that in 1928 some 20,000 tons of home killed beef and veal passed through the wholesale market at Manchester, which serves a population of 4–5 million. This was about 4% of home production. See also the figures for Smithfield given above (p. 98).

account for some part of his high margin. The cooperative movement handles at present a very small part of the trade—less than 10% of the home killed meat and between 2 and 3% of the imported—so that it is not easy to envisage a solution of the problems of retail distribution along this line.

6 BACON

The bacon for breakfast habit seems to have been a well established one; since it persisted despite the steady rise in retail bacon prices which took place prior to the outbreak of war. Sir William Crawford, investigating family budgets in the winter of 1936–7, calculated that the consumption was as follows in working class families:

Income	Amount spent per head per week (pence)	Quantity purchased per week (ounces)
£250–£499	5·8	6·1
£125–£249	4·0	4·5
Family income under £125	2·8	3·6

One out of three families in the poorest group had bacon for breakfast.

The Merseyside Survey gives rather a similar indication of the popularity of bacon. The consumption of it increased with advancing economic prosperity. Even in the lowest group of all, with family incomes below £2 a week, three families in five managed to afford bacon. Since that survey, and even since Crawford's inquiry, the retail price of bacon rose, and it is likely that this reduced the consumption in working class households.

The Reorganisation Commission 1932

The prohibition of imports of fresh pork into this country in 1926 forced those countries which had previously sent pork to Britain to concentrate on bacon instead. The result was that, according to calculations for the year 1930, only one quarter of the British output of pig meat was sold as bacon. The fall of prices in the years before 1932, partly due to the depression, partly to the increase of imports from $9\frac{1}{2}$ million cwt in 1927–9 to 12 million cwt in 1932, led to a demand for an inquiry into the industry and for a revival based on restriction.

There were two sides to the industry which the Reorganisation Commission [1] came to examine in 1932—the farming side and the processing side, the farms and the factories. There were some 2½ million pigs in the country, but no one could be sure what quantity would be available for bacon at any particular time. There were two markets into which the pig farmer might sell his animals; and these two markets —one for pork and the other for bacon—were unconnected and alike unregulated. A really good pork pig differs in breeding and feeding from a really good bacon pig; but most farmers tended to produce an animal which could be sold in either market but was not ideal for either.

Again, pigs breed very fast—a sow may litter twice in a year and produce between seven and ten piglets in a litter. Pig production follows a cycle. Pigs are few and dear, feedingstuffs are cheap because the demand is slight, and as a result more farmers are attracted to pig raising and the numbers of pigs produced increases. As a result, feedingstuff prices rise and pig prices fall, and farmers decide to reduce their future output of pigs. They can do this, however, only by increasing the number of pigs which they put on to the market immediately. Not until this phase has passed do pigs fetch a good price again and farmers plan for a larger number. This cycle, which is complicated by a number of factors and is still the subject of controversy,[2] takes a period of four years.

The bacon curing was done in some 600 scattered factories. Many of them were small—half had a weekly throughput smaller than the economic minimum under English conditions. The larger ones complained of supplies which were often inadequate and always fluctuating. A medium sized factory, for example, might receive 350 pigs one week and 800 the next. Not only was plant left unused for part of the time, but large staffs had to be kept to cope with the occasional rushes. The Reorganisation Commission collected information about costs from one factory which showed

[1] The Reorganisation Commission for Pigs and Pig Products (England, Wales and Scotland). The chairman was Colonel Lane-Fox.
[2] See articles quoted in Astor and Rowntree: *British Agriculture, The Principles of Future Policy* (1939), p. 216.

that over a year's working the costs per cwt were 9/2 when the average kill was 684 per week and 7/9¼d when the average kill was 902. The average weekly throughput of many of the Danish factories was about 2,000, whereas half the British factories had a throughput of less than 500 pigs a week.

In addition it was doubtful whether pigs got to the market by the most direct route, and the consumer of home cured bacon had to bear the burden of all the expenses incurred in auction markets as well as profits, commissions and salaries of the factory agents and the dealers.[1]

The Commission therefore proposed an organisation of the bacon industry for the purpose of (1) increasing the pig population and the production of bacon and hams, (2) raising the price to the producer and improving the quality of pig production, (3) raising a steady supply which would enable the curers to work economically, (4) improving the marketing of pigs.

The Establishment of the Marketing Scheme

A Pigs Marketing Board and a Bacon Marketing Board were set up in July, 1933, and a Bacon Development Board in 1935. First a figure was to be taken for the total supply of bacon required annually. This was fixed in 1933 at 10,670,000 cwt [2] (although the consumption in the previous year had been 12 million cwt) and imports drastically cut so that no more than that total should be on the market. Total imports went down from 11 million cwt in 1931 to 6·6 million in 1936 while the imports from the Empire, which stood at less than half a million cwt in 1931, rose to 2·25 million by 1937. Home production, however, rose only from 1·6 million cwt (the estimated figure for 1930) to 2·4 million cwt in 1937. Thus the total supply of bacon available was considerably reduced in the course of six or seven years. With supplies from abroad restricted, prices went up, but quality was so often poor that many working

---

[1] This was based on the view of the Pig Industry Council.

[2] The estimate of supplies required has been raised a little in the course of the operation of the scheme. But the actual supply of bacon and hams (home production plus imports) has been below 9,800,000 cwt since 1932, and in 1936 was as low as 7,200,000 cwt.

class housewives, instead of taking cheaper bacon, gave up buying it altogether.

The method of organising home supply which was introduced was that of buying on contract by the curers. The producer contracted with a curer for the supply of a certain number of pigs within a given period (the first contract period lasted four months—from November, 1933, to February, 1934, inclusive). He was permitted to exceed the number by 5% or to fall short by the same percentage. Apart from this tolerance the producer was liable to a fine of £1 for each pig for which he had contracted which he failed to send. The payment the producer received varied, first, with the quality of the animal. There were four weight classes, the first three of which were divided into five grades according to fat measurement. The 'basic price' was that of a Class I Grade C pig, and bonuses and deductions determined the relative prices of pigs of other weights and fat measurement.[1]

In addition, however, there were the variations in the price of feedingstuffs to consider—for these must be taken into account if the farmer was to be assured of a price to cover his costs. The basic price was therefore to vary with the rise and fall of feedingstuffs. When the price of a standard ration of feedingstuffs was 7/6 per cwt the minimum basic price was to be 12/- per score—i.e. 67/- per cwt. From the prices which he contracted to pay the curer was entitled to deduct 1/5 per pig; of which 3d was for insurance and the balance went to the Pigs Marketing Board.

Although a price could be guaranteed to the farmer, it could not be guaranteed that the curer would be able to sell the bacon when it was cured. In fact the curers could not dispose of their supplies, despite the import restrictions, and they were involved in heavy losses for which they were compensated. Nor did the further restriction of imports secure the curers' markets; the consumer not able to afford Danish bacon and not liking the English that he got at the price did not buy bacon at all. The curers' losses could not

[1] The details of successive contracts can be found most conveniently in the Agricultural Register.

permanently be met from the loans to the Marketing Board; so in the second contract period the co-partnership system was introduced. The formulae which determined the price the farmer received were made still more elaborate; the retail price of bacon was introduced into the calculations and the farmer had to bear part of the losses of the curers.

This elaboration largely destroyed the point of the original formula; for it meant that the farmer was no longer guaranteed a price which covered his costs of production. In December 1934, when the contracts were being negotiated for the following year, farmers were very reluctant to promise their pigs. The prices of pork were rising, and there seemed to be better profits to be made outside the Bacon Scheme. No more than 1,670,000 pigs were contracted for, and the Bacon Marketing Board declined to proceed with the negotiations unless 450,000 more pigs were forthcoming. The Pigs Board thereupon had to invite farmers to enter into contracts on the same terms with the Board itself; such contracts would have the further advantage of making it possible to level up the supplies between different curers. A little over 200,000 more pigs were forthcoming, and the curers agreed to proceed—but a second supplementary contract had to be issued for the provision of further pigs after May. The required number, however, were not forthcoming; and the Pigs Marketing Board agreed that curers should buy in the open market.

Under the terms of the second contract the curer had to pay a flat rate of 1/8 for each pig which came to him under contract. An undertaking had been given that all pigs moved more than five miles would be transported, either by road or rail, by the railway companies. The contract terms for the year 1935—the third contract period—were still more complicated than had been the terms for the latter part of 1934. Producers were obliged to contract to deliver not less than 25% of their total number of contracted pigs within the months January to April, and not more than 45% in the months September to December. A bonus was to be paid on all pigs delivered in the first four months, the bonus to come from a fund to which curers contributed

2d for every pig delivered to them in the course of the year.

Negotiations for 1936 contracts began in the middle of 1935 and occupied three or four months. The agreement reached slightly improved the position of the pig producer. Again, however, too few pigs were offered, and the curers had to be permitted to buy in the open market. And the breakdown of the scheme was completed when an attempt was made to arrange terms for 1937. From the beginning of that year, in fact, buying in the open market had to be permitted. All that remained of the bacon scheme was the regulation that pigs for bacon purposes must be bought by registered curers from registered producers and must be graded in accordance with the measurements outlined in the contract now voided. The curer and producer were left to settle their own prices.

The Bacon Development Board

Meanwhile a further part of the machinery proposed by the 1932 Reorganisation Commission was set up in 1935—the Bacon Development Board. It had representatives of both producers and curers under an independent chairman; and its functions were to control factory construction and extension, regulate conditions of operation of factories, and carry out research and education. All curers who had been established before the Development Board came into existence had a right to a licence for two years. This period expired in the autumn of 1937; and the Development Board would thus have been within its powers in refusing to renew the licences of factories which it considered redundant or badly sited. Owing to the breakdown of the contract scheme, however, the Development Board renewed all licences for the year 1938.

This Development Board was the centre of the new organisation proposed by the Government and embodied in the Bacon Industry Act (1938). The Board was strengthened by the appointment of new independent members and was to devote much of its energies to the elimination of small and inefficient factories.

The basis of the new plan was a price for bacon guaranteed by the Exchequer. It was fixed as 94/9 per cwt, payable on an increasing quantity of home produced bacon each year up to a maximum of 2½ million cwt in the third year. By the end of this period it was hoped that the rationalisation of the curing side and the cheapening of production by eradicating disease would have gone so far that further government assistance would be unnecessary. The details of the plan allow for a reduction in the degree of assistance in the second and third year.

The price which was to be guaranteed to the farmer was 12/6 per score when the feeding ration cost 8/6 per cwt. For every 1/- that the feeding costs rose above 8/6, 10¾d was to be added to the guaranteed price. Producers might specify the curer to whom they wished their pigs to go, but if they were prepared to make an open contract not naming any curer, they were to be paid a bonus of 2/- per pig. In any case the pigs they sent might be allocated to another curer, in which case the producer received a bonus of 6d per pig.[1]

The method of regulating imports remained substantially the same. The estimate of the total amount which the British market could absorb was raised from 10,670,000 cwt to 10,818,000. The Pigs and Bacon Marketing Board were to make an estimate of the amount of this which would be provided from home sources. The rest was imported under a quota system operated by the Board of Trade. Each importing country was entitled to send a certain percentage of the total quantity to be imported. The largest share was provided by Denmark, which was entitled to send up to 64% or so of the total amount imported.

This new scheme, however, was no more successful than its predecessors. Feeding stuff prices were high, and as a consequence the number of pigs in the country was reduced in the autumn of 1938. The high prices which seemed to be in prospect and the lack of confidence in marketing

---

[1] The eagerness of the farmer to name his own curer is probably due to a desire to avoid having his pigs sent to a distant factory. The feeding and finishing of pigs is a skilled business, and they lose in value if, when they leave the farmer's hands, they are transported too far by rail or van.

schemes for bacon pigs made farmers chary of concluding elaborate twelve month contracts. The result was that the number of contracts concluded was smaller than on any previous occasion; and bacon pigs actually realised at 10/- to £1 a head more when sold in the open market than when disposed of through the scheme. The effect of this was that the curers were getting pigs well below market price and were, therefore, under the terms of the scheme, due to pay a fairly large sum to the Exchequer; they were, in fact, feeling the disadvantage of the guaranteed margin which the Government had offered them.

Effects of the Bacon Scheme

What has been the effect of the attempt at organising the bacon trade?

First, the pig population of Britain was increased from 3,370,000 in 1932 to 3,883,000 in 1937. The peak was reached in 1935, when the number of pigs was reckoned at 4,074,000.

Second, home produced bacon provided a larger percentage of the total consumption of the country.

TOTAL SUPPLY OF THE UNITED KINGDOM

	U.K. Output in cwt	Net Imports in cwt	Total Supply	Bacon put in Cure by Curers registered under Bacon Marketing Scheme in cwt
1932	1,760,000	11,998,000	13,758,000	—
1933	1,760,000	9,930,000	11,690,000	—
1934	2,230,000	8,365,000	10,595,000	1,736,000
1935	2,953,000	7,580,000	10,533,000	2,377,000
1936	3,590,000	6,537,000	10,127,000	2,757,000
1937	3,115,000	6,870,000	9,985,000	2,448,000
1938	3,236,000	6,800,000	10,036,000	2,517,000

Supplies of pigs certainly fluctuated less from month to month under the scheme. The Report on Marketing Schemes 1936 quotes index numbers of monthly variations in deliveries of pigs for the years 1934–6. The limits of variation were 151 : 53 in the first year, 129 : 72 in the second, 119 : 82 in the third.

The average of monthly prices per score of bacon pig was 11/11 in 1934, 11/1½d in 1935, and 11/5 in 1936. The price was higher in 1937; although it is not easy to get figures exactly comparable with those per score of basic pig in the years preceding.

Last, there was a considerable increase in the amount of tank curing in the country as opposed to dry curing. From the economic point of view the main difference between the two processes is that dry curing takes about 21 days, whereas tank curing takes 8–9. Since the same plant can with comparatively small alterations be used for either process, the total output of tank cured bacon which could be secured is a good deal larger than that of dry cured.

Retail prices rose steadily since 1932, as far as can be gathered from the Ministry of Labour Cost of Living figures. In these the following prices are quoted for bacon (per lb).

1932	1933	1934	1935	1936	1937	1938
10d	11½d	1/1¼	1/1¾	1/2¼	1/2⅜	1/3 5/17

At the same time very little appears to have been done to lower curers' margins. The number of factories actually increased. During 1937 the number of licences for the production of bacon increased from 770 to 819. This increase was due to an expansion of business on the part of small curers, who thus just came within the limits of the scheme. After that, however, there was a sharp fall in the number, and in March 1939 there were 582 curing units licensed by the Development Board. Eighty-eight of these were large, producing an average of more than 100 cwt a week, 241 had an output averaging less than 15 cwt a week, and the remaining 253 were medium sized. Altogether it was calculated that they could handle four million pigs a year.[1]

The main piece of organisation carried out on the curing side of the industry was the sales quota scheme—a restrictive device. Each registered curer was allotted a basic quota

---

[1] According to a statement on behalf of the Minister of Agriculture made in the House of Commons, 22 March 1939.

normally equal to one-half of his total output during two years ended November 1935. Then in any year the sales quota which a curer was allowed to sell was the same percentage of this basic quota as the aggregate amount all curers were allowed to sell was of the total of the basic quotas. The Bacon Marketing Board devised a system for regulating the quantity which any firm might market. It appears to be true to say that the average firm was just managing to get along, but the large curers who were able to work economically were making very good profits. The largest firm of all, Marsh and Baxters, which controls a number of other concerns and probably controls upwards of 40% of the total output of bacon, is a private company.

The price structure for first quality streaky bacon on the outbreak of war was something like this:

Price paid by consumer (1/4 a lb) .	149/4 cwt
Retailer's margin (25%) . . .	37/4
Therefore retailer pays the curer .	112/–
Of this the farmer receives between .	96/– and 104/–

A pig of liveweight 200 lb will produce a dressed carcase of just over 150 lb, and a carcase ready for curing of about 120 lb—or, allowing for shrinkage, about 1 cwt. The farmer got an allowance for insurance, but usually had to pay, it seems, 1/– out of 1/6 of the premium himself. In addition there would be a transport deduction of 2/3 per pig. The curer would get 9/– to 10/– for the offals of which he disposed, and so might reckon on a gross margin of 16/– up to 25/–. According to the Lane Fox Commission, the costs of dry curing even with a throughput of no more than 500 a week should not exceed 10/– a pig.

The Retail Trade in Bacon

As in the case of meat the tendency now is for the retailer of bacon to buy his supplies already cut into pieces although in addition he may purchase one or two sides for cutting himself. These pieces have to be sliced by machines into rashers and the amount of waste which arises in this way depends on the practice of the individual grocer. The methods of cutting followed by the wholesalers from whom the provision dealer buys may vary and so may the margin on which the wholesalers reckon to work, though it was probably 5 to 7% of turnover in most cases prior to the war. From these variations in the practice of wholesalers and retailers and from the fluctuations in demand for different cuts from month to month arose the difficulty of estimating the retail margin on bacon. It depended on the scale of the retailer concerned and upon the class of customers for whom he was catering as well as upon the time of year and method of dividing the side. To take an example on the basis of prices in the summer of 1939, when a side of Green Continental Bacon would cost the retailer about 94/- per cwt delivered to his premises. A side weighing 56 lb would therefore cost about 47/- and would realise about £2 14s 6d.

	Weight	Wastage	Saleable weight	Price per lb	Realisation
Back	16 lb	1½ lb	14½ lb	1/4	19/4
Hock	8 ,,	sold whole per lb.	as joint	at 8d	5/4
Collar	8 ,,	1 lb	7 lb	1/2	8/2
Streak (Flank included)	8 ,,	—	8 ,,	8½d	5/8
Gammon . . .	16 ,,	sold at of 1/-	an average per lb.	price	16/-
	56 lb				£2/14/6

Therefore a profit of 7/6 was made on a turnover of £2 14s 6d. This was approximately 14%.

This represents a low estimate of the retail margin and it should be noted that it includes little if any allowance for meat wasted because unsold. In some cases it would rise to 25% on turnover and 20% may be taken as a fairly common figure. But the margin, it must be emphasised again, was very variable, depending on a number of complicated factors. For example the retailer could sometimes make more money by cooking the gammon; but the demand for this is small at certain times of the year.

The Effects of the War

Changes likely to have permanent effect have been made in the bacon trade since war broke out. A new company, called the Bacon Importers National Defence Association and closely linked with the Ministry of Food, has come into existence. Such an organisation was planned by a committee of business men in the bacon import trade, working with the Food (Defence Plans) Department months before the war broke out. Under the scheme the Ministry of Food is the only importer of bacon—but relies for the distribution of it upon the firms established in the trade and consolidated in this Defence Association. The function of this organisation is to divide the stocks which are imported between the firms in the trade in proportion to the volume of business which they did before the war. There is a datum period for the trade as a whole and each importer is allocated by the Defence Association a share of the total amount of bacon brought into the country in proportion to the business done in that datum period. The total volume of imports has very materially diminished and the smaller firms have had to form themselves into groups in order to get representation on the Defence Association.

So far as the home bacon industry is concerned, a director of a firm of curers which is linked with Marsh and Baxters has been made Controller of Bacon Supplies.[1] In the early days of the war a definite price was fixed for pigs—13/- per score lb dead weight up to 200 lb. As *The Times* pointed out,

> The all-round price . . . fixed for pigs of all weights, porkers as well as baconers, is clearly intended to increase the nation's supply of pig meat by inducing the farmers to carry their pigs on to the bacon weight of about 150 lb rather than to sell them at the pork weight of 80 lb to 100 lb. Normally prices for bacon pigs are about 2/- per score less than pork prices.

This price was forced up subsequently by the pressure of the farmers, who were able to plead increasing costs as their justification. At the same time swift steps were taken towards

---

[1] J. F. Bodinnar, chairman of C. and T. Harris (Calne). He had been a prominent member of the Bacon Development Board before the war.

the rationalisation of the curing trade. It was announced that 'small curers' (that is, those curing on an average less than 15 cwt per week, later 5 cwt), who made up some two-fifths of the concerns in the trade, would be refused the necessary licence to cure bacon. Again under the full control scheme, it was announced, the farmer would be obliged to hand over his pigs at a Government or at a bacon factory which would be specified for him.

After only a few weeks of war the Ministry of Food took powers to requisition a proportion—which was sometimes as high as 50%—of the output of British bacon factories. This is distributed through the trade channels through which imported bacon normally passes. The reason which the Ministry gave for assuming this power was that an appearance of unfairness was being given by the greater abundance of home-produced bacon; for this meant considerable advantage to those traders who had formerly been accustomed to handle this rather than the imported.

Conclusions

The experiment in the organisation of the bacon trade prior to the war was a sad failure, and in suggesting any alternative there are various considerations to be kept in mind.

The nationalisation of the curing side of the industry and the closing of small factories should make it possible to reduce curing costs very considerably. The small curers are in fact being crushed out of existence at present in the interests of the large would-be monopolists. A nationalisation scheme should ensure them reasonable compensation and concentrate production in larger and more economic units. Denmark has set an example; most of her bacon is produced in factories with a throughput averaging 2,000 a week, and there seems to be no reason, provided that the factories were carefully sited, why most of British curing should not be done on a similarly large scale. The Reorganisation Commission quoted an estimate of a large bacon factory: with a kill of 2,500 a week it could produce a cwt of bacon at a cost of 5/1. It did not state whether this was dry cured or tank cured bacon; presumably it was the former, since very little tank cured bacon was being produced at that time. Thus, allowing 6d per cwt profit and 3/- per cwt for transport, and deducting 9/- realisation price of the offals, it should be possible to sell bacon wholesale at 100/- per cwt when the price of feeding stuffs stands at 8/6 per cwt. This would mean a retail price of about 130/-, or just about 1/1 per lb instead of the present figure.

The concentration of curing would make it possible to utilise offals more economically. At present costs of collection from the large number of small units are so high that a good deal is wasted. This is certainly the case with pigs' blood; and it is probably the case with much edible offal. The delicatessen trade is not developed on a large scale in this country (except to some extent in the North) as it is for the utilisation of such edible offal abroad. Again little use is made of gland offal, which, if it could be collected cheaply, would probably yield some return at present unrealised.

On the farm side there seems to be a good case for the regulation of marketing by an organisation resembling the Pigs Marketing Board. This would negotiate with the government representatives and so fix a guaranteed price related to the costs of production. Farmers would sell their pigs on contract to the Government. Bonuses and other inducements could be used, as under the Marketing Schemes, to secure level deliveries month by month.

There still remains the problem that the pork market is unregulated and supplies are liable to be diverted into that if prices are higher than in the bacon market. A good many of the difficulties, however, have been due to the fluctuation of the pig cycle; which would be very much affected by control of feedingstuff prices and guaranteed prices for baconers.

The raising of pigs for bacon is not closely linked with other branches of agriculture. For the most part pigs are fed on meals manufactured mainly from imported grain. ' If rationalisation were pushed to its logical conclusion we might formulate a picture of pig feeding carried on in large buildings adjacent to mills on the quaysides of our principal ports, where imported cereals would be passed from ship to mill to pig and out as bacon pig to curing factory in one continuous process.' In the Great War the pig population was expanded very rapidly, and pork was a regular standby for provisioning because pigs multiplied so rapidly. But if more tonnage is absorbed in bringing feedingstuffs for pigs than is saved by raising pigs in Britain there is no case on the ground of war needs for protecting and expanding the home bacon industry.

Perhaps the most important question of all, however, is that of quality. Apart from the very best Wiltshire bacon, the English product cannot compete successfully with the Danish. Here the process is likely to be slow; education on breeding and feeding alone can raise the general standard of English bacon. In the interim, however, the lower price which will be made possible by nationalisation of the curing factories should make it possible in peace time to increase consumption of bacon and to admit foreign bacon in larger quantities.

7 SEA FISH

In the past twenty years fried fish shops have increased in number and in respectability. Perhaps as much as 70% of the white fish of the country reached the consumer in this way before the war [1]; and in consequence it is exceedingly difficult to calculate the total retail value of fish consumed. Feavearyear puts it at £66 million (from which it is necessary to deduct £9–10 million on account of tinned fish). Sir William Crawford in *The People's Food* gives the following estimates of average weekly expenditure per head on fish in the lower income groups:

Family Income	Expenditure (in pence)
£250–£499	7·0
£125–£249	2·9
Under £125	2·3

His complete estimates of expenditure give a total of £40 million a year; but Crawford leaves out fish eaten in restaurants and fried fish shops (although he includes fried fish eaten at home). If £10 million are added to cover this the total is still well below Feavearyear's estimate.

How much of this £50 million goes to the fisherman? Feavearyear's figures relate to 1936 and Crawford's to the winter of 1936–7. During 1936 the value of fish brought by British or foreign ships direct to British ports was £16¼ million. £3,150,000 worth of fish was landed at foreign ports and shipped to Britain. On the other hand, nearly £4 million worth was exported. Thus the fishermen and the importer got less than £16 million out of the £50 million paid over the counter by the consumer.

Large distributive charges have become a feature of the trade since the last war. The retail price of fish has risen very sharply; far more sharply than has the price paid to

---

[1] 50% in 1927 according to the Food Council *Report on Fish Prices*. The trade has grown considerably since then.

the fisherman. The average price of a hundredweight of fish at the port in 1913 was 12/5; in 1938 it was 15/9. The fisherman was getting a little over 1/3 in 1938 for what would have fetched a shilling in 1913. The housewife on the other hand, as the index of retail fish prices [1] shows, was lucky if she paid no more than two shillings for what would have been a shillingsworth of fish in 1913.

Some 34,000 persons are insured as fishermen in the United Kingdom. This figure appears to include some of the shore staff as well, since it is a good deal larger than the number returned as 'operatives' in the fishing industry in the 1931 Census. In addition some 12,000 persons were returned in the Census as fishermen 'working on their own account'. A number of Scottish fishermen in particular have not come under unemployment insurance because they receive not a fixed wage but a share of the earnings of the boat. Even in peace time unemployment among fishermen is high. At no time in 1938 were less than 17% of the workers in the industry out of employment; and in several months the percentage was as much as 32–4%. So on the one hand the productive resources—which in this case consist above all of the skill and experience of the 50,000 fishermen—remained only partly used while on the other fish was dear and scarce in the inland centres of population. A Royal Commission appointed in 1933 examined the problem [2] but neither Government nor opposition has produced a courageous and boldly conceived plan for this neglected industry.

The sea fish industry, as the Royal Commission found, can be divided for purposes of examination into two parts—the white fish industry and the herring industry. Both are in a state of depression, more serious in the latter case. Although the solution to the problems of both parts must be sought along the same lines, each requires separate examination.

[1] Ministry of Labour Cost of Living figures.
[2] Sea Fish Commission for the United Kingdom appointed under the Sea Fishing Industry Act, 1933. *1st Report (The Herring Industry)* 1934. *2nd Report (The White Fish Industry)* 1938. The chairman of the Commission was Sir Andrew Duncan.

SEA FISH

WHITE FISH

The bulk of the United Kingdom's supply of white fish is caught in home waters. Since 1933 imports of white fish have been limited to a total of 1¾ million cwt—compared with approximately 15 million cwt landed in Great Britain— and have been subject to quota regulations. In 1938 imports of fresh white fish fell to slightly over one million cwt because some countries did not fulfil their quotas.

The industry is centred mainly in five ports—Hull, Grimsby, Aberdeen, Milford Haven and Fleetwood. These ports handle no less than 85% of the total quantity and 79% of the total value of British white fish. Their relative importance is shown by the following table:

Port	Landings of white fish 1938		Average price per cwt
	Quantity in thousand cwt	Value in thousand £	
Hull	5,625	3,692	13/1
Grimsby	4,069	3,915	19/4
Aberdeen	1,608	1,762	21/11
Fleetwood	1,200	1,365	22/9
Milford Haven	644	861	26/9

As these figures show, Hull specialises in the cheaper lines for frying; costs there are kept down by efficient trawling and a measure of cooperation between trawler owners. This port grew rapidly after 1918, increasing the number of its trawlers and so enlarging the total fishing capacity of the country. Trawlers have been getting larger— so that even when there has been a decrease in their numbers, the number of fishermen has shown a slight increase.

Total landings have increased considerably since the Great War, and the result has been that the more accessible grounds have been fairly thoroughly fished over with nets of smaller mesh than had previously been customary. Many of the fish caught were too small and were thrown back into the sea in the hope that they would live. This was inevitably a wasteful process likely to deplete the fishing fields. Trawlers had been driven further afield—to the Barents Sea off the northern coast of the Soviet Union, the seas surrounding

Iceland, and the seas off the west coast of Norway to the north of the Faroes. The effects of this in the case of the most popular sorts of fish are very marked:

Fish	% of total supply derived from distant waters	
	1913	1938
Cod	32	81
Haddock	15	38
Plaice	21	25
Hake	8	—

While total landings grew, the elaboration of the distributive machinery raised prices so sharply that the additional supplies could not be absorbed by the market. The fisherman's price remained low—kept down by the keen competition between different ports and between different firms of trawler owners in the same port. Between 1928 and 1938 the value of a hundredweight of cod at the port slumped by almost half, while the price of other fish fell by about a quarter. Over the same period the quantity of cod landed rose by 50%—until it became about twice what it was before the war. The quantities of other white fish landed have been much more constant.

The Fishing Fleet

There is a good deal of variation from one port to another in the organisation and condition of the fleet. The Royal Commission in its Report on the White Fish Industry went into this problem carefully on the basis of 1934 figures. It found that apart from Hull, where special conditions applied, only 12% of the country's trawlers had been built since 1918. The Hull fleet, however, was much more modern —half of it was built since 1918. It was, too, in the hands of far fewer companies than were the fleets at other ports; more than half belonged to companies owning 20 or more boats, and apart from this, although probably as a result of it, cooperation between all trawler owners in the port had developed a good deal further than in any other part of Great Britain. In running trawlers as in most other enterprises there are economies to be effected by working on a large scale and buying requisites in bulk; and to some extent these economies can be gained by cooperative buying.

As a general rule the crew of a trawler consists of a minimum of nine or ten men; though big trawlers making trips to distant grounds have a larger complement. Men are signed on for a complete voyage made up of a number of trips; and are paid a small wage of 40/- or 50/- a week plus a share of the catch.[1] The first engineer will probably get a little higher wage—perhaps 50/- plus a share; while the skipper and mate generally receive no wage but get 10% and $7\frac{1}{4}$% respectively of the net value of the catch.

These shares are calculated only after a number of deductions covering the expenses of the voyage have been made from the sum realised by the sale of the catch, the cost of coal consumed, the cost of ice for packing, and so on. The items deducted vary from port to port [2] but the system from its nature involves the workers in the risks of the voyage and the still greater risks attending the marketing of the catch. The length of voyages and therefore the time for which a man is continuously employed vary from port to port and according to the seas where the trawlers go to fish. When he is not actually employed a fisherman is eligible for unemployment benefit or unemployment assistance.

As in the course of years the prices paid for fish at the ports fell, there was at first a tendency to try to keep up the aggregate returns by beginning to fish earlier in the year and by continuing after the season had passed. The result was that a number of immature or spent fish came on to the market. This has been met under the 1933 Sea Fishing Industry Order by a prohibition of fishing in distant waters in certain months of the year.

More recently there has been an endeavour to keep up returns by restricting the number of trawlers engaged;

[1] Fishermen remunerated partly but not solely on a share basis are insured against unemployment.

[2] Until recently they varied with each trawler company; this naturally led to endless disputes. As a result of trade union representations there is now a standard settling sheet for each port, approved and printed by the Board of Trade, on which the deductions which may legitimately be made are listed.

since the higher costs which journeys to the distant waters involved made low prices particularly fatal. In the autumn of 1937 Hull and Grimsby, where ownership is concentrated in comparatively few hands, agreed to lay up one-fifth of their distant fishing fleets in an endeavour to raise the price. In the spring of 1938 the British Trawler Owners' Federation published the following figures [1]:

	Trawlers laid up		Fishing	
	Home waters	Distant waters	Home waters	Distant waters
Aberdeen	12	—	241	7
Fleetwood	6	3	124	25
Grimsby	40	20	298	100
Hull	—	47	27	188
Leith	1	—	58	—
Lowestoft	28	—	62	—
Milford Haven	4	—	119	—
North Shields	3	—	57	—
Total	101	70	986	320

The producers' side of the industry continued to discuss restriction on landings and a plan was put forward for a compensation fund which would make it possible to lay up 400 boats. This policy is disastrous to the men actually engaged in the fishing. The agreement between Grimsby and Hull affected 600 or 700 men in Grimsby and probably 800 in Hull. But it should be noted that Fleetwood, which was reported to welcome the decision made by Grimsby and Hull to restrict fishing so drastically, very soon saw the launching of a scheme backed by the merchants of the town for the purchase of ten up-to-date trawlers able to fish in the Atlantic. Fleetwood was said to be suffering from a shortage of fish supplies; and it was hoped that these trawlers would add £100,000 to the annual turnover of the port.

The Duncan Commission on Sea Fish, working on 1934 figures, concluded that trawler owners were making profits of something like 5% on turnover in Hull, 4% in Milford

[1] Quoted in the *Fish Trades Gazette*, 30 April 1938.

Haven and 1% in the other principal ports. Expenses were high and did not depend upon the size of the catch to any important degree.

There is one item of expenditure where there are, in the view of the Commission, possibilities of economy. That item is coal, which absorbs some 20% of the turnover of vessels trawling in distant waters and up to 28% in near and middle waters. It is in fact the largest single item, except for wages and shares paid to seamen, and the Commission was led to remark that the considerable variations in the price at the different ports could not be ' wholly explained by insurmountable difficulties such as distance from coal fields '.

The gap between the price which is paid to the trawler owner for his fish at the port and that which is paid by the consumer inland is very large. The Duncan Commission reckoned that it was roughly half the retail price, and a comparison of aggregate retail prices with landing prices suggests that this is an underestimate. This is accounted for not by the profiteering of a particular powerful group as is the case in some commodities, but by the large number of competing concerns—many working on a very small scale—at each stage of the distributive process. This means that price fluctuations and overlapping of distribution are regular features of the trade.

The Trade at the Port

Most fish goes first into the hands of a wholesaler at the port where it is brought to land. The quantity landed varies very much from day to day, and since fish is a highly perishable commodity and there appears to be no adequate system of refrigeration at the ports, both supply and price fluctuate very rapidly. So a staff which appears excessive may have to be retained by the trawler owners to deal with the large quantities which come on the market at particular times.[1] The fish is disposed of by employees of the trawling company or by salesmen who work on a commission of about 5%, pay the trawler owner in cash the full price

[1] According to a writer in the *Fish Trades Gazette* (11 December 1937), it is reckoned that three men are employed in the port for every fisherman.

realised and themselves allow credit at discretion to the buyers.

These buyers are a mixed lot. Port auctions are open to any one and some fish may be sold to a wholesaler for transport to an inland market, some to a merchant doing a wholesale and retail trade for distribution to retail shops in that part of the country, some to a retailer doing a local trade and some even direct to a consumer who wants a bargain. The number of merchants who do a wholesale business at the ports has grown in the past few years, since the trade is easy to enter, requires little capital, and calls for no more experience than can be gained from working as the employee of a wholesaler already established. In Grimsby, for example, the number of port wholesalers increased between 1913 and 1934 from 510 to 729 although the quantity of fish handled fell by almost a third in that period.

The consequence of the chaotic conditions at the port auctions is that there is little concern for preserving the distinction between fish of the same kind taken from different waters and therefore of varying qualities. This is likely to have a bad effect in the long run, because consumers cannot feel assured of the quality of the fish they buy. Cardiff is the sole example of a port where one firm owns all the trawlers and in addition conducts the market and carries on a wholesaling business—apparently with very satisfactory results.

The margin taken by the port wholesaler was reckoned by the Sea Fish Commission (who worked on the basis of the accounts of a number of firms in different ports) to be 17–19%; but to be much higher in the case of wholesalers in Hull, who not only took a much larger net profit than did their opposite numbers in other ports, but also had to spend appreciably more on carriage to the consuming centre.

The Transport of Fish

Transport is a fairly substantial item in the distributive costs of fish. In 1934, for example, 45% of Fleetwood's catch went to London and only 41% to the five principal towns of Lancashire, its natural market. A good deal more might be done to ensure that there is no unnecessary carting of fish about the country and that each consuming centre depends as far as possible on the nearest port. Railway transport for fish, as for other foodstuffs, is better than road when it is a question of long distances, although the government reports hint, more in sorrow than in anger, that the railways might really lower their charges a little, since it is in their interest that the industry of the country should prosper. Road transport has developed a good deal in recent years, especially for weekend supplies. Some fish is sent by lorry from Aberdeen on Saturday to arrive in London for market on the Monday. Road transport is generally cheaper especially as the sender does not have to meet charges for carriage to and from the railway station. The railway companies have not regarded the development unmoved; and early in 1938, to take an example, sought by opposition to the granting of licences to prevent the expansion of an Aberdeen road haulage business. The haulage contractor ran a trunk service twice a day from Aberdeen to Liverpool and other Lancashire towns, bringing fish boxes and fruit on the return journey. The railway companies, who argued that they could provide the necessary facilities, lost their case. To take another example from the same centre, the continued importance of rail transport despite the use of lorries is shown by the statement of the President of the Aberdeen Fish Trades Association that a 5% increase in railway rates would mean £10,000 a year in extra transport costs to the fish trade of Aberdeen.[1]

The Inland Wholesale Markets

Prior to the war there were five large inland markets serving the main consuming areas. The largest is Billingsgate, which is reckoned to serve a population of 12 million in Greater London, and to which incidentally go most of the supplies from the smaller fishing centres and a large proportion of the imported fish, as well as considerable quantities from the main ports. Just over 4 million cwt of fish passed through Billingsgate in 1937. The quantity

[1] *Fish Trades Gazette*, 12 February 1938.

has declined since the war despite the increase in the total supplies of fish, owing to the increasing tendency to head and fillet fish at the ports instead of transporting valueless material to the wholesale markets. The other wholesale markets are situated in Glasgow, Manchester, Liverpool and Birmingham.

The markets are controlled in every case by the city authorities, and are the field of operations of a second set of wholesalers. These 'inland' wholesalers buy from the port wholesalers and distribute to the retailers. Some of them work, partly at any rate, on a commission basis, but it appears that this is decreasing, and it is more common for them to buy and sell on their own account. The margins on which they work are smaller than those of the port wholesalers, and were reckoned by the Sea Fish Commission as about 15% of turnover. As in the case of other foodstuffs, there are a number of wholesalers—possibly up to half of those who have stands in the market—who specialise in splitting up large quantities into small lots for sale to retailers. In the case of Billingsgate, there are a number of very large wholesalers, so large that, according to the Royal Commission report

> it may well be that 10% of the businesses (that is 20–25 firms) account for nearly one-half of the total trade.

In the provincial markets the numbers of wholesalers have remained fairly constant. The largest number is 55, in Manchester. The total number of people registered with the White Fish Commission as wholesalers is 3,000.

The Fishmonger and Frier

From the wholesaler the fish passes to the retailer. Varying estimates have been made of the number of shops disposing of fish direct to the consumer, but there was agreement that the fish friers were more numerous than the ordinary fishmongers; and surveys taken of changes in retail trading in the years 1901–1931 disclosed a very marked increase in fried fish shops. The White Fish Commission, compiling its register of those engaged in the fish trade at the beginning of 1939, settled the matter by showing 20,000 fishmongers and the same number of friers.

The Duncan Commission were able to furnish no figures of returns and margins for the fried fish shops; but for the ordinary fishmonger they calculated a difference between the prices at which he bought and sold amounting to 26% of the latter. The fish friers have been badly hit by the restrictions placed by the trawler owners on landings and have made representations to the Food Council about their difficulties in getting supplies. They also have a grievance in that in some wholesale markets a group of merchants make a point of cornering the supplies of fish which friers buy and selling to them at a considerable profit. This was the case in Glasgow; but the local association of fish friers made such a persistent complaint that the market authorities put a stop to the practice and the friers were subsequently able to claim that the price of fish had been cut by one-third.

Most of the retail trade is in the hands of very small concerns, since such a perishable commodity is not easy for large chain shops to handle. There appears to be a definite demand for small and handy shops—as is shown by the fact that the answer most frequently given by housewives for not buying their fish at their cooperative stores was that it was too far from their homes.[1]

The fried fish trade is also an affair of small units, and is not as yet well organised. There exists a National Federation of Fish Friers, but despite the fact that it has been in existence for over a quarter of a century, it has not organised anything like half of those engaged in the trade. Frequently people set up in the trade on credit from the manufacturers of ranges and the manufacturers of fat, give very lavish portions in an endeavour to establish themselves and are not able to stay the pace for long. All the usual characteristics of small-scale shopkeeping—the pathetic eagerness to escape from wage earning and to achieve some degree of independence, the absorption of the energies not merely of the husband but of the whole family, the large turnover of personnel and the dependence on the large manufacturers who supply

[1] See *Consumers' Cooperation*, p. 362.

the goods for retailing—can be found in the fried fish trade. On the other hand there is no doubt that there are a substantial number of fish-friers who have built up sound businesses and who incidentally have done a lot to improve the appearance of fried fish shops and the quality of the goods they sell.

It has been calculated by some in the trade that as much as £1 million a year is wasted on the wooden containers in which the fish (herring as well as white fish) is transported, for many of them are not returned by the fishmonger to whom they have been sent but are broken up for firewood. Some wholesalers have endeavoured to get them sent back by making a definite charge to be refunded on return but have found that this is very unpopular with retailers, and may mean loss of custom. Consequently they have tended to set this loss of containers down as a necessary part of their costs and to raise their prices to cover it. Whoever bears the direct loss the effect is to raise prices generally; and the waste, since it is estimated at so high a figure, accounts for quite an appreciable part of distributive costs.

Unilever

A word must be said of the one large-scale business in the fish trade—MacFisheries. This private company is a subsidiary of Lever Bros and Unilever. It controls some forty other companies, thirty of them directly. They include firms operating in each branch of the industry—trawler companies, wholesalers and retailers.[1] One of the most important subsidiaries of MacFisheries is the herring firm of Bloomfields.[2]

Nearly four hundred retail branches throughout the country operate as MacFisheries or under the name of one of their subsidiaries, and must have a turnover in fish and poultry running into millions. The company originated in a project of the late Lord Leverhulme. Having bought all

---

[1] These include Aberdeen Steam Trawling and Fishing Co Ltd, MacLine, Orford Oysterage Ltd, Grocetaria and Muirhead and Willcocks (a retail chain with a central establishment in Manchester and seventeen branches in Lancashire and Cheshire).

[2] See section on 'The Herring Industry'.

SEA FISH

that could be bought of the islands of Lewis and Harris, he wished in his benevolence to bring prosperity to the inhabitants by providing them with an outlet for the fish they caught. For this purpose he bought up a small number of retail fish shops; but the fishermen did not take kindly to the new Lord of the Western Isles and obstinately continued to sell their fish by auction in the traditional way. His Lordship finally sold the shops—which had been his private property—to the firm of Lever Bros who developed them into the present MacFisheries.

The firms controlled by MacFisheries in different lines of trade operate quite separately. Thus a trawler owned by MacFisheries bringing its fish to port may sell it to a wholesale firm controlled by MacFisheries—or it may not. Similarly a wholesale firm may sell to the retail side of MacFisheries—or it may not. It seems probable that the company handles a larger amount of fish for retail than at any previous stage. Their share of the other trade is, however, tending to increase—Associated Fisheries which is linked with this group recently bought up two fleets of trawlers consisting of 27 vessels in all.

Distribution—A Summary

The Duncan Commission on White Fish stated that the margin on fish amounted to just about 50% of its retail price and drew up the following price structure:

```
Amount paid by Port Wholesaler to Trawler Owner    .    .    100
   Port Wholesaler :—
      Wages and Salaries        .   .   .   .   .   .    8
      Carriage and Packing      .   .   .   .   .   .   11
      Other expenses and net profit .   .   .   .   .    4
                                                        ──
                                                        23

Amount paid by Inland Wholesaler to Port Wholesaler .   .   123
   Inland Wholesaler :—
      Wages and Salaries        .   .   .   .   .   .    8
      Carriage    .   .   .   .   .   .   .   .   .      6
      Other expenses and net profit .   .   .   .   .    7
                                                        ──
                                                        21
```

Amount paid by Fishmonger to Inland Wholesaler	144
Fishmonger :—	
Wages and Salaries	27
Carriage and Packing	6
Rent, Rates, etc.	9
Other expenses and net profit	10
	52
Amount paid by Consumer to Fishmonger	196

As the comparison between the aggregate landing price and the aggregate retail price showed, the tendency of the Duncan Commission was if anything to minimise the percentage of the retail price which was taken up by distributive costs. Public institutions buying on contracts can effect very remarkable economies by short cutting this elaborate distributive process. Thus, to take one example, early in 1938 there was great indignation in the fish trade because the Bristol Public Assistance Committee was buying fish on contract from a merchant in Grimsby, and paying a flat rate of 2d a lb *including transport from Grimsby to Bristol*. Again, the L.C.C., which buys 30,000 cwt of fish a year and takes it direct from the port wholesalers in Hull, Grimsby and Yarmouth, is able in this way to effect ' substantial economies '.

The Herring Industry

' There is unquestionably a wonderful nutritional story to be told regarding the herring,' says Sir William Crawford. ' It is certainly not widely enough appreciated at present.'

Figures bear out the latter part of Sir William's statement. Although there was some improvement in home consumption between the slump and the war it is still below pre-1914 level. Here again it is a story of a big gap between the producers' price and the consumers price and of prices at the ports which are only a fraction above those of 1913. The average port price of a hundredweight of herring in 1913 was 6/4. In 1938 it was 6/3. On the other hand there is the additional difficulty that the retail fishmonger has no great enthusiasm for the herring. It is too cheap and therefore unremunerative.

The price of herring in the port of landing is subject

to much more violent fluctuations than that of white fish, as a result of variation in the supply available. The movement of the herring shoal may cause part of the fleet to come in lightly laden; the fish will fetch a good price because it looks as though there will be a scarcity and regular orders must be punctually despatched by train. Then the rest of the fleet comes in, perhaps with a good catch, the price slumps and considerable quantities are used for fish meal. Wireless is now used to inform dealers of the catches being made, so that fluctuations arising from ignorance of supplies are less violent; and on the whole it is likely that this has had the effect of depressing prices.

The fish when brought to land is sold by the cran—which amounts to $3\frac{3}{4}$ cwt. It is auctioned usually on sample; and the salesman as in the case of white fish takes 5% and pays the owner cash. The buyers are curers and kipperers, canning companies, hawkers who sell 'fresh' herring and dealers who cater for the export trade.

The Sea Fish Commission Report and the Herring Board

The herring industry seemed to have touched bottom in 1933, when it was the subject of an investigation by the Sea Fish Commission. Home consumption had declined, and the export trade, which disposed of about two-thirds of the catch, had been badly hit by the development of the herring fisheries in continental countries. The Herring Report of the Sea Fish Commission summed up the matter as follows:

> From 1911 to 1913 the total quantity of herring sold amounted to an annual average of about 10,800,000 cwt which realised on landing £3,700,000. . . . From 1931 to 1933 (the smallest output falling in 1933) the average was only 5,100,000 cwt sold for £2,100,000. Stated in another way, over a twenty year span the total export of herring has dropped by about 55% and the sale for home consumption has dropped by about 45%.

Over the period of 1913 to 1933, however, the number of steam drifters (which accounted at both dates for the bulk of the trade) had fallen only from 1,470 to 1,088.

The fact that far fewer fish were handled in 1933 than in even so recent a year as 1929 by practically the same number of vessels meant little short of ruin to the fishermen in the trade. Figures collected and compared by the Sea Fish Commission suggested that, whereas the average gross takings of Scottish steam herring drifters in 1929 were £2,208, the average four years later in the case of the same vessels was £1,080. Running expenses, however, absorbed £824 (76·30% of the takings) in 1933, as compared with £1,132 (51·27%) in the earlier year. There was so much the less for the owners and for the men whom they employed —as was the custom of the industry—on a share basis.

The tendency was to begin fishing earlier in the season and try to continue later in an endeavour to increase the takings; but the effect of this was to cause immature or spent fish to be brought to port, and so for the public taste to be to some extent prejudiced against herrings—a development likely to worsen conditions still more.

As a result of the report of the Sea Fish Commission, a Herring Commission was appointed in March 1935 under the Herring Industry Act. It had at first a chairman and seven members, the chairman and two other members being unconnected with the industry. The Scottish herring fishers at once protested that they were inadequately represented and another Scot was added to the Board.

The job of the Board was to be the reorganisation of the industry, and it was envisaged that it might take powers for market development, for buying up redundant boats and limiting their number, for building new ones and repairing old where that was necessary, for fixing prices and buying and selling stocks to stabilise prices. In addition it might dispose of surplus herrings, levy fees on people in the trade and inspect boats and premises.

The industry over which the commission came to exercise their functions was not organised in quite the same way in England and in Scotland. The Scottish herring fleet is run on much more individualistic lines than the English. There are fewer companies, and in many cases fishermen own their boat and their gear or have a part share in it. As the Board pointed out, one of the main difficulties of the Scottish drifter fleet was the poor financial backing of the individuals

SEA FISH

or groups who owned vessels.[1] Bloomfields Ltd, a private company and a subsidiary of MacFisheries, which handles the herring side of the MacFisheries group, controls a number of firms in both England and Scotland.[2] Neil Mackay, the chairman of Bloomfields and a managing director of MacFisheries Ltd, was a member of the Herring Board.

Since 1934, the figures of total landings have been:

Year	Landing in cwt
1935	5,680,235
1936	5,557,853
1937	5,515,674
1938	5,387,202

The latest figures available for the size of the herring fleet show it to consist of 747 steam and 274 motor drifters.[3] A little has been done by the Board in the direction of buying up fishing vessels for destruction. Up to March 1937 they brought up a total of 116 drifters for this purpose.

The Export Trade since 1933

As far as the export trade was concerned, the Herring Board pointed out that—

> there is no physical reason why British fishermen and curers should not produce cured herrings at a cost which would enable them to compete successfully with the Dutch,

but they seemed to be so impressed by the difficulties of securing more efficient management of the curing and exporting branches of the industry that they believed that the industry should be reorganised so that the volume of trade would not be greater in the future than it had been in the preceding years of depression.

Export markets, particularly in Germany and Russia,

---

[1] Herring Board, Second Annual Report (for year ending 31 March 1937), p. 11.
[2] Bloomfields Ltd controls A. Brenner and Co, Bloomfields Overseas Ltd, George W. Green Ltd, Great Yarmouth Ice Co Ltd, James More Ltd, J. Slater Ltd, Norfolk Cold Storage and Ice Manufacturing Co Ltd, W. E. Shreeve Ltd, Walter J. King Ltd, William Low (Fraserburgh) Ltd, and Duncan and Jamieson Ltd.
[3] Herring Board, Third Annual Report.

have gradually been lost. The situation to 1933 may be summed up as follows:

NUMBER OF BARRELS OF HERRINGS EXPORTED TO PRINCIPAL IMPORTING COUNTRIES (IN THOUSANDS)

Period	Total	Germany	Russia	Poland
1911–13 average	2,424	1,319	1,105	—
1929	1,679	697	11	609
1933	727	396	2	201

These countries and others such as Estonia, Finland and Holland have all developed their herring trade in recent years, so that the Herring Board was forced to conclude that prospects of recapturing lost markets abroad were not so bright even as they appeared in 1934, and that there was no reason to believe that the export trade would recover. The most that could be expected was that the Soviet Union would take some small quantities at a low price. The total export to all countries in 1938 was about 820,000 barrels as compared with 789,000 in 1933.

The herring for export are handled by the curers who are in a strong position, taking as they do a large share of the total quantity landed. The landing price of herring as compared with the export price has been as follows:

Year	Average landing price per cwt (England and Wales)	Average Export price per cwt	Total Quantity Exported (thousand cwt)
1935	6/6	13/4	3,068
1936	8/6	15/4	2,755
1937	7/2	15/9	2,379
1938	6/2	14/10	2,734

There could be no clearer example of the strong position of the curers, who are able to maintain, and even raise, their selling prices when landing prices fall.

The curers have not hesitated to threaten a strike when anything contrary to their interests has been proposed. Thus when the Herring Board attempted to abolish buyers' discount (in accordance with the recommendation of the Sea Fish Commission) and increase salesman's charges, objection was raised by the buyers and particularly by the curers, who threatened to abstain from buying unless the rules were withdrawn. As a cessation of this trade would have inflicted great loss on the fishermen the Board decided to withdraw the rules.[1]

The curing trade is divided between about two hundred firms of varying size. Between 1929 and 1933 the output of barrels by a curing crew of four fell from 575 in the Scottish summer season and 625 in the English autumn to 275 and 335 respectively. Unless the total output were increased, either the number of the crews must be cut down (this the trade had been slowly doing during the previous two or three years) or the less efficient firms must be eliminated. The latter course, in the view of the Herring Board—

> although more rational and likely to produce all round efficiency, would probably meet with serious opposition.

The Herring Board has propounded restriction on landings and on curing as a remedy for the industry. The export trade is marked by the excessive numbers of firms engaged on the distributive side. ' There is no doubt that there are considerably more salesmen than are required. . . . ' says the Herring Board in its report for the year ending March 1938; and later it states that there are—

> undoubtedly far more licensed exporters than are necessary to handle the trade, but the great bulk of the business is in fact transacted by a few firms who . . . are able to operate more cheaply and efficiently than the others.

Since ' the others ' remain in business, it seems that the large firms must be in a position to make quite substantial profits.

The course of action of the Herring Board has not met with general approval. It appears to have allowed itself to be the agent of the curers, and of the larger curers at that. In one case in East Anglia a local committee was set up to restrict the hours of curing so long as the price of fresh herring exceeded 25/- per cwt,

[1] See Herring Board, Second Annual Report.

the object being to restrict purchases by curers and so limit the effect of their competition in inflating prices.

This action was taken as a result of a threat on the part of the curers that they would stop curing because of the prevailing high prices.

The Home Market

The possibilities of expansion lie in the home rather than the export market. Between 1933 and 1937, partly as a result of publicity organised by the Herring Board, the home consumption of British caught herrings increased by about 25%. During the same period the consumption of herrings imported out of season fell by over a third. Of the 596,000 crans consumed in 1937, 328,000 were kippered as compared with 41,000 treated in other ways and 227,000 eaten fresh. Thus in fact almost all processed herrings consumed in the United Kingdom are kippered. The trade has been affected by the expansion of the fried fish market which has taken place since 1918, and by the increased popularity of white fish which has gone along with this.

As in the case of the export trade there are more firms than are necessary involved. The Herring Board in their report for the year ending March 1938 stated that—

> there are undoubtedly a greater number (of kipperers and bloaterers) than would be sufficient to supply the market's demand,

although it went on to express the view that no economy would necessarily be effected by 'mere reduction of their numbers'.

This redundancy, together with the tendency of the retail fishmonger to charge a higher price for herring than is necessary, because a sale at too low a price would tend to diminish the demand for more profitable fish, accounts for the large gap between the price which the fisherman receives and that which the housewife pays.

Throughout the Board's existence there appears to have been friction with the Scottish fishermen. Perhaps because of their small scale methods and lack of capital they demand grants instead of loans and many of them were in fact unable to repay money which the Board had lent. The Board finally found itself faced with a refusal to cooperate on the part of many fishermen. In its final report (for the year ending 31 March 1938) it attacked them as follows:

> It would appear that a considerable proportion of the industry ... do not desire regulation, reorganisation or the planning of their business upon an economic basis. What they do desire and have repeatedly asked for is that they should be enabled to continue on their old uneconomic lines, and that the losses consequent upon their so doing should be met by Treasury grants and subsidies which ultimately fall upon the general taxpayer.

The Herring Board was dissolved in the middle of 1938; its end was rather sudden, and members of the industry criticised the government for an abrupt dismissal of which no explanation had been given. By the outbreak of war the new Board which took its place had not got much further than touring the ports and being assured that it would have the full cooperation of the industry.

CONCLUSIONS

For obvious reasons the war has interrupted fish supplies; and the trade was the object of the early attentions of the Ministry of Food. The attempt at control was a fiasco and had to be dropped after a very short time. With the end of the war, however, energetic action will be needed to set the fish trade on its feet again and direct it towards well based prosperity.

The problems of herrings and of white fish are in some respects different; but common to both industries are the excessive distributive costs which have had the effect of limiting the market and forcing the productive side into restriction schemes in the hope of raising port prices.

To bring the general level of consumption of fish up to the optimum would involve increasing the present supply by at least 40%. There would be little difficulty in providing this additional quantity without importing any more. It would involve the fuller utilisation of the fishing fleet and still further reliance on distant waters. It might be necessary to draw a larger proportion of our supplies from the Atlantic fisheries than hitherto. But these problems would not be hard to solve once a market for the fish was assured.

It is equally essential to devise ways and means of getting the fish to the consumer and retailing it at a price which she can afford to pay. The figures given by Sir William Crawford show how the amount of money spent on fish rises as the income available for buying food increases. There would be no difficulty about absorbing all that the present fishing fleet can catch if only the retail price were lower. The first step in restoring prosperity to the industry in peace or war would be to bring retail prices a little nearer those prevailing at the ports.

There seems to be no reason to believe that measures contemplated under the Sea Fish Industry Bill will narrow this price gap. A White Fish Commission was set up to deal with that side of the industry. It confined itself to compiling a register of those engaged in the production and distribution of white fish. All branches of the industry were to be encouraged to organise and present their schemes to the Commission; and the usual lip service was to be paid to consumers' interests by setting up a Consumers' Council. Experience shows, however, that such organisation is unlikely to mean lower prices. When war broke out an inter-trading plan was in course of preparation, and its sponsors hoped to have it operating in the spring of 1940. Under these plans no fishmonger or fish frier who was not a member of his appropriate association was to have been allowed to buy from a fish merchant who belonged to the wholesale merchants' association. Since organisation among these wholesalers is practically 100%, all fishmongers and fish friers would have to join up or go out of business. Organisation, whether of this kind or under a governmental scheme with its usual bases of regulation and restriction of entry into any branch of the trade, shows how completely the day of *laisser faire* is past not only in the basic industries but in the distributive trades as well.

A quarter of the distributive margin is made up of costs at the ports. The port auctions are the field of operation of the agents of the large inland wholesalers as well as of small men who have acquired some knowledge of the trade when employed by an already established merchant. What has to be done at the ports is to allocate supplies to the different inland centres; and a margin of 2/6 in the £ seems an excessive charge upon the retail price for the performance of this function. The trade is easy to enter; but there seems every reason to suppose that entry will be less easy after registration has been imposed under the Sea Fish Industry Act. The fluctuations in supply and the need to dispose of fish as quickly as possible mean that large staffs have to be kept at the ports—three times as numerous as the men who actually do the fishing. More refrigeration stores would enable supplies to be evened out and short-term price fluctuations avoided. It would mean that restriction orders would be still less defensible because there would be no possibility of a glut and the destruction of the market when good catches were brought in.

To provide adequate refrigeration, however, is only the first of the changes which should be made at the ports. From it would follow a reduction in costs of marketing, but the function performed at the port—that of allocating supplies to inland centres—still remains one which could be as effectively and more cheaply performed by the officials of a cooperative organisation of producers. Such an organisation would be the proper body to control the refrigeration stores. Its officials could allocate supplies to the various markets in the urban centres just as satisfactorily as does the present elaborate machinery.

There already exists a definite tendency to by-pass the large wholesale markets. This may well have the effect of keeping prices down; certainly there seems to be no reason why much more fish, particularly that intended for the fried fish trade, should not go direct from the port to district centres without the expenses involved in passing through the wholesale market.

Any such changes in the distributive mechanism *might* lower prices; there is no guarantee that they would. Essential to any large-scale reorganisation, if it is to lead to lower prices and not to a better living for such middlemen as continue in the trade, is a White Fish Board appointed by the Ministry and assisted by an Advisory Council representative of the various branches of the industry. Such a board would not be primarily a trading board; although it might usefully have power to buy fish if it felt that this step was necessary. Its essential functions would be the general supervision of the industry, power to limit the entry into any branch, the fixing of prices and margins after enquiry into the trade, the administration of a fund for loans to such sections of the industry as needed assistance and the management of general publicity. For these functions to be satisfactorily performed the Board should have the clear objective of reducing retail prices and should not be composed of men of straw who yielded the real direction of the whole industry to save particular section or interest within it.

Reorganisation along such lines should have the effect of lowering prices and increasing consumption especially if reductions in costs were effected by buying coal and other requisites cooperatively and by transporting fish in bulk. This increased turnover should make possible a fairly substantial reduction in the fishmongers' margins, which account already for half the difference between the price paid by the housewife and that received by the fisherman.

In the case of herring fisheries cooperation between producers, particularly in the case of the Scottish fishermen working with small capital, should be encouraged; and an elected Board on a national scale might well be established. A fund should be established by the Government from which grants and loans—according to circumstances—should be made to fishermen. In the years of depression little money has been available for replacements and the equipment of the fleet has deteriorated. In particular money could be well laid out on small motor-boats which have the advantage over steam drifters that they can be used for white fishing out of the herring season. Once the emphasis of the industry is shifted to increased production there should be less difficulty about the financing of improvement.

The pessimistic views of the Herring Board on the export trade seem to be largely justified. The Board emphasised, however, that competition with the Dutch presented no physical impossibilities, and given efficient organisation it seems reasonable to suggest that some of the foreign markets might be regained. The curers seem to be in the best strategic position in the trade at present and strict control should be exercised over them, either by a government agency or by the producers' board. The trade seems to be carrying an excessive number of exporters at the present moment and entry to this stage of the trade might be limited. Germany and Russia, however, are developing their own fisheries and it seems illusory to hope for increased trade there even in peace. Sweden and the United States both take fewer herrings from Britain than they did.

There seem to be great possibilities in the canning of fish which has so far been little developed in the United Kingdom. Some £10 million a year is spent on tinned fish in the United Kingdom but 90% of the supplies so consumed are imported. The most important source remains Japan who sends cheap tinned salmon; although the United States is also important as an exporter.

Canning offers a particularly valuable outlet for herrings since the process softens the bones and makes the fish easier to eat. Canned herring in consequence would probably prove popular if it were put on the market with a large advertising campaign to tell ' the wonderful nutritional story of the herring '. Other forms of herring have increased in sales as a result of advertising in the last few years and would probably continue to have a small and steady market. But canning, it seems reasonable to hope, would very much increase the demand and revive the prosperity of the herring ports.

There would, of course, be difficulties which would have to be resolved in practice. They would arise from the attempts to secure level supply (required for the economical running of a cannery) in view of the seasonal character of the herring fishing and the movements of the herring from north to south. Much the same difficulty arises in connection with fruit and vegetable canning ; and probably the most satisfactory solution would be to have one or two fish canning centres based on the present seats of the industry. This would, it is true, involve fish being transported considerable distances—from the north of Scotland, for example, for canning. Since the canneries would be comparatively near the main consuming areas, however, it would be largely a question of the fish being transported part of the way along a route that it would have in any case to follow.

8 VEGETABLES AND FRUIT

The organisation of the supply of vegetables and fruit, on which the consumer spends nearly £190 million a year,[1] has remained substantially unchanged by the war. The Potato Marketing Scheme has been suspended and the import of some luxury fruits prohibited to save shipping space; but the broad outlines of organisation remain the same as before the war. The fruit and vegetable trade is very complex because of the variety of commodities included under that title, the varying quantities available at different seasons of the year and the fluctuations in supply and price which may be produced by a sudden and comparatively slight change in the weather. 'A hot summer's day,' to quote the Linlithgow Report, 'will treble the supplies of home grown lettuces and marrows at Covent Garden.'

The remarkable fluctuations which may take place from year to year and from month to month in the case of one vegetable may be illustrated from the following table of the average monthly price of lettuce (per doz.) during four consecutive seasons.

Month	1st year	2nd year	3rd year	4th year
March (frame lettuce)	2/–	1/6	1/3	1/1
April ,, ,,	2/3¼	1/9	/10	1/1
May (outdoor lettuce)	1/3	1/9	1/1	/11
June ,, ,,	–/8	1/9	–/6	–/9
July ,, ,,	—	2/4	–/4	—
August ,, ,,	–/5	2/1	–/5	–/6
September ,, ,,	–/5	–/9	1/2	–/5
October ,, ,,	–/7	–/3¼	–/6	—
November ,, ,,	–/4	–/5	–/9	—

Fluctuations in price occur indeed from day to day and even from hour to hour; so that the farmer can rarely be sure what his produce will fetch Not only does supply vary with weather but so does demand. In addition, different vegetables

[1] From an unpublished estimate for 1936 by A. E. Feavearyear. He calculates that £45 million was spent on potatoes, £42 million on other vegetables, and £100 million on fruit.

and fruit compete with one another; an increased supply of tomatoes, for example, may cause a falling off in the demand for strawberries.

It is not easy to give accurate and up-to-date figures for the country's production of fruit and vegetables. The most recent detailed figures relate to the years 1930–2 [1]; and perhaps the best indication of the scale of vegetable and fruit production is provided by the figures for farmers' gross receipts. These figures show a steady increase since 1933, and in 1936–7 amounted to just over £9 million for fruit, £17 million for potatoes and nearly £16 million for other vegetables. This totals more than £42 million—some 16 to 17% of the total value of agricultural produce.

The position has been summed up on the basis of figures for 1934–6 [2]:

UNITED KINGDOM CONSUMPTION OF FOODSTUFFS—AVERAGE OF 1934–6
(FIGURES IN THOUSANDS OF TONS)

Commodity	Home Production		Net Imports Less Exports	Total Consumption
	Quantity	% of Total		
Apples	343	53·3	301	644
Oranges	—	—	488	488
Bananas	—	—	283	283
Other fresh fruit	253	47·0	274	527
Dried fruit	—	—	158	158
Canned fruit	*	—	197	197
Nuts	5	7·4	63	68
Dessicated coconut	—	—	15	15
Potatoes	4,395	96·0	181	4,570
Green peas and beans	206	99·0	2	208
Other vegetables (including tomatoes and rhubarb)	1,650	79·0	439	2,089
Preserved vegetables	*	—	41	41

* Included in fresh fruit and vegetables.

The principal vegetables imported are onions and tomatoes. Onions account for more than half the total import of vegetables and come mostly from the Netherlands, Egypt

[1] These will be found in Appendix I of the Ministry of Agriculture Economic Series, *Marketing of Vegetables*, published in 1935.
[2] From Report of Food (Defence Plans) Department of the Board of Trade.

and Spain. Tomatoes are a third of the total and come from the Netherlands and Canary Islands. There are no quotas on any vegetables (except potatoes) but they are all subject to import duties, and in the case of tomatoes and carrots there is a period of maximum duty in each year to protect the market when British supplies are most plentiful. Similarly most fruits are subject to import duties varying with the season of the year.

As is the case with so many foodstuffs, the amount spent on fruit and vegetables rises steadily with the family income available. Sir William Crawford [1] gives the following figures of expenditure per head per week (in pence):

Family Income	Fresh Fruit	All Fruit (incl. tinned)	Potatoes	All Vegetables
Over £1,000	15·3	19·3	6·1	16·4
£500–£999	12·9	17·2	4·4	12·9
£250–£499	9·9	12·9	4·5	9·7
£125–£250	3·9	5·5	4·1	7·4
Under £125	1·7	2·5	3·9	6·2

The average total consumption of fruit per head of the population fell very sharply in 1935 from the 1934 figure of 95·8 lb per annum to 79·3 lb. It was higher in 1936 and again in 1937, but even in the latter year it was still 10 lb per head less than in 1934. The lower figures are very largely due to a smaller consumption of apples.[2] The high consumption in 1934 was probably the result of the very good crop of British fruit and the consequent low prices. On the other hand the crop in 1937 was on the whole not so good as that of the previous year, and the prices—at any rate those received by the producer—were generally higher; but nevertheless the consumption was higher. Thus it is probably fair to conclude that in general the price and consumption of fruit is determined by the supply available from abroad as well as from home orchards; but that an exceptionally good home crop (such as 1934) will bring down prices and raise consumption.

[1] *The People's Food*, pp. 246–263.
[2] *Weekly Fruit Intelligence*, 25 June 1938.

Potatoes

The problems of potato supply and marketing originate in the variability of the yield per acre. In 1934–5, for example, 7·1 tons per acre were produced; while in the next season the figure was 6·3. The variable yield can be shown even more clearly by comparing figures of average production calculated on a county basis. Thus in one recent year the figure for Bedfordshire was 3·6 tons and for the adjoining county of Huntingdon 6·8.[1] At the same time the demand is comparatively inelastic and a slight excess of supply over demand is sufficient to produce a glut and sharp price cutting.

It was to mitigate the sharpness of fluctuations which inflict considerable hardship on the farmer that the Potato Marketing Scheme was devised in 1933. It was submitted to the Ministry of Agriculture by the National Farmers' Union, and having been given the blessing of Parliament was put into operation at the end of the year. Potatoes are the only vegetable of which the supply is regulated by a marketing board.

The essence of the scheme is the maintenance of prices through control of supplies. There was less difficulty in applying this in the case of potatoes than in the case of other foodstuffs because imports are so unimportant a part of the supply. The total consumption of potatoes in the United Kingdom (allowing for the produce of allotments and gardens which does not come on to the market) is calculated at 4,576,000 tons, of which no more than 4% are imported.[2]

Imports

Imported supplies consist mainly of early potatoes—coming from the Channel Islands and, even in 1937, from Spain. Under the 1933 Agricultural Marketing Act the Board of Trade are vested with power to regulate imports by order and to set from time to time a limit upon the total. This quota is fixed after consultation with the Market Supplies Committee, which in its turn confers with a special

---

[1] 1935 figures.
[2] This figure is taken from Appendix III of the Report of the Food (Defence Plans) Department already quoted.

committee of nominees of interested parties including the Potato Marketing Board. The Board of Trade makes over the greater part of the quota to the Potato Importers' Association, which divides it among its members. Allocations are made on the basis of past imports, but a share of the import quota is held by the Board of Trade for newcomers to the trade.

The Board of Trade does not announce what quota it imposes, although it has stated that its quotas are not in all cases filled. The reason given for this reticence is that if it were known what quantities would be admitted it might bring down prices in the home markets. Thus it may be seen that supplies from overseas are closely controlled, and even shipments from Northern Ireland, where the scheme does not apply, are limited by voluntary agreement.

The Control of Home Supplies

The peacetime control of home production rested on the basic acreage and the 'riddle'. The basic acreage was the area that a farmer might plant with potatoes without paying an excess acreage levy. It was determined under the scheme in one of three ways—which one, the individual producer might choose for himself. It might be the acreage which he planted in 1933 (if this was still in his possession in 1934), the average acreage of the years 1931–3, or—if it did not exceed seven—the maximum number of acres planted in those three years. If a farmer moved to another farm he could not take a right to a certain acreage of potatoes with him. Those rights are attached to the farm on which potatoes were grown in 1931–3 (or in respect of which Excess Acreage Levy has been paid). If any producer wished to increase his acreage he might do so on paying what amounted to a fee of £5 for each additional acre.

In addition, a standard of size was set to regulate the quantity of potatoes coming on to the market. Any potato small enough to pass through a square mesh called the riddle must be cast aside and not offered for sale for human consumption. The standard size of this riddle was $1\frac{1}{2}''$; but from time to time the Board made a survey of stocks available in the hands of registered producers [1] and authorised merchants, and if it believed they were large enough to cause a fall in prices might increase the size of the riddle.

Shortly after the Board came into existence in the spring of 1934 a regulation was issued prohibiting the sale for human consumption of potatoes of less than $1\frac{5}{8}''$ or $1\frac{3}{4}''$ diameter according to varieties. The regulation was terminated at the end of July. Although the main crop did not look as though it would be above the average, it was found necessary to reimpose regulation in December and to forbid the sale of potatoes that would pass through riddles varying from $1''$ to $1\frac{3}{8}''$ according to varieties and districts. On two occasions the Board imposed a maximum limit and so, for example, forbidding the sale of potatoes weighing 1 lb or more. The reason given for this was that since the types and sizes of potatoes were varied, it was a penalisation of some districts to hold stocks off the market by a minimum limit alone. The result of the operations of the Board was a very steady rise in the prices received by growers. For English potatoes the average price per ton received by the growers for the seasons 1933-4, 1934-5, 1935-6, and 1936-7 were respectively 59/-, 75/6, 113/-, 135/-.[2]

The estimated production in England, Wales and Scotland (to which the Potato Marketing Scheme alone applies) amounted in 1938-9 to 4,404,000 tons. Not all, however, was produced under the Scheme, for growers with less than one acre under potatoes, as well as growers who sell none of their crops except for seed purposes, are excluded.

Many of the registered producers failed to plant the full acreage allowed under the scheme. This is shown by the fact that the aggregate basic acreage of the registered producers for the year 1938 was 655,000, only 537,000 acres of which were planted.

[1] The usual method of storage is in 'graves' on the farms. The potatoes are put in a broad shallow trench and covered with straw and clay. They are then dug out as required for marketing. The price rises in the spring—particularly in April—and this rise provides the inducement for farmers to hold on to their stocks and bring them on to the market at that time.

[2] Ministry of Agriculture, Report of Agricultural Marketing Schemes for the year 1937.

VEGETABLES AND FRUIT

Not all the home potato production is available for human consumption. Before the Potato Marketing Scheme was introduced it was calculated that some 10–15% of the production was usually retained on farms for feeding to stock, and that seed potatoes accounted for about another 10–15% of the total. After the scheme was introduced the tendency was to feed to stock potatoes which were not large enough for sale under the regulations of the Board.

The Distributive System

The bulk of the supplies of main crop potatoes are, then, home grown; and the growing is concentrated in a few areas—around the Wash, Lincolnshire, Cambridgeshire and Bedfordshire, Yorkshire, Lancashire and Cheshire, Ayrshire and Northern Ireland. The main consuming areas are the big industrial centres, London, South Wales and the North of England. So far as England and Wales are concerned it has been said that—

> the distributive system must link up two groups of areas, the one producing about 70% of the home grown supplies and the other covering about the same proportion of the population. The distributive problem, however, is not simply one of linking up a consuming area with the nearest producing area. Local variation in the quality of produce has its counterpart in local preference for potatoes of particular qualities.[1]

Most of the producers of potatoes operate on a small scale, often combining the growing of potatoes with other crops. Half the producers plant less than five acres of potatoes each; while another quarter plant less than ten acres.

The quantity of potatoes sold by the farmer direct to the consumer is very small over the country as a whole. As in the case of other vegetables the time which it takes for the producer or some of his family to hawk the goods from door to door in a nearby town makes this an expensive way of disposing of produce; and again as in the case of other vegetables there are the difficulties of maintaining a steady and reliable supply.

The bulk of the crop is disposed of through the local market, where growers and merchants meet and settle prices.

[1] Ministry of Agriculture Economic Series, *Marketing of Potatoes*.

From there the potatoes may be sold by the wholesaler to a retailer or, more usually, to another wholesaler in an urban centre. Thus merchants operating in the London markets or in such an 'importing area' as South Wales (to which potatoes are brought from the Fen country, for example) will get their stocks partly direct from the growers with whom they may have contracts (or with whom they may deal through their agents in the producing areas) and partly from merchants who themselves have bought from the growers. These country markets in the producing areas vary considerably in size and importance. The most influential one is that at Wisbech, whose prices are watched by dealers all over the country and made the basis of the Ministry of Agriculture's calculations. Recently Peterborough has rivalled Wisbech in importance.

Rail transport charges upon potatoes are fairly high, although they fall sharply in the case of large quantities. Thus from Ormskirk to London the rates are 44/4 per ton in the case of loads of less than 2 tons, but 20/6 per ton if the consignment is more than 5 tons. From Peterborough the corresponding rates are 24/3 and 14/2. During 1937 more than 800,000 tons of potatoes were carried by the British railways at an average charge of 15/- per ton.[1]

The margin on which the merchants are usually reckoned to work is 20/- to 25/- a ton; but where they are passing on to other wholesalers the margin may be much lower, and where long distances and heavy transport costs are involved, much higher. Of this margin probably as much as 10/- will be absorbed by costs of collection from the farm.

Thus, to take the figures for one month (November 1938), King Edwards (Silt and Reds) were selling at Covent Garden [2] at an average of about 140/- a ton, at Manchester at an average of 145/-, and at Bournemouth (which may be taken as an example of a town which is neither the centre of an industrial area nor situated in a producing area) 150/- a ton.

[1] Railway Returns for 1937.
[2] Covent Garden prices are not always representative. Generally they are slightly above the prices ruling in other London markets—usually 3d a cwt.

These prices charged by wholesalers to retailers may be compared with the growers' prices at Wisbech, Boston and Spalding, where these potatoes were selling at an average of 113/9, 105/- and 111/3 respectively. Other King Edward potatoes, which were fetching 121/3 at Covent Garden, 115/- at Manchester and 140/- at Bournemouth, were being bought from the growers at an average of 87/3 at Ely, 90/- at Peterborough, 98/3 at Ormskirk, 100/- at Warrington Exchange and 115/- at Exeter. Or, to take another potato, Majestic Black Greys were fetching an average of 82/6 wholesale at Covent Garden, 73/4 at Manchester and 105/- at Bournemouth, while growers were receiving 56/9 at Ely, 62/6 at Ormskirk, 57/6 at Peterborough and 66/- on the Warrington Exchange.

It can be seen from these figures, which are not unrepresentative (Majestics and King Edwards between them accounted for more than half the total acreage of potatoes), that there are considerable variations in the wholesale margins. Although for transactions within a comparatively small area the margin was 20/- to 25/-, it rose in some cases to 30/- or even 40/-. The variations depend upon the number of times the potatoes are handled by different middlemen and the transport costs for different journeys.

Before the formation of the Marketing Board the distributors rather than the producers appear to have been the dominant partners; at any rate in times of glut and consequent low prices it was not they but the producers who bore the burden. Indeed there was actually some tendency for distributors' margins to rise because of the strong position of the wholesaler negotiating with competing producers.

But the Marketing Board did a great deal to extend its control—and so the control of producers—over wholesaling. First the Board made it clear that it would require registered producers to include certain items in all contracts which they signed. They must insist that the net price to be paid to the grower should be named in the contract, and they must include a clause that the contract should be unenforceable for any class of potato the sale of which the Board should prohibit after the contract had been concluded. Then it forbade sales on commission which had been a common way of disposing of potatoes to the wholesaler. This step was taken after a vote of the registered producers had approved it; commission sales had often in the past meant very small returns to the grower.

The Board then extended still further its control of the wholesale trade. It passed a resolution prohibiting any registered producer from selling potatoes to any merchant who was not 'authorised' by the Board; the avowed intention was to rationalise the wholesale trade for the benefit of the producer. A number of exceptions to this rule were made, to cover direct sales by the grower to the retailer or the consumer, sales of seed potatoes, sales for manufacture and so on.

Any merchant seeking authorisation had to show financial stability and knowledge of the trade, and to demonstrate that the needs of the district in which he wished to set up were not already being satisfactorily served. Some 3,600 merchants have been authorised by the Board. Many of them operate on a small scale; probably the majority do not handle more than 500 tons of potatoes a year although on the other hand there are large firms which do business involving 10,000 tons and upwards annually. Many dealers become authorised because they buy from farmers who bring some potatoes to market with other vegetables and fear they will lose this custom if they are unable to buy potatoes.

A further step made by the Board was the encouragement in different districts of Market Plans Committees to represent the authorised merchants trading in that region. Later adherence to the regional committee where one existed became for merchants a condition of authorisation by the Board. The plan originated from the experience of merchants in the Glasgow district, where there was an experiment by the distributors in the voluntary regulation of their margins. These Market Plans Committees fixed the wholesale margins for their respective regions—usually at 10/- to 15/- per ton—and from time to time issued a figure for the 'arrived price'—that is to say the average price to the merchant of potatoes delivered to his warehouse, consisting of the grower's price plus the costs of collection from the farm, which probably amount to about 10/- per ton. The minimum price for sales to a retailer was thus fixed, at the arrived price plus the approved margin.

By the end of 1935 such Committees existed in about 40 districts; but in the following season, despite the encouragement of the Board, only 19 recommenced operations. Later the Board established in some districts Price Recommending Committees consisting of representatives of producers; and developed these, principally in Lancashire and Cheshire, to the point where Potato Exchanges were set up as meeting places of representatives of producers who could advise producers about the prices they should ask. The purpose of these organisations was to stabilise the margins and to prevent fluctuations; they proved more satisfactory than the Market Plans Committee and increased in number.

There was a danger that such marketing devices might be used to keep up merchants' profits and to maintain the less efficient firms in business; and the Food Council, while it stated that allegations of abuses in connection with these schemes had not been proved, was of the opinion that—

> producers would be well advised to abandon all attempts to secure minimum margins either for wholesalers or retailers, more especially as no powers to do so were specifically included in the Potato Marketing Scheme.

Retailing and the Bishop Auckland Experiment

Potatoes are sold with other vegetables and fruit, and the same remarks with regard to retail margins apply. There has, however, been one example of the distribution of surplus potatoes at differential prices. This was the experiment made by the Potato Marketing Board at Bishop Auckland in January and February 1935. The essence of the scheme was that potatoes which were being sold retail at sevenpence a stone were made available to the families of unemployed men at fourpence a stone, provided the customers came and fetched them from the distributing centre which the Board set up. The potatoes were bought wholesale at a little over fourpence a stone—in fact at 59/- a ton. Altogether 182 tons were disposed of at a cost of £111 for warehouse distribution and £65 to cover the difference between the market price and the price paid by the buyers, as well as the loss in weight in bagging the potatoes. This total expense of £176 in disposing of 182 tons of potatoes works out at about three-halfpence a stone. So in fact to buy and distribute the potatoes in this way cost fivepence halfpenny a stone—three-halfpence less than the prevailing retail price. Against this economy must be set the inconvenience of this scheme to the customer who had to fetch the goods from the warehouse, which was open only two days in the week.

On the other hand, if we are comparing this *ad hoc* distributive machinery with normal retailing from the point of view of costs and efficiency, it must be borne in mind that the Potato Board was dealing in one class of vegetable only and therefore had a very small turnover out of which overheads had to be met. The principal conclusion which the Board drew from this experiment was 'that it was possible to devise machinery for the distribution of cheap surplus supplies without endangering the existing price structure or destroying the retailers' contact with their customers'. This had been done and the goodwill of retailers ensured by arranging for a payment to them of 1d per stone on all the potatoes distributed through the scheme. The retailers did very well out of this, since the consumption of potatoes increased very considerably and they received their 1d per stone with no effort on their part.

The fish and chip trade deserves some special attention as a method of retail distribution. It was calculated in 1931 that some 15% of the potatoes which passed into domestic consumption did so as chips, and there is no reason to believe that the proportion has decreased. The proportion varies in different parts of the country; it is substantial in London and other industrial districts and has been estimated to be as much as 60% in Lancashire. The Potato Marketing Board has recently entered into relations with the National

VEGETABLES AND FRUIT

Federation of Fish Friers Ltd. 'It is too much to expect,' says the Report of the Board—

> the Board and the National Federation always to see eye to eye in regard to potato price levels, although to be fair the Federation have consistently advanced the view that at no time do they wish the price of potatoes to be so low as to yield to the producer a figure below his costs of production.[1]

The Board also concerned itself with the question of the surplus which might not under its regulations be sold through the ordinary trade channels. Some was fed to stock as in the past; and experiments were made to see whether the apparatus used for grass drying could not also be used for the drying of potatoes.

One method of disposing of the surplus is that which was tried by the Board at Bishop Auckland—sale at special cut rates in parts of the country where large numbers of people are existing on insufficient diets. The Board has also had in mind the eventual possibility that this country might become a potato exporting country and have had a report prepared on the potentialities of the South American market. But most attention has been given to ways and means of putting the surplus to an industrial use. The difficulty is that there must be a regular supply if a factory is to be established and plant installed; and the surplus varies in size from year to year. The only purpose for which the surplus has been found satisfactory so far is the manufacture of cattle food. A factory at Wisbech used 3,500 tons of the 1935 crop in this way, paying usually at the rate of £1 a ton. The quantity used in this way has increased, and the 1937–8 season was the first in which the plant ran continuously from September to July, processing an average of 280 tons a week.

Production and Prices under the Board

The Board has had a good deal of criticism levelled at it for restricting production and raising prices. The acreage and output of potatoes in Great Britain have been as follows.

[1] Report of the Potato Marketing Board.

Year	Acreage in thousand acres	Output in thousand tons
1932	655	4,450
1933	671	4,550
1934	627	4,464
1935	594	3,765
1936	589	3,791
1937	591	4,062
1938	609	4,404

It is by no means proved that the Marketing Board has permanently raised retail prices above their previous level. Between 1934 and 1937 retail prices rose steadily but in 1938 they were lower. The annual average of monthly retail prices of potatoes since 1928 has been as follows [1]:

Year	Pence per lb
1928	1·16
1929	0·94
1930	0·80
1931	1·17
1932	1·23
1933	0·78
1934	0·86
1935	0·92
1936	1·08
1937	1·09
1938	0·96 (provisional)

The Food Council compared the season 1936–7 with the season 1927–8 when production was almost the same. They found that between September and May 'the average growers' price was 15/6 per ton higher than in 1927–8 (about 13%); the average wholesale price was 12/6 per ton (about 9%) higher; and the average retail price was 17/- per ton (about 8%) lower. In 1936–7 the apparent distributive margin was thus substantially less than in 1927–8 and the grower appears to have received a greater proportion of the retail price. Again if these 1936–7 prices are compared with 1935–6 it emerges that growers got better prices in the later year (135/- per ton as compared with 113/-), wholesale prices were higher (153/6 as compared with 136/6), but

[1] Based on the Ministry of Agriculture monthly figures of retail prices.

retail prices per 7 lb according to the Ministry of Labour were 7d as compared with 7¼d in 1935–6.¹

VEGETABLES

The main centres of vegetable growing are the Eastern Counties—East Anglia, Cambridgeshire, Lincolnshire and Hertfordshire; the West Country—Somersetshire and Worcestershire; Kent and certain parts of Yorkshire. Since the last war there has been a considerable increase in the supply coming from East Anglia and from Hertfordshire.

Large quantities of vegetables are produced by the specialist market gardener working either on a small scale with family labour or on a large scale with ample capital for machinery and other aids to increased production. But, in these new areas especially, much of the supply has been produced by general farmers who have continued other lines at the same time.

The large scale market gardener is at a considerable advantage compared with the small family farmer. He may work as much as 2,000 acres of land, can afford to manure the land adequately and regularly, can economise labour by the use of machinery and can save money by the bulk purchase of requisites.

The general farmer who grows vegetables has considerable advantages too, for experience has shown how well the cultivation of vegetables can fit into the rotation of crops and the routine of the farm. Vegetables are not grown every year on the same soil; and the general farmer does not have to buy in fertilisers in the same quantities as those specialists who have no livestock. The general farmer who has taken up the cultivation of vegetables can utilise his labour all the year round—for some of his crops will now mature in what was the slack time in the winter.

Home grown market produce may pass along any one of a series of chains of middlemen between the grower and the consumer. There does not seem to be any way of arriving at an accurate estimate of the proportion of home grown

¹ Ministry of Agriculture, *Report on Marketing Schemes, 1937*.

vegetables which pass directly from the grower to the consumer or the retailer. With the development of motor traffic the quantities sold by the growers setting up stalls on the side of the road has increased. There are some indications that in particular districts and at special seasons a fair amount of this direct trade is done in vegetables, and competition is keen. For the grower to hawk his produce either to housewives or to shopkeepers or to sell it in his own shop takes, however, a good deal of his time and a large share of the proceeds in costs. It is unsatisfactory too because the producer dealing directly cannot maintain the variety or the regularity of supply which the retailer, relying himself upon a wholesaler, can ensure. A few growers have permanent contacts with buyers—usually retailers some distance away; but the favourite way of marketing produce direct is by growers' stalls at retail or wholesale markets.

In the aggregate, however, not much of the produce is distributed in this comparatively direct way, and the Linlithgow Report in 1923 described fruit and vegetables as 'unique in the number and variety of intermediaries who may at times be engaged in handling the produce, and whose sole service is that of distribution'.[1] There were cases quoted of as many as sixteen to twenty handlings of the same produce, including packing, carting on and off trains and exposing for sale at different stages of the process of distribution; but these cases were rare and in general one or two intermediaries handle produce grown near the consuming centre. In the case of specialised producing areas, such as the Vale of Evesham or the Lea Valley, the chain of intermediaries is usually a little longer. According to the Linlithgow Report again, half the produce from these areas passed through the hands of three or four middlemen before reaching the consumer; while three-quarters of the remainder passed through the hands of two intermediaries.

The general effect of the string of middlemen and the high distributive margins which are to be expected where

---

[1] *Report of the Linlithgow Committee.* Despite the fact that this report is seventeen years old the general description of the distribution of vegetables is still applicable.

there are so many factors affecting supply and price is well known. While market gardeners complain of their small returns, housewives complain of high prices of vegetables. For each shilling received by the vegetable grower the housewife pays at least two shillings; and usually a good deal more if she buys from the high price shops and has her goods delivered. Sir John Orr drew particular attention to the shortage of minerals which extended to the diets of groups even quite high up the scale of incomes; so that an increase in the consumption of green vegetables and raw fruit, which are particularly rich in minerals, is very desirable from the point of view of national health. The experience of a retailer in the South of England was that if the price at which cauliflowers are offered can be reduced from 4d to 2d the sales may be expected to multiply five or six times; clearly not very much can be deduced from the experience of a single man operating under competitive conditions (especially as housewives probably tend to compare prices with greater care when buying fruit and vegetables and to be influenced less by the habit of going to a particular shop than in buying other goods), but, especially when taken in conjunction with the results of the potato marketing scheme in Bishop Auckland, it does indicate that given lower prices through distributive economies, housewives would need neither exhortation nor advertisement campaign to induce them to bring the national consumption of fruit and vegetables nearer to the national optimum.

The Local Market

How are these margins divided up between the different stages of the distributive process? The first function which must be performed is the assembling of the produce of the growers, who usually work on a small scale. This assembling is necessary if the units are to be large enough for them to be transported fairly cheaply. At one time marketing by smallholders acting as individuals and therefore dealing with small quantities at irregular intervals was still possible; but any smallholder who persists in doing this still is likely to find that his profits have slumped because of the increased efficiency and speed of transport (which means that the average distance which supplies are sent to the market is increased) and because of the heavier supplies which are now available. This function of assembling is one which can be performed by cooperative associations of the farmers themselves. This is the work which such societies as the Littleton and Badsey Growers Ltd perform, but such cooperatives are few in number, and the function is more usually carried out by the country agent of the market salesman working on a commission basis. This is in fact at present the commonest method adopted by the growers of disposing of their produce to the wholesaler.

There is this reservation to be made—that at times a conveniently situated grower will take a large part in the distributive trade. This is pointed out in the Ministry of Agriculture Economic Handbook on the *Marketing of Vegetables*, which gives as an instance the fact that

> at the height of the outdoor cabbage lettuce season few Covent Garden salesmen handle the crop, the bulk being disposed of by growers direct; the same is true of late summer and autumn cauliflowers marketed at Birmingham and of the summer cabbage and natural rhubarb at Liverpool.

There is one drawback to the method of sale to the wholesalers through an agent working on a commission basis. There is a danger that when prices are low he will resort to a minimum charge per package for the goods he handles, thus receiving a larger percentage than in normal times.

In addition to the commission of the local agent there is another important item of expense falling on a consignment as it passes from the grower to the wholesaler. That is the cost of transport. In the years after the European war the overwhelming proportion of the vegetables went by rail. Facilities were often poor and rates stood, even after a reduction, at 50% above pre war. The Linlithgow Report commented that such rates could not be maintained unless the fruit and vegetable trade in many districts was to perish. The situation has been materially altered, so far as the growers comparatively near the large consuming centres are concerned, by the development of road transport. The outside limit at which the lorry can compete with the railway train, however, is a hundred miles; and it seems likely that for some time to come it will be cheaper to send the goods by rail if the distance is greater than that. Kent, Hertfordshire, Cambridgeshire and parts of Lincolnshire and East Anglia all are vegetable growing areas which are within a radius of a hundred miles of London. Cases have been known of growers in Cambridgeshire who wished to send vegetables to Leeds and found it best to send them by road to London first and then north again by rail. The advantages of road transport are greater flexibility, the reduction of the number of handlings and usually more punctual delivery; and these advantages heve secured the definite predominance of road transport for vegetables.

The Small Grower and His Handicaps

In marketing as in production the small man is at a disadvantage. The large grower is better able to maintain a stall in Covent Garden through which he may dispose of his own produce—and perhaps of the produce of his smaller neighbours. Even when the goods are sold by agents on a commission basis the small lot gets much less consideration than the large lot which is probably more carefully sorted and attractively packed.

In respect of transport again the small man has special difficulties if he retains an interest in the consignment after it has left his district. The large man who has a holding near a centre of population will run his own lorry into the market; but the small man must pay the comparatively high rates which the railways charge for carrying small quantities.

The disadvantages lead to the situation in which the small grower sometimes finds that the price which his goods have realised does not cover the cost of transport and the agent's commission, let alone the cost of growing and harvesting the crop. Difficulties either when the yield per acre is too small for the grower to make ends meet or the supply so large that the price slumps may lead the grower to get an advance from a wholesaler—as have for example many growers in the Lea Valley who have not received enough for their produce since to pay off the loan. They are tied to one wholesaler by this indebtedness. In the Vale of Evesham there have been examples of men who would have disposed of their goods through cooperative channels but were not able to do so because they were in debt to the local auction market. Again some growers mortgage their crops in advance and others sell in advance to vegetable canning firms.

The wholesalers' margins do not appear to be excessive. The Linlithgow Report quoted a sample which showed a gross profit of 9·67% and a net profit of 1·84%. This may be an underestimate, especially since the investigation is now fifteen years old; but it may be taken as an indication that the wholesalers cannot be said to be guilty of gross profiteering. More recently one such firm in the North of England had a turnover of £80–90,000 and a net profit of about £900 on one year's working.

The Wholesale Markets

The focus of the wholesale trade is of course the large wholesale market. Particularly important is Covent Garden, which deals in home grown and imported fruit and vegetables; but conditions are unsatisfactory and the market has been described as—

> wholly inadequate to deal efficiently with the amount of produce handled. In no other market in the country is the accommodation so deficient and the congestion so acute. Indeed from the standpoint of the facilities offered the market is a confused and unorganised anachronism.

Most of the firms dealing on Covent Garden work on a small scale. So sensitive is the market that comparatively large firms—such as George Munro and Co and Pouparts—although they have only a small share of the total trade are in a dominating position.

Proposals have been made for the establishment of a ring of suburban markets to replace Covent Garden; and one such market has grown up on the west of London at Brentford. But it appears that there will always be a need for some central market fulfilling some of the essential functions which Covent Garden now inadequately performs. Unless it is possible to improve access to it, however, it seems desirable to reduce the quantity of goods which actually pass through the present central market, since both delay and depreciation may be caused by additional handlings. Some of the unnecessary and uneconomic reconsignment which took place in the past has now been cut out despite the strong opposition of vested interests. The Linlithgow Report, which drew attention to the extent of uneconomic reconsignment in the years after the war, also gave examples of reconsigned goods from Covent Garden being dumped on provincial markets to discredit direct consignment.

Despite such difficulties, however, progress has been made; but there is one genuine obstacle to the further reduction of apparently clumsy and wasteful marketing. That is the sensitivity of local markets, which is inevitable under the present competitive organisation of the trade. They handle comparatively small quantities, and any increase is likely to cause a quick and catastrophic fall in prices.

Although, owing to variation of price from season to season and from month to month, it is difficult to generalise, it seems that the wholesale price is frequently as low as half of the retail price. The price structure may be illustrated from these figures:

	English tomatoes at beginning of season (pence per lb)	English tomatoes early season (pence per lb)	Cucumbers (pence each)
Price received by grower	5·03	2·94	4·23
Agent's commission	0·60	0·37	0·50
Transport to Covent Garden	0·16	1·02	0·17
Other selling expenses	0·21	0·67	0·10
Wholesale price in Covent Garden	6·00	5·00	5·00
Carriage to other markets	1·19	0·75	0·70
Wholesaler's other costs	0·75	0·16	0·45
Wholesaler's profits	2·66	1·09	0·67
Retailer's buying price	10·00	7·00	6·92
Retailer's selling price	15·00	10·00	10·00

Retailers' margins in the fruit and vegetable trade are large. Most of the shops which deal in this class of goods are small; there is indeed only one chain of any size, and it is questionable whether that is large enough to affect conditions in the trade. Some big chain stores like Marks and Spencer skim the cream off the trade by buying up at a favourable moment large quantities of fruit which is easy to handle and which shows little wastage. Fairly large quantities of oranges, to take one example, are disposed of in this way. To quote the Ministry of Agriculture Economic Handbook on the *Marketing of Vegetables*.

> The average selling price for various reasons often represents an addition of about 50% to the general purchase price of the vegetables sold. In general the gross profit appears to range from 25% to 33⅓% on all sales.

It goes on to quote extensively from the report of the 1923 Linlithgow Commission, saying that there is no reason to believe that its conclusions were not broadly true in 1935.

The reason for the high margins taken by retailers was stated by the Linlithgow Commission to be the numerous services which the retailer had to perform and the liberal allowance which had to be made for waste of various kinds. 2½% to 5% of goods arrive in bad condition; some 5% on all turnover must be allowed for short weight given by growers; up to 5 or 6% is inevitably lost in weighing out, say, a hundredweight of apples into 1 or 2 lb lots; and retailers lose an amount, which varies according to the size of their turnover and the equipment of their shop, by goods deteriorating while in their hands. This last item, which was calculated at 19½% by private traders, was reckoned at no more than 8½% by cooperative societies.

Fresh Fruit

According to the calculations of the Food (Defence Plans) Department of the Board of Trade about one quarter of peace time supplies of fruit are home grown. The percentage of course varies in the case of different fruits; all our bananas and oranges are imported and about half of our apples, pears and other fresh fruit come from overseas.

Home Production

As in the case of vegetables there have been some changes in the areas of home production. The West Country—Hereford, Devon and Somerset—still provides a large part of the home grown supplies; but since 1918 Kent, Norfolk and the other Eastern Counties have increased enormously in importance as fruit growing counties. Similarly there has been a tendency for soft fruits to leave the traditional areas for East Anglia. Unlike vegetable growing, however, the growing of fruit is still the province of the specialist farmer; but even small scale fruit growing is comparatively highly capitalised.

As in vegetable growing the large scale producer enjoys advantages in growing and marketing over his small scale competitor. The markets for fruit are uncertain, and this has led many fruit farmers to supply the retailer direct. It is calculated that as much as 30 or 40% of home grown fruit is marketed in this way. Apart from this percentage, however, a certain amount of fruit is sold either in the market or on contract to the canning firms, and some goes to the jam manufacturers. Ten or fifteen years ago the amount disposed of to the jam manufacturers was very large, as much as 90% of the blackcurrant and raspberry crop, 60% of the strawberry crop and 40% of the plum crop, according to the Linlithgow Committee. Recently, however, imported fruit pulp has to a very large extent replaced home grown fresh fruit as the raw material of jam manufacture.

Apart from the supplies disposed of in this way, the home grown fruit passes through much the same distributive machinery as home grown vegetables. It is very difficult to estimate the margins because prices vary so much from year to year and fluctuate so sharply in any one season. It appears, however, to be true to say that the public pays 100 to 150% more for home grown fruit than the producer receives for it. When there is a glut there occur cases of the fruit grower finding that the price which is paid for his produce does not cover the cost of marketing and that he is in debt to his agent. The agents often work on a commission basis but have a minimum rate per package which maintains their living but hits the grower whenever prices are particularly poor.

The quantities available from year to year vary so much that to give an account of the home production of fruit it is desirable to give the figures for four seasons.

	Plums	Pears	Cherries	Straw-berries	Apples (other than cider)
1934	3,177	585	380	549	8,059
1935	385	307	188	247	1,417
1936	2,388	727	329	369	6,300
1937	2,310	217	189	574	2,511

Produce in thousand cwt. In each case the yield per acre, or the yield per tree, fluctuates very sharply from year to year. In the case of apples, for example, the yield per tree was 72·5 lb in 1934, 12·7 lb in 1935, and 37·9 lb on the average in the ten years 1927–1936.[1]

The Seasonal Supplies

In the case of apples and pears home supplies are plentiful only during part of the year—from August until the end of December. Out of season the market is supplied almost exclusively by imported apples. The variations in supplies and prices of these may be shown by the study of prices in a single year.[2] In the early summer imported apples from New Zealand, Australia and Tasmania formed the bulk of the supply at 11/- to 14/- a case of 40 lb in the London market. The prices in the provincial markets to which the apples have to be transported are a little higher— say 6d or 1/- a case more in a market like Birmingham. The early English apples appeared in late July or in August at prices like this: London, 1st quality 3/6, 2nd quality 3/-; Manchester, 1st quality 5/6, 2nd quality 4/- (per twenty pounds). As the autumn advanced more varieties of English apples came into the market and imported supplies came in from the United States and Canada. The prices of the English apples varied from week to week. First quality Grenadier or Warners King, for example, commanded

---

[1] These figures are taken from the *Agricultural Statistics*, 1937.

[2] 1938 has been taken. Of course prices as a whole vary from year to year. To take one year, however, is valuable as showing the prices of different grades and at different markets as the months pass.

VEGETABLES AND FRUIT

between 3/6 and 5/- per 20 lb in the London market. Prices tended to rise in November and December; such expensive varieties as Cox's Orange Pippin fetched up to 20/- per 20 lb.

Nova Scotian apples were put on the market in November and December at the wholesale price of 3/6 or so for 20 lb. The United States apples appeared slightly dearer, while British Columbian were comparable in price with home grown varieties. In the high class shops best quality foreign apples were being priced at about 8d a lb—i.e. 13/4 for 20 lb. In early December, when wholesale prices of English apples were between 5/6 and 7/- for 20 lb the retail price was between 10/- and 13/- in the high class shops and therefore probably about 7/6 to 9/- in the lowest priced shops and 8/6 to 11/- in the medium priced.[1] For an apple of really good quality and flavour the price was as high as 25/- per 20 lb (Cox's Orange Pippins), compared with a wholesale price between 14/- and 20/-.

Imports

A calculation of the proportion of imports which came into England prior to the war [2] shows imports, despite the imposition of tariffs, to be surprisingly little affected by whether the corresponding home grown fruit is in season.

The United Kingdom takes its imports of fruits from different countries at different times of the year. It takes its apples, as has been shown, from North America in the winter and from Australia and New Zealand in the summer. Spain and Palestine [3] are the most important sources of winter supplies of oranges; while South Africa, Rhodesia, Brazil, and to an increasing extent California, send summer supplies.

The supply of fruit from abroad is largely controlled by

---

[1] This relationship between prices in fruit shops catering for different classes of customer is suggested by Colin Clark: what costs 2/- on the stalls and in the cheap shops costs 2/4 in the medium priced and 2/8 in the high priced establishments.

[2] See *British Agriculture*, p. 167. The calculation is based on the years 1934–6.

[3] Palestine increased its acreage under oranges tenfold between 1922 and 1936.

large importing companies which buy from the producer and frequently own their own lines of steamers specially equipped for the transport of fruit. The case of bananas, on which it happens that fairly full information is available, may be taken as an example of the supply of fruit from overseas.

85% of the supply of bananas for the United Kingdom market come from Jamaica. This trade (which has been materially assisted by a duty of 50/- a ton on all bananas coming from countries outside the Empire) is almost entirely in the hands of Elder and Fyffes, a subsidiary of the American United Fruit Company. This company together with another firm, the Standard Fruit Company, also American, dominates the island of Jamaica. Ten years ago a cooperative Jamaica Banana Producers Association was set up 'to promote competition among the exporting buyers',[1] to protect the small producer and to prevent the domination of the island by foreign trusts. Supporters of the association pointed to the rise in prices immediately after its establishment as a proof of its success.

This Association bought bananas principally from the smaller growers but it was soon shown to be at a disadvantage when compared with its capitalist competitors. It engaged to pay for bananas at 2/- a count (of twelve 'hands' with a minimum of nine bananas in each 'hand') and, despite the fact that a dividend paid later brought the price up to 2/2½d this was still below what the United Fruit and Standard Fruit could offer. Many members of the association broke their contracts and surreptitiously sold bananas to the capitalist exporting firms. The government refused to give to the association the special legislation for which it asked to prevent this, on the ground that such legislation would force a lower standard of life on the smaller producers.

If the exporting companies could overbid the cooperative association at the producing end they could also undercut it at the marketing end. The association, although it owned a small fleet of ships, could not always make up full cargoes

---

[1] To quote a report on the Jamaica Banana Industry made by Mr. Jack to the Fiji Legislative Council in 1935.

to Europe. It could not use the devices of the capitalist companies—buying in the open market (whence the United Fruit Company drew 20% of its supplies in the period 1930–35) or regulating the cuttings on plantations which it owned, nor could it maintain a level supply in Europe by making use of sources in Central America as did the private companies. The association was unable to compete successfully because of these handicaps and finally shed its cooperative principles. It was reconstructed as a trading company and made an arrangement with the United Fruit Co whereby when its cargoes were short the United Fruit Co should complete them, whereas when they were too large the United Fruit Co should take over the excess.

The price paid to the growers is about 2/6 a count. And the cost of collection, transport and distribution were calculated by the 1936 Commission of Inquiry as follows:

	Cost in pence per count
Handling	10·15
Loading	1·17
Freight	25·65
Discharging	3·90
Distribution and marketing (in U.K.)	8·47
Overheads	2·01
Management	0·98
Total cost of collection, distribution, and transport	52·23

These figures were based upon the accounts of the producers' association which probably had freight charges a good deal higher than have the private companies now; so that the cost to the importing company of getting a count from the producer to the retailer is probably about 4/–. 2/6 has been paid for the fruit, so that the total cost is about 6/6. These bananas are sold at about 1d each, that is to say a count will fetch at the very least 9/–. If 2/– is reckoned as the retailer's margin, a minimum of sixpence is left as net profit to the importing company.

The condition of labour in Jamaica is illustrated by the

following passage from a report by a representative of the Fiji government who visited the country in 1935:

> At the wharves the carrying labourers, mostly women, may number as much as 500. These are paid 1/9 per 100 stems, and they usually earn about 5/- or 6/- per day which may last for as much as 18 hours. On the ship the stems are passed from hand to hand very speedily along a chain of men down to the final position of the bunches in the hold. These chains of men usually number about twenty men and there are usually about ten such gangs at work when a ship is being loaded—the men in these gangs are paid 2/6 per 100 stems and are generally reckoned to earn 7/- to 8/- per day. They work quickly and must handle between 300 and 400 bunches in the day, and an average bunch would weigh some 40 lb at present (low because of adverse weather as already mentioned). Any labourer who happens to drop a bunch is immediately sacked, but such an occurrence is very rare.

This example illustrates the strong position of the fruit importing companies and their ability to impose wretched conditions upon the unorganised labourers in the country of supply.

CANNED FRUIT AND VEGETABLES

The popularity of canned fruit and vegetables has grown a great deal since the European war. According to Sir William Crawford the expenditure per head per week on tinned fruit is as follows:

Family income	Expenditure in pence
Over £1,000	2·3
£500 to £999	2·4
£250 to £499	1·7
£125 to £249	0·9
Below £125	0·4

The aggregate value of the tinned fruit consumed in the course of a year must be over £10 million. This is distributed through grocers and chain stores, and a good deal of it is imported. In 1938 the imports of tinned and bottled fruits were valued at about £6½ million, while the value of that produced in the United Kingdom was probably about £1½ million.[1] The United Kingdom is in fact the largest importer of canned fruits, and the bulk of its supplies are from the United States. Australia, South Africa and Canada also send supplies, although the quantities which they export to the United Kingdom are not comparable with those from the U.S.A. Malaya is important as a source of tinned pineapples, sending more than 90% of the quantity consumed.[2]

Half the U.K. consumption of canned vegetables is met by home produced supplies.[3] The value of imported supplies during 1938 was about £1½ million, a large range of vegetables are canned in the U.K., but the largest single item is peas, which are marketed in cans 'fresh' or 'processed'.

Fruit and vegetables for canning must be of good quality and of suitable varieties—not all varieties are suitable for canning even when good specimens are available. The fruit sent in must be of good size and odour and must be got fresh to the factory. Factories are frequently placed in the growing area, although it is now established that if proper precautions are taken fruit can be transported quite long distances.

The canning company naturally desires level supplies of good quality, and contract buying has become common. The usual procedure [4] is for maximum and minimum prices to be fixed and for them to be varied from year to year on the basis of an agreement that the price shall be so much above or below the price quoted in the Agricultural Market Report. Prices paid for produce delivered on contract are generally low. This system has, however, proved more satisfactory in the case of vegetables than in that of fruit. Already more than a quarter of the total acreage under peas is to provide raw materials for the canning factories. In the pea growing area many farmers buy their seed from the

---

[1] It is not possible to speak more precisely. There are no reliable figures for the value of U.K. output later than those for 1933 in the Import Duties Act Inquiry (see A. Plummer, *New British Industries* 1937), which show the value as being £1,354,000.

[2] 1934–7 average quoted in the Imperial Economic Committee *Survey of the Trade in Canned Food*.

[3] This was the case in 1935, the last year for which figures are available.

[4] See Ministry of Agriculture Bulletin on *Canning*, published in 1933.

canning factories. New potatoes, specially selected, are also beginning to be tinned. On the other hand, the variations in yield of fruit from year to year make it difficult to forecast supplies and so arrange contracts ahead.

Canning is a seasonal trade; and this too adds to its difficulties, because it means heavy overheads and the existence of suitable labour which can be called on at the right time. Safe transport methods for fruit which is to be canned are naturally helping to solve this problem; and probably the best solution to the general problem is for the factories to handle as wide a variety of food products as possible. Cold storage can be used for some fruits to smooth out short term fluctuations in supply. The off season can be used for such products as ' processed ' peas, baked beans and fruit salad (made by reprocessing imported canned fruits); and some firms have sought to keep down overheads by setting up sales organisations which market other goods as well as canned fruit and vegetables.[1]

There may well be a big future for canning. Tinned products as they have grown popular have not displaced fresh fruit and vegetables but have had the effect of lengthening their season. Fruits may be preserved for varying lengths of time in gas storage—apples for example can be kept in this way throughout the winter—but tinning offers a method of preserving any fruit for a longer period of time. At the same time the tinned goods are easier to handle; and the housewife likes them because they are quickly served and there is no waste.

The industry is a highly organised one, and its leading members have attentively studied American methods. In 1924 the National Food Canning Council was formed, with representatives of all interested parties—the Minister of Agriculture, the tinplate manufacturers, the fruit growers and the existing canners—and the period which followed was one of modernisation of plant and revision of old methods. In 1931 the National Canning Co was formed to acquire an existing canning factory at Wisbech and to build others

---

[1] See Imperial Economic Committee *Survey of the Trade in Canned Food*, section on the *Local Fruit Canning Industry in the United Kingdom*.

in fruit and vegetable districts. The CWS owns two food canning plants—at Lowestoft and Wisbech—and five other factories which are engaged in producing preserves and pickles as well as some canned fruit.

The majority of canners have brought themselves voluntarily under the provisions of the National Mark scheme, and are therefore subject to inspection to maintain high standards of quality. These standardised products sold well; in the first year 11 million cans of fruit and 6 million of peas and beans bearing the National Mark were sold. Most canned fruit is distributed direct from the canners or, in the case of imports, from their agents, to the retailers, and sold under a branded name. The retailers' margin is usually about 33%.

CONCLUSIONS

Even at peace time price levels working class families cannot afford vegetables and fresh fruit in the quantities that they need. Provided the price could be reduced there is every reason to suppose that consumption would rise rapidly. Supplies available to the public must be increased and prices cut.

Potatoes deserve separate treatment because here production and distribution are already controlled. Nothing is to be gained by going back to the old unregulated methods of production and marketing; the Potato Marketing Board has undoubtedly improved the growers' position, and it does not seem that it has made prices any higher than they were before the Board was established. What is very unsatisfactory, however, is that the surplus of potatoes is being disposed of for industrial purposes when the Advisory Committee on Nutrition is recommending potatoes to replace some of the sugar and 'highly milled cereals' in the ordinary diet because of the minerals and vitamins that potatoes contain.

An opportunity to consume the 'surplus' potatoes would be welcomed by many families in the distressed areas. Distribution along the lines of the Bishop Auckland experiment could be arranged as an emergency measure, pending some form of organisation which does not involve the payment of an unearned income to the retail distributor and does not emphasise to quite the same degree the distinction between the employed and unemployed worker. In these two respects the Bishop Auckland experiment was unsatisfactory; but something along the same lines would be better than using the surplus potatoes for cattle feed. The farmer gets 20/- a ton for his potatoes put to industrial uses. That could be raised by 50% or 100% without involving the Board in any loss (the potatoes at Bishop Auckland were bought at the wholesale market price, which was nearly 60/- a ton, and the Board was involved in a comparatively small loss on the period of special distribution). The only person who would be hurt would be the wholesaler, who would sell fewer potatoes to the retailers in the district where the emergency scheme operated.

What seems desirable in the long run is a scheme under which a trading board of independent persons with an advisory board representative of interests buys at a guaranteed price all the potatoes which the farmer grows. This board would perform the wholesaling functions and in addition would supervise the distribution of potatoes at special rates to institutions and to any special classes of consumers.

This, however, is only half the problem of vegetables, and the other half is a good deal more complex. The production and distribution of roots and green vegetables is unorganised; as a result far less is being grown than might be, and the price to the consumer is a good deal higher than it need be. If the diet of the whole population is to be brought to the optimum the supply of fresh fruit and of green vegetables must be increased by something like 50%. Although some of the fruit must be imported, this means expanding the actual home production both of fruit and vegetables by something like that figure, and at the same time reducing the cost to the consumer by means of economies in distribution and perhaps in production.

Let us take the distributive side first. The present arrangements are chaotic and wasteful, and ensure neither a good price to the producer nor a cheap and fresh supply for the consumer. The first step seems to be to see that the producer, whether of fruit or vegetables, is allowed to concentrate upon the job of production instead of being constantly distracted by anxiety about the price which his product is going to fetch.

This could best be done by the encouragement of cooperative organisations of producers on a local basis. The farmer would deliver his produce to the depot—or alternatively have it collected from his farm, whichever method proved to be the most economical in view of local circumstances. It would then be graded and packed, and the farmer would receive a credit note for it. The association would be responsible for having the produce transported to the wholesale market (securing favourable terms from the railways because the goods were sent in bulk) and sold there from the association's own stall. The farmer would be paid at the average price which produce of the type and quality he had offered fetched over a week or fortnight. Thus short term fluctuations could be prevented and the disadvantages and losses in which a large number of small sellers are involved when operating in the same markets or obliged to operate through agents, some of whom may have similar produce of their own which they wish to sell when demand is small, would be brought to an end.

Clearly there would be difficulties in such a scheme. Cooperative associations have been tried in the past, and whereas some operating on a small scale and undertaking limited functions have secured a fairly stable position, other more ambitious efforts have had initial success and then collapsed because the number of participants and consequently the throughput were not large enough to bring the charge in respect of overheads so low that the sceptical were attracted. The organisation would have to be used by all the producers in an area if it were to produce the best results; and the only method possible would be to take a poll of registered producers of fruit and vegetables in certain scheduled areas. A managerial board should be elected and given a monopoly of all sales in the area, although it should be open to the committee to decide, subject to the approval of the Ministry of Agriculture, that sales direct to the consumer and/or sales in certain specified local markets to local retailers might be exempt from control by the cooperative. Very small producers—with little more than an allotment—should certainly be exempt from control ; it is unlikely that they would attempt to send to the wholesale market individually in competition with the cooperative.

These cooperative associations would clearly assume other functions beside that of marketing organisation. They should have general charge of increasing fruit and vegetable production. By acting as information centres and linking the various advisory and specialised services provided by agricultural colleges with the actual small scale farmer they would be filling a need which everyone who studies agricultural research and the dissemination of information notices. They should be able to make small advances to farmers (indeed if any attempt was made to average prices over a longish period it would be essential that they should be able to allow the producer something on account) and they might well act as the representative of individual farmers who wished to avail themselves of state facilities for long term credit. Although the existence of a fairly large number of small producer retailers who would be ruined if they were suddenly forbidden to sell their produce from house to house must be recognised, it should be the policy of the local associations to encourage these individuals to expand their production so that all their time could usefully be employed in it and the association be able in the course of years to take over the local trade as well as that in the distant wholesale markets.

Such proposals, however, do not solve the problem of long term fluctuations of price and sudden slumps in the wholesale markets, against which it is desirable to protect particularly the small producer. The best way to give protection would be to extend public control over the already well organised canning industry and to regard it as the function of this industry to step into the market in the event of a threatening slump in price to buy fruit and vegetables for canning or for storage. The canners would not rely for the greater part of their supplies upon this method of buying but would contract probably with local associations—as they do at present with individual producers. Although further research needs to be done on the point, there are no indications that any serious loss of nutritive properties takes place when fruit is canned.

The canning industry, however, could not alone absorb the occasional surpluses in addition to its normal requirements; for canning factories must have fairly level supplies and the extent to which they can use exceptional quantities is limited. It might be necessary for some kind of government control to be exercised in the central markets; this could be done if the Government, or some specially constituted organisation controlled by it, had command of storage. The period for which fruits can be stored varies; but in the cases where storage for a period of time was technically possible the Government might buy to put a bottom in the market. Where storage for a period is not possible the Government should seek to distribute the surplus supplies at cut prices to local authorities for feeding schoolchildren and for other purposes. As far as storage is concerned the Government would have an advantage over private producers because of the larger quantities which they would handle. At present gas storage, although technically possible for a large range of products, is not an economic proposition. A store of 50 tons capacity, however, forms a serviceable unit; and such stores could be established under the control of the local producers' associations or of an administrative board.

Such a marketing system would have the effect of ensuring the position of the farmer to a much greater extent than at the present time and so, while probably slightly lowering prices paid by the retailer (since there would continue to be in the central markets competition between the different local associations with which the canning corporation would only interfere on exceptional occasions), would tend to encourage the production of more fruit and market garden produce. Each local association and its officials (responsible to their members) would be anxious to get a reputation for sending produce of good quality.

These methods, however, although they would lessen the waste involved in present marketing and would improve the position of the small farmer, would not produce a very large or a very speedy increase in the quantity of fruit or vegetables available; nor would they over a short period appreciably cheapen production. A certain amount could be done by bulk buying of fertilisers by producers' associations and by government attempts to control the prices of these and other farmers' requisites.

In the United States there has been some development of large scale production of vegetables with the use of agricultural machinery of a special type. For example, the production of lettuces has been very highly organised in California and the price brought down by mass production. The seeds are planted by what is described as ' a new kind of tractor drawn power equipment which ploughs, harrows and levels the soil in one operation '. The only stage which requires a large quantity of labour is the thinning of seedlings to distances of 14 inches. There is one case in which fertilisation is done from an aeroplane at a cost of 3/- an acre. Methods of packing and distribution are equally highly organised and cheap.[1]

It is doubtful how far it would be possible to go in this direction here; although a start in that direction has been made. There seems to be no reason on the face of it why experimental farms under government auspices should not attempt this large scale production of green vegetables with the use of agricultural machinery, and stimulate cooperative farming on a large scale by its example. At present, however, the tendency is for vegetables to be produced on general farms; and for some time this is likely to be prevalent. The immediate thing to concentrate upon therefore, seems to be more economical marketing by which the price can be brought down without the farmer suffering.

Imports account for a large part of the peace time fruit supplies of the United Kingdom and boards with trading powers should be charged with their regulation. The New

---

[1] See W. F. Darke, ' Lettuce Growing in California,' *Journal of Ministry of Agriculture*, 1938.

Zealand Labour Government has already set an example by taking under government control the importation of bananas and oranges. This trade had previously got into the hands of a small number of importing companies with a virtual monopoly. The result of government control has been a spectacular reduction of prices and a large increase in consumption. How much could be done to lower prices is uncertain since some of the profits of the present importers would have to be used to raise the standard of living of the Jamaican producers and transport workers.

The retail shopkeeper is a difficult problem. His costs mount up because he has to put up an impressive shop front, and to keep errand boys for delivery, and because so many small items, like waste and loss on weighing-out, nibble away his gross margin. The largest economies which could be effected in that 50% of retail price which is added after goods have left the wholesale market are in respect of transport, of waste (the cooperatives with their possibly rather larger and steadier turnover allow less than half as much for waste as do the private greengrocers and fruiterers) and as a result of larger turnover and steadier supplies.

These proposals taken together might well mean a cut of about 33% in the retail prices of home grown fruit and vegetables in the course of a comparatively short time.

9 TEA

The consumption of tea, as far as can be discovered, does not vary greatly from one social class to another. Crawford's figures (which were based upon investigations in the colder months of the year) are as follows:—

Family Income	Amount spent per head per week (pence)	Quantity purchased per head per week (ounces)
Over £1,000	8·6	4·5
£500–£999	7·1	3·9
£250–£499	6·0	3·3
£125–£249	5·2	3·4
Under £125	4·5	3·4

The poorer members of the working class do not drink less tea; they drink cheaper tea. It is a mild drug and 'revives you'; it has the additional merit of being cheap—one tenth of a penny a cup. Old age pensioners, unemployed—in fact members of all the lowest income groups—will cut down on tea last of all, and may in some cases subsist very largely on sweet tea and bread and margarine.

The experience of the trade is that working class women demand good tea and quickly detect any worsening of quality. It is on sale at a series of prices. Normally the cheapest is 1/10 per lb, and more expensive blends are available up to about 4/– or 5/– per lb. Fancy prices can be paid for other kinds of tea; but these expensive blends do not account for any large proportion of the total consumption.

The total retail value of tea sold was, according to Feavearyear, £44 million in 1936. In that year the value of tea imported was £26·5 million and the value of re-exports £4·5 million. Thus there was a gap of £22 million between the c.i.f. value of net imports [1] and the retail value of the tea. The tea tax accounted for about £6 million, and the retailers probably received for their services some £8 million. Thus

---
[1] c.i.f., cost, insurance, freight.

TEA

the wholesalers, brokers, blenders, advertisers, etc., probably accounted for some £7–8 million.

The United Kingdom consumes practically half the tea exported from the producing countries. Net imports in 1938 were as follows :—

	Value in in £000	Quantity in 000 lb
TOTAL NET IMPORTS	26,179	460,598
India	14,356	256,704
Ceylon	9,153	148,356
Dutch East Indies and Netherlands	1,013	21,808
China	337	5,970
Other countries, including Japan, Nyasaland and Kenya	1,320	27,760

About 92% of the supply by weight and a rather larger percentage by value was produced in the British Empire. In 1937 about 12% of the Indian supplies came from Southern India and 88% from the North.

Conditions of Production

The low and medium priced teas come from the plantations of India and Ceylon. Although nominally independent, the plantation companies fall into a number of groups for marketing and general management. Their policies are determined by boards of directors who live in Britain; and such firms of merchants as James Finlay and Co, Octavius Steel and Co, George Williamson and Co, Rowe, White and Co, are each of them agents and secretaries of six, eight or more companies concerned in planting tea and rubber in India, Ceylon and Africa. Frequently directors of these merchant firms sit on the boards of several planting companies.

The cultivation and picking of the tea requires a good deal of unskilled labour which is obtained very cheaply as a result of the strong organisation of the planters.

> The tea industry in Assam is probably the most highly organised in the country and the India Tea Association ... represents about 90% of the total area under tea cultivation in Assam. ... The Association has been able to enforce what are known as 'wage agreements' among its members in order to secure, as far as

practicable, uniformity in the matter of wages and to prevent one employer from paying substantially higher wages than his neighbour.[1]

The result of the poor organisation of the workers is that the whole family has to work—women, children and all, in order to keep alive.

> On the plantations nearly all the members of a worker's family are wage earners, and even children of tender years are out with their parents to increase the family earnings. There are thus comparatively few non-working dependants in a working class family. The effect of this on the standard of earnings is important for, even with low individual earnings, the total family income may be sufficiently high to prevent the worker from feeling the pinch of poverty.[2]

The earnings vary considerably, since payment is made on a piece work basis; but the following are suggested as average monthly earnings in the Assam Valley:—

(In rupees: the rupee is about 1/8.)

Men	13
Women	11
Children	7

These represent the earnings of the average worker if he does not absent himself on a single working day. Since the average worker has some days of absence per month these figures make the position seem better than it is. On the other hand most workers receive free housing and firewood and often a patch of land for private cultivation. Similar conditions prevail in other parts of India. Wages are kept low by the strong organisations of the employers.

The young shoots are picked by hand from the tea bushes and are sent as quickly as possible to the factories. There they are withered and fermented; and the tea is packed in chests for transport to the market.

The Control of the Tea Trade 1930–38

The export of tea is regulated by a scheme which first came into existence in 1929 and had the effect of maintaining

[1] *Report of the Royal Commission on Labour in India*, 1931, p. 385.
[2] *Report of Royal Commission*, pp. 398–9.

prices at the beginning of the slump. It reduced output by some 50 million lb; while bad weather effected a further reduction of some 22 million lb. Even with this restriction of supplies the price of common teas throughout 1930 stood at 8½d to 9½ per lb, and the weighted average wholesale price in the London market was 1/3¼d as compared with 1/5 in 1928–9 and 1/7¾d in 1925–6.

At the beginning of 1931, just when the tea firms were congratulating themselves that 'tea, of all the great agricultural industries, had suffered least during the great slump', the collapse came. Negotiations for the renewal of restriction broke down and prices went down to 4d a lb for common tea, while in one week in July the average weighted price of *all* tea sold at Mincing Lane was 8½d per lb (according to the Food Council).[1] The price of common tea rose in the course of the year to 7d. Prices towards the end of the year appear to be near the cost of production, since the authoritative comment was made that 'seventy-five out of every hundred pounds of tea sold in 1931 lost money to the producer'.

The tea planters had learnt their lesson, and in the following year a new restriction scheme was agreed upon by associations of Indian, Ceylon and Dutch East Indies producers. It was to last for five years and the export in any year was to be a given percentage of that of the datum (which was the export in 1929, 1930, 1931 or 1932—each national association being at liberty to select the year of maximum crop). Since new estates came into bearing after the datum years and had to have a share in the trade, any previously established estate had its export quantity restricted to less than the agreed percentage. The agreed percentage for the first year was 85.

1934 was the first full year in which the scheme operated. The results were disappointing to the planting companies because of quotas carried over from the year before and unexpected supplies from China and Formosa which were

---

[1] Food Council *Report on Tea Prices*, published July, 1931. Retail prices had not fallen with wholesale prices, and the margin according to the Food Council rose from 6d per lb in 1925–6 to 8·8d in 1929–1930.

outside the scheme. Average prices varied from district to district but were in all cases higher in 1934 than in 1933.

Cheap tea was in demand—it was reckoned that 70% of the tea drunk in Great Britain was retailed at 1/6 per lb. Imports of countries outside the scheme subsequently fell, but prices of the common teas did not show much improvement. The average price in the London market rose in the course of 1935 from 11½d to 1/0¾d per lb. During 1936 it was remarkably steady at between 1/- and 1/1, and it could be stated that 'producers do not desire the price of low grade tea to be further advanced'. Average prices per lb in some districts over the years 1933 to 1938 were as follows:—

	1933	1934	1935	1936	1937	1938
	s. d.	s. d.	s. d.	s. d.	s. d.	s. d.
Assam	1 0·55	1 1·72	1 1·58	1 1·56	1 3·46	1 2·91
Darjeeling*	1 1·69	1 3·20	1 4·27	1 3·14	1 5·27	1 4·55
Ceylon*	1 1·48	1 1·96	1 2·37	1 2·08	1 4·00	1 3·34
Cachar and Sylhet	9·23	1 0·40	10·79	11·88	1 1·86	1 0·42

* *Note.*—Ceylon accounted for a very large percentage of supplies imported into England. Darjeeling may be taken as an example of prices of finer quality tea.

The year 1938 was a fairly tranquil one for the trade. The average price of all tea in the London auctions being round about 1/1 or 1/2 per lb. It was probably true that as in the previous year on the distributive side, competition was keener than ever; dividends, cash returns, coupons, and radio advertising playing important parts in drawing public attention to particular brands.[1]

The dividends of tea planting companies, which had been very high (20–30% before 1929 in most cases) and had fallen heavily during the slump, have recovered but do not in most cases approach their earlier levels.

The London Tea Market

London is the world's principal tea market. No country

[1] The account of tea supplies 1930–7 is based upon the annual 'letter to the trade' issued by Brooke Bond and Co Ltd. Any figures and facts quoted are derived from this unless another specific source is quoted. This publication originated in the annual letter sent to *The Times* by the founder of the firm.

consumes so much tea as Britain, and in addition a large quantity is re-exported from London. Of the £30,799,000 worth of tea imported into the United Kingdom in 1938, £4,620,000 was re-exported to a number of European countries (including the Soviet Union), to Canada and to the United States. In recent years Amsterdam and Calcutta have developed a little as tea markets; but they do not rival London.

Tea is consigned to London by the estates and put into the hands of selling brokers in the tea market at Plantation House. The selling broker works on a commission of 1%, and the buying broker on a commission of ½%. One firm may carry on both buying and selling brokerage business. Sometimes in the market a selling broker on the rostrum will knock down a lot to a partner on the floor; sometimes a selling broker will bid himself for the lot which he is auctioning. The firms which do this business are old established and are few in number—on the buying side there are not more than a dozen—and it would be difficult if not impossible for an altogether new firm to be set up.

As well as acting on the instructions of a purchaser a broker may buy on his own account and sell later in smaller lots to purchasers who could not handle large quantities; the tea which is ' bought over ' in this way is catalogued and disposed of to the small dealers and blenders who rely on this method of acquiring their supplies. Probably less than 25% of the brokers' purchases are made without orders. A broker must pay a 20% deposit on any tea which he buys, so that speculation is to some extent limited. There appears to be a very real danger of abuse, however, in the case of firms which act for large purchasers. When these brokers speculate they can always treat unlucky purchases as carried out on behalf of the firm for whom they are accustomed to act. The case is particularly serious when one partner acting as selling broker deals with another partner who is buying for a large blender or dealer. The tea market is very sensitive, and the Food Council in a report published in 1926 described an unpleasant case of a broker whose prophecies in the trade press would have suited his own business very well, but were based on very slight evidence and were in the event shown to be false.

Some of the largest purchasers, who act of necessity through brokers, are the proprietary tea firms such as Lyons and Brooke Bond. It is calculated that they take as much as 20% each of the cheap tea. Allied Suppliers,[1] who buy tea and other groceries for Home and Colonial, Pearks, Liptons and other chain stores, probably account for another 20%; while the Cooperative Wholesale Society handle about 25%. Lyons, Brooke Bond and Allied Suppliers all buy through the same firm; while there was, at any rate until recently, another firm which invariably acted for the CWS. Thus two firms of buying brokers handle between them four-fifths of the total supply of tea for the mass market.[2]

While the tea is being sold in the market it remains itself in the bonded warehouse in the Port of London. It remains there not only until it is sold but until the purchaser wants it. It may stay there months; before the restriction scheme was introduced it was quite a regular thing for tea to remain in bond nine months.[3] If properly packed it does not deteriorate in that time; and the warehouses seem to be sufficiently capacious to store several months' stock without difficulty.

The Tax on Tea

It is only when the tea comes out of bond that it pays duty. This duty stands since the 1938 budget at 6d per lb on Empire tea and 8d on foreign tea. The effect of the attempt to give protection to Empire tea in this way was rather different from what was expected. Prices of all foreign

---

[1] Allied Suppliers, registered in 1929 as a private company in which 75% of the shares are held by Home and Colonial—which is itself a subsidiary of Lever Bros and Unilever Ltd. The firm are described in the Stock Exchange Year Book as 'tea blenders and packers and wholesale grocery and provision merchants; ... own (*inter alia*) the tea packing and blending businesses of Home and Colonial, Liptons, Maypole Dairy, Meadow Dairy, and Pearks Dairies'. It has a direct controlling interest in S. Frost and Co.

[2] The Imperial Economic Committee stated in 1931 that they were informed 'that about 70% of the home distributing trade is now in the hands of four combinations'.

[3] The Food Council in 1931 worked on the assumption that tea remained in bond for an average of about three months.

teas fell 2d below Empire. Foreign exporters had lowered their prices because, as the Brooke Bond letter to the trade pointed out when this preference was first introduced, ' the world's residue of supplies must come to London '— even if prices have to be cut to dispose of them there.

The tax on tea has a long history. It was first imposed in the seventeenth century at so much a gallon. It later stood at 5/- per lb. It stood at a shilling per lb in the war and post war period ; was gradually diminished until just before the election of 1929 it was abolished altogether by Winston Churchill. To Neville Chamberlain belongs the distinction of having revived it in 1932, when he put 2d per lb on British teas and 4d on foreign. Since then it has been twice increased. There is probably no more regressive tax bringing contributions to the British Exchequer. It is felt most by the poorest consumers, who spend a larger proportion of their income on tea than do the rich. It does not vary with the retail price of the tea, and it is therefore proportionately far heavier upon cheaper brands.

Blending and Distribution

Before the tea can be sold to the consumer different types, each with their own characteristics, must be blended to give satisfactory colour, taste and ' body '. Sometimes as many as eight different originals will be used to get the required blend. The blending is done by machinery and in the case of the proprietary teas (Brooke Bond, Lyons, etc.), the packeting is done at the same time.

In other cases the tea may be sent elsewhere for packeting. A small and decreasing quantity of tea is sold by the grocer from the canister [1]; and a certain amount is distributed to grocers in their own packets printed to the design of their choice and bearing their name.[2] The blend will be varied to suit the water with which the tea has to be made ; and tea of the same price bearing the same label will vary in blend according to the locality.

Most tea after it leaves the blenders passes through the

---

[1] The canister trade is much more prevalent in Ireland than in England.
[2] This may be the same blend as is offered in proprietary packets by a large distributor.

proprietary tea firms or through the CWS. One of the proprietary firms—Brooke Bond—was in peace time accustomed to distribute tea only to independent grocers and used an elaborate distributive machine. 800 vans visited grocers once a week, bringing new stocks for which payment had to be made there and then. Coop tea is of course retailed only by coop stores; and the packets labelled with the names of the grocery chains—Home and Colonial, Pearks, etc.—are also sold only through their own stores.

The other teas, such as Mazawattee, Hornimans, Salmons and Lyons (who do not rely on their chain of restaurants to get their packet tea to the public) are distributed by wholesale grocers who are said to reckon upon a margin of about 2½%. From the wholesale grocer the retailer can buy 2/- tea at 1/10, 2/6 tea at 2/2 to 2/3½d, and 2/8 tea at anything between 2/3 and 2/5 (delivered to the retailer). In general it seems that the retailers' margins are smaller in the case of Lyons tea, which is extensively and expensively advertised. Some wholesalers will give a discount of ½d a lb on orders of 24 lb and over in the case of the less popular and less advertised brands. This discount applies in the case of such teas as Mazawattee and Doctor's China. The latter, which is retailed at 4/8, 4/2 and 3/6, is sold wholesale at 3/11, 3/7 and 2/11½d. The retailer's margin may rise to a little over 20% of the wholesale price and may fall, in the case of the cheaper proprietary teas, to 10%. Brooke Bond, who deliver in their own vans weekly, allow about the same margins (no discount and cash with order).

It seems probable that the chain grocery stores secure about the same margins, although there is a tendency to cut them in order to keep up quality and attract custom. As in the case of eggs and other foodstuffs which vary in price it seems worth while for the chain stores to cut margins for the purpose of increasing the total turnover. If a housewife goes to a particular shop for her tea or eggs it is likely that she will buy her Shredded Wheat, Quaker Oats and so on at the same place.

The tea trade is clearly dominated by the large distributors of tea—CWS, Brooke Bond, Lyons and the firms represented by Allied Suppliers. They handle the bulk of the tea drunk by the working class and middle class; they could if they so desired push down prices in the London Tea Market [1]; they do already decide when the fluctuations in market price are to be reflected in the price which the housewife has to pay. The trade has a very healthy respect for the discrimination of the working class housewife as far as tea is concerned, and no firm is willing to lower the quality of one of its blends for fear of losing custom. Hence when tea prices move up or down they do so by agreement. The Tea Control Committee meets informally once a month to review prices and to decide on any necessary changes.

Conclusions

The Food Council in 1931 compared the average price of tea at Mincing Lane with the average retail price as indicated in the *Ministry of Labour Gazette*, less current duty. They found that the distributive margin had risen from 6d per lb in 1925–6 to 10d per lb in 1930–1. If the same method is applied to the end of 1937 the figures are as follows :

	per lb
Average prices at Mincing Lane in latter part of the year [2]	1/2·03d
Average retail price (latter months of 1937 and first quarter of 1938) [3]	2/2·50d
Current duty [4]	4·16d
Therefore Margin	8·31d

Although the margin is appreciably higher than in 1925–6 it is appreciably lower than in 1931. The price structure was roughly as follows :—

Value of tea landed	100
Paid by blender	135
Paid by wholesaler	154
Paid by retailer	158
Paid by housewife	186

No lowering of the price at which the broker sells can be looked for; the conditions of labour in the plantations are

---

[1] There is of course the complication that a number of tea planting companies are controlled by distributors in this country. Had it not been for this and for the effective organisation of the planting interests the market price would probably have gone down a good deal in the last few years.
[2] Derived from Brooke Bond ' letter to trade ' for 1937.
[3] From *Ministry of Labour Gazette*.
[4] Reckoning that 92% of tea consumed is British.

so bad that any cut in profits should result in better wages rather than lower prices.

One step which should unquestionably be taken to lower the price of tea is the abolition of the tax, at any rate on the cheaper grades. As a revenue expedient it is unsatisfactory because it bears equally upon all tea no matter what its price and because it is levied upon what is a necessity to the poorest section of the population. As a protective duty it has been a failure. At the same time the experience of 1929–30 should be borne in mind. When the duty was removed in the spring of 1929 the consumer gained an immediate relief. In 1930, however, the distributive margin rose precisely to the extent that the consumer was relieved of tax, and in 1931 rose again. Prices paid for tea at the auction fell further than the price which the housewife paid; this situation arose from world causes outlined above rather than from the tax changes, but the course of prices suggests that in the present state of organisation of the tea trade increased distributive costs might swallow up any benefits of reduced taxation.

10 SUGAR

Sugar is unlike most other foodstuffs in two important respects. First, some 40% of the total pre-war supply was used industrially and so was bought by the housewife not as sugar but as syrup, jam or confectionery. Second, it is not necessarily a matter for congratulation that the consumption of sugar per head in the United Kingdom was higher than in almost any other country. The League of Nations Commission stated that ' the increasing habit in certain countries of large sugar consumption tends to lessen the amount of protective foods in the diet and is to be regarded with some concern '. The Advisory Committee on Nutrition emphasised the energy value of sugar but declared that it lacked protective nutrients.

The amount of money actually spent upon sugar (as distinct from that spent on industrial products of which sugar is an important raw material) is not large nor does the quantity of sugar consumed vary much from one social class to another. Sir William Crawford calculated the weekly expenditure and consumption prior to the war to be:

Family Income	Amount spent per head per week (pence)	Quantity purchased per head per week (ounces)
Over £1,000	3·2	17·6
£500–£999	3·0	17·9
£250–£499	2·7	17·2
£125–£250	2·6	16·8
Under £125	2·3	15·2

The amount spent directly on sugar is thus so small that it seems scarcely worth while to examine the possibilities of reducing its cost; but the amount spent on various kinds of confectionery and jams is likely to be quite considerable in the case of the lower income groups and to be maintained despite poverty. Further, the consumer does not pay for sugar only over the counter; since 1923 he has paid for his sugar as a taxpayer—and has paid very heavily—through the exchequer contribution towards the cost of growing beet. The question of sugar supply and distribution deserves attention on those grounds alone.

The Source of Supplies

Practically the whole British supply of white sugar goes through the refining process (which renders it white and ready for the consumer) actually in this country. The raw sugar which these refineries use is derived from two main sources; some from beet grown in this country; the rest overseas from cane grown there. In 1937-8 the production of raw sugar from British beet amounted to nearly 391,000 tons (equivalent to 377,000 tons of refined white sugar), while imports of raw cane sugar totalled 2,377,000 tons (2,103,600 tons of refined) made up as follows :—

	000 cwt		%	%
Union of South Africa	4,298		9·1	
Mauritius	5,638		11·8	
Australia	7,616		16·1	
Fiji	1,536		3·2	
British West Indies	3,493		7·3	
Other British Countries	1,391		2·9	
Total British Empire		23,970		50·4
Dutch East Indies	2,895		6·2	
Cuba	12,068		25·3	
St Domingo	5,452		11·5	
Other Foreign Countries	3,158		6·6	
Total Foreign		23,573		49·6
Total Imported Supplies		47,543		100·0

The total c.i.f. value of this sugar was £18,867,000, but the supplies coming from British countries were valued at £12,442,000 of this. Cuba sends the largest quantity of cheap sugar—12,068 thousand cwt valued at £3,274,000.

Even before the last war sugar was taxed for revenue purposes; but since an attempt has been made to establish a sugar beet industry in Britain itself a protective element has entered into the sugar taxation policy. The import duty is complicated by variations according to the degree of polarisation of the sugar and preferences given to Empire sugar, and by the international restrictions at present imposed on the trade. In the financial year 1938-9 the Exchequer received £12,985,000 net in respect of the sugar duties and it is anticipated that the increased rates will produce a total return of £15½ million in 1939-40.

World Sugar Production and Experiments in Restriction

Costs of production of imported cane sugar vary considerably from one country to another. In 1930 the Royal Commission on the West Indian Sugar Industry, reviewing the world position, quoted a table which illustrates these variations. The situation has changed a good deal since then but the table is still worth quoting as illustrating the contrasts in costs between one country and another.

Countries in order according to production costs	Per cwt*
Cuba	8/4½
Java	9/3
Fiji	12/3
British West Indies	12/4¾
South Africa	15/8¼
Australia	24/3

* f.o.b., but excluding depreciation and interest on capital.

Cuba gained its advantage and its large share of the British market by its low costs of production and the high degree of organisation of the industry. The same Royal Commission drew attention to the existence of a single sales agency which handled all Cuban sugar exported. At that time there were already several factories there capable of grinding 100,000 tons of sugar a year—a figure which then exceeded the production of any single British West Indian colony.

Before 1914 a considerable part—as much as 50%—of the world's supply of sugar was derived from beet; these supplies were interrupted by the war, and cane producing countries, particularly Java and Cuba, took the opportunity of expanding their exports. When the war ended the beet exporting countries set about recovering their share of the world market, although more labour was required to produce a given quantity of sugar from beet than from cane, and wage levels in the beet producing countries were higher. Nevertheless beet became increasingly important as a source of supply—the proportion of beet sugar to total world supplies rose from 27% in 1920–21 to 40% ten years later; but this could be done only by an elaborate system of subsidies and export bounties in the beet producing countries. At the same time some consuming countries were giving encouragement, by preferential tariff, to cane sugar growing in tropical countries; and the efficiency of cane production was increasing. Consumption of sugar was increasing slowly, but increased production of cane and beet sugar outstripped it, and by 1929 stocks of unsold sugar had begun to accumulate in different parts of the world.

This naturally meant a sharp fall in price, and created a situation very grave for such territories as the British West Indies which were almost exclusively dependent upon sugar export. At this time too the Labour Government in the United Kingdom was proclaiming its intention of abolishing all taxes on food and so robbing West Indian sugar of the preferential position which it enjoyed. Some of the islands declared that it would be impossible for them to maintain essential services if this took place, and that they would be obliged to apply for a grant in aid from the British Exchequer. The recommendations made by a Royal Commission that the preference on sugar should be increased and a single purchasing agency set up for the United Kingdom which would guarantee a price of 15/- a cwt for imperial sugar were not accepted; but on the other hand the preference was not removed and the West Indian sugar industry survived the crisis although the world price continued to fall.

Low prices and excessive supplies, however, were a general complaint, and an endeavour was made in 1931, by means of the Chadbourne agreement between certain producing countries, to reduce supplies and improve the price, which then stood at about 6/4 per cwt as compared with 25/- eight years before. Germany, Czechoslovakia, Poland, Hungary, Belgium, Cuba, Java and Peru were the principal countries which participated. Production was reduced in these countries by 6·4 million tons between 1929–30 and 1933–4; but on the other hand the countries outside the agreement increased their production by 4·2 million tons. British possessions were the worst offenders—India, Australia, South Africa, Mauritius, Fiji and the West Indies all increased their production by anything up to 50% by 1933–4; and have all increased it still further since then. Such additional supplies flooding the market made the Chadbourne agreement unworkable; and although stocks were reduced prices remained almost as low as ever.

Between May 1937 and September 1939 the world supply of sugar was limited by an elaborate system of quotas based upon the quantity exported by the various countries in the year ending 31 August 1937. The Agreement, which was supervised by the International Sugar Council, covered all the important producing countries except Argentina and Canada; the United Kingdom as part of the scheme guaranteed to maintain those parts of the Sugar Industry Reorganisation Act (1935) which limited the total production from beet in the country; and there was, within the general agreement, a special position assigned to the British Colonies, the Union of South Africa and the Commonwealth of Australia as British Preferential Suppliers (with aggregate basic export quotas amounting to just over 1½ million tons [1]).

The sugar exporting industries in the countries which supply the United Kingdom are for the most part highly organised. The South African industry has developed rapidly since the formation of the South Africa Sugar Association in 1919—and in the last decade increased efficiency has doubled production. An attempt has been made to limit production because of the heavy supplies produced as a result of increased efficiency; but most of the mills exceeded their quotas. The Australian industry has also expanded recently and there is an agreement between the government and the growers whereby a high retail price

---

[1] The quotas increase or decrease from year to year in proportion to the increase or decrease of the estimated quantity required by the U.K. in the year in question compared with requirements in the year ending 31 August 1937.

is fixed for home consumption so that sugar can be exported below cost of production. Through the use of these methods Australia has secured a high quota—approaching the peak export figures—under the 1937 International Agreement.

Neither of these countries, however, is so exclusively dependent upon sugar export as are the British West Indies where sugar plantations have existed since the eighteenth century. These countries did not supply more than 7 or 8% of the United Kingdom imports of raw sugar; but the islands were almost exclusively dependent upon this trade and upon their sugar export to Canada. Because of the large share which this one crop plays in their economy, they have been seriously hit by world excess production; and the sugar industry in this area constitutes one of the principal economic problems of the British Empire.

Difficulties arose in 1939 as a result of the decisions of the International Sugar Council in the previous year. By a cut of 5% in the quotas and by voluntary surrender of quotas by some countries the Council adjusted the supplies forthcoming to the estimated consumption. This adjustment, however, was upset by the poor crops in India and Europe and by the hoarding of sugar in several countries as a result of unsettled political conditions. The result was a shortage of sugar which drove up prices.

The Refining Industry in the United Kingdom

Before 1928 a considerable proportion of the sugar supplies of the United Kingdom was refined abroad and brought into the country in that state. In 1928, however, the Finance Act lowered the duties on raw sugar as compared with refined. The British refiners agreed to lower their price to the consumer in accordance with the reduction in duty; this reduction the foreign refiners, of course, could not imitate and so the British refining industry secured a monopoly of the home market. Under the Industrial Agreement concluded in 1933 by the sugar manufacturing companies on the one hand and the refiners on the other an elaborate quota system regulates the refining both of home produced beet sugar and imported raws.

Five-nineteenths of the pre-war refining was done by the Corporation (subject to certain conditions and qualifications about the amount which is refined during the beet season) and the remaining fourteen-nineteenths by the refiners. There are seven refiners registered with the Ministry of Agriculture, and they divided the fourteen-nineteenths among themselves as follows :—

	%
Tate and Lyle Ltd	74·965
Martineau Ltd	1·229
MacFie and Sons Ltd	5·501
The Sankey Sugar Co Ltd	5·482
John Walker and Co (Sugar Refiners) Ltd	4·654
The Westburn Sugar Refineries Ltd	5·735
The Glebe Sugar Refining Co Ltd	2·434

The table makes clear the predominance of Tate and Lyle in the sugar trade; but that predominance is even greater than it appears here, for Tate and Lyle have bought up MacFie and Sons, closed it, and assumed its quota, already control John Walker and have a 50% interest in the Glebe Co. The firm, which has a capital of £8,600,000,[1] was founded in 1921 on the amalgamation of the two large and old established houses of Henry Tate and Sons and Abram Lyle and Sons, acquired an interest in a number of beet sugar factories and to-day has a large holding of shares in the British Sugar Corporation, which controls these enterprises under government auspices.

The firm has interests too in the West Indies, where it controls Caroni Ltd., with its 19,000 acres of cultivated sugar in Trinidad, and the West Indies Sugar Co Ltd. At the annual meeting in December 1938 Sir Leonard Lyle referred to—

> excellent results from the manufacture of such articles as tins, wooden cases, packing containers, and also from our road transport company, which has not only functioned most efficiently, especially during the recent crisis, but which has shown us an excellent return on the money invested. We are concentrating still further

[1] The capital stood at £4½ million in 1932 (3,400,000 ordinary shares of £1 and 1,100,000 6½% preference shares of £1). The ordinary share capital has been increased by two bonus issues of 40% each.

on the production of essential materials used in the manufacture of our articles.[1]

Under an agreement between Tate and Lyle and the Government made in 1936-7 the effective refining margin is limited to 13/- per cwt.[2] In addition, however, Tate and Lyle reserved the right to increase the margin if costs rose above the 1935 level; and according to the Ministry of Agriculture costs had risen at least 2½d per cwt. This provision was agreed upon in correspondence between Sir Leonard Lyle (President of the firm) and the Treasury; the published agreement makes allowance for the margin to rise in accordance with changes in another respect—a rise in the cost of raw sugar. The refiners are entitled to raise the margin 1d per cwt for every 1/- by which the price of raw sugar exceeds 4/6. The refining margin, however, appears to cover Tate and Lyle's costs fairly adequately, as they showed a net profit after payment of tax of £1,260,590 in 1938. Between 1934 and 1938 the dividend on ordinary shares was never less than 18%, and bonus issues, of 40% on each occasion, took place in 1935 and 1938. The net profit for 1938 after payment of tax was £1,260,590. In the following year the net profit was £1,319,788, but large sums were put to reserve and a dividend of only 13½% was declared.[3]

The British Sugar Beet Industry

The British sugar beet industry, which supplied nearly a fifth of the total sugar requirements of the United Kingdom on the outbreak of war, was not firmly established until a government subsidy scheme was introduced in 1924. For ten years or more before that attempts had been made

[1] *The Times*, 9 December 1939.

[2] This margin is not easy to estimate precisely, because it is apparently to be calculated, not upon the difference between the average of daily raw sugar prices and the 'Tate and Lyle granulated ex-refinery' price quoted daily in the newspapers, but upon the difference between this average and the price actually realised by the firm for refined sugar. A controversy arose on this point between Sir Leonard Lyle and the City Editor of the *Daily Herald*, who had stated that the refiners' margin tended to average more than the 13/- per cwt agreed upon. (See *Daily Herald*, city page, 9th January, 1939.) Included in this 13/-, it should be noted, is the excise duty.

[3] This was on 49 weeks' working instead of 52, since the company deemed it advisable to end its financial year prematurely on the outbreak of war.

to set up beet factories; but despite government grants and remission of excise duty (in 1922), they had been unsuccessful. The 1924 scheme was largely justified in the House of Commons on the ground that it would benefit agriculture—for the price given by the factories for beet would mean at least one profitable crop for farmers. The factories received a subsidy on every cwt of sugar they produced. All that they were required to undertake was that three-quarters of their machinery should be British. Their accounts were to be placed annually in the hands of the Minister of Agriculture, who was authorised to make public only the aggregate trading profits.

This scheme, although expensive (£34 million was paid in direct subsidy and £15 million allowed in duty remission between 1924 and 1935), did not solve the problem. The number of factories and the acreage of sugar beet increased rapidly; but trouble began to be caused by the refiners, who felt their competition, for the factories refined the sugar which they produced. Pressure by the refiners upon the Government resulted in a provision in the Finance Act of 1928 which reduced the duty on raw sugar below that on refined.[1] This meant that the refiners, although not protected against the factories, were protected against sugar which was refined outside the country altogether; and in return they promised to reduce the price to the consumer by 2/4 per cwt, which was the extent of the protection given to them.

This concession, however, introduced a new complication. The excise duty—that is the payment made by the factories on the refined sugar which they produced—was reduced only by a fraction of a penny over 1/6 per cwt. If the factories produced raw sugar, however, they got the advantage of the full reduction by 2/4. The consequence was that the factories tended to produce raw sugar—which they passed on to the refineries—and themselves set about refining sugar which had been imported raw; a system calculated to waste the maximum amount of money on handling and transport. Keen competition followed, in which the refineries

---

[1] This was rather a complicated business, because a given quantity of raw sugar produces approximately ·9 of that weight of refined sugar.

proper, such as Tate and Lyle, who were building up their powerful position in the industry, had the big advantage of a large throughput. Moreover, under the original scheme the subsidy rate, which had come down in 1927, was reduced once more in 1930, and this, combined with the complications arising from the 1928 Finance Act, put the factories in a very bad financial position. The aggregate trading margin, as published by the Government, fell heavily; and in an endeavour to avoid the granting of further government aid, the Minister of Agriculture negotiated early in 1933 an Industrial Agreement between the factories and the refineries. It was based on a total consumption in the country of 1,900,000 tons, of which the factories were allocated a total of 500,000 and the refineries 1,400,000. Any excess of beet sugar over the current campaign quota had to be produced as raw sugar. The refiners undertook to provide an assured market for what the factories produced over and above their quota. By the operation of this agreement, competition was brought to an end and the trading position and profits of the refiners as well as of the factories improved thereafter.

In 1935, after a great deal of inquiry and negotiation, a new scheme of organisation of the British sugar industry was produced.[1] It was ten years since the Government had begun to give indiscriminate subsidy to sugar beet manufacture without demanding any substantial control in return. Within ten years, the more optimistic advocates of the subsidy had argued, the industry would be on its feet; but at the end of that period there came instead a new scheme based upon further generous grants from the Exchequer. The sugar factories were amalgamated into the British Sugar Corporation, with three out of its eleven directors appointed by the Government, and individuals who had had shares in these established enterprises received holdings in the Corporation. The Treasury guaranteed a basic dividend of 4% on a share capital of £5 million, and in addition, as an incentive to more efficient working, the shareholders were to have distributed to them a percentage of the economies effected

[1] See *Report of the Committee of Enquiry into the U.K. Sugar Industry* 1935. The Committee was presided over by Sir Wilfred Greene.

on amalgamation by use of more modern machinery and by improvements in marketing.[1]

The Incentive Agreement, intended to provide an inducement for the Corporation to make economies, suggests that those who framed the scheme did not put much reliance on the power of three government nominees on the Board of Directors to influence the policy of the industry; and the Sugar Commission of independent individuals set up under the 1936 Act is a more serviceable instrument of control. This Commission had the general functions of supervising matters relating to the production and marketing of sugar in the United Kingdom; and further it was its duty to calculate in accordance with the provisions of the Act the subsidy to be paid to the Corporation in a given year and to decide upon the price to be paid for beet if the Corporation and the National Farmers Union (which acts as representative of the growers) cannot agree.

Since the Act came into force the amounts of sugar produced and of assistance paid have been as follows:—

	Sugar produced, white equivalent (tons)	Payments made to farmers for beet	Direct assistance from the Exchequer
		£	£
1936–7	521,963	6,853,000	2,562,113
1937–8	377,133	5,230,000	1,231,810
1938–9	289,435	4,947,000	1,730,048

To produce a ton of beet costs normally between 20/- and 30/- and the average price paid by the factories for delivered beet was 40/6. From this ton three cwt of sugar can be manufactured. Factory costs are not easy to estimate; they are no longer published, but in 1933–4 they stood at 4/3 per cwt of sugar. Taking 4/- as the present figure the total cost of producing 1 cwt of raw sugar from beet is about 16/-, whereas the price of raw sugar manufactured from cane ranged during 1938 between 4/- and 8/5 per cwt.

[1] The percentage which they were to receive of economies affected after 1936 was to be calculated in accordance with a complicated table. Broadly speaking the larger the economy the larger the share that the Corporation got; but in successive years this share in respect of economies made was to diminish.

The Distribution of Sugar

The wholesale side of sugar distribution is dealt with mostly by dealers doing a general trade in groceries, but the wholesalers of sugar do not in most cases touch the sugar itself. It is sent from the factories to the retail distributors and the wholesaler merely takes his discount. The main reason for this is the tradition of the days when the refineries found it easier to hand over the task of finding the retailers to a middleman.

The precise terms of sale by the manufacturer vary with the quantity taken. A standard price, known as the ' list price' is quoted by the refiners, and discounts are allowed which vary with the quantity purchased. For example, $4\frac{1}{2}$d per cwt is allowed on 100 tons, 3d on 10 tons and $1\frac{1}{2}$d on $2\frac{1}{2}$ tons. The larger wholesalers sell to the retailer at the list price less discount, and their profits consist of the difference in the discount obtained on the larger quantities bought by retailers. Cartage is charged in addition. Smaller wholesalers charge up to 6d per cwt above list price. A few retailers who take sufficient quantities can buy direct from the refineries, but on the whole buying is done through the wholesalers. In London and South Wales the terms of sale are maintained by agreements between the wholesalers. The general conclusion of the Greene Committee seemed to be that the wholesale business is operated on a ' small but comparatively assured margin of profit '.

The retail trade, however, has no such assured margin of profit. In peace time conditions retail margins were extremely small, and it was a common practice for sugar to be sold by retailers at less than the cost price to them, with the object of attracting custom. For example, when the refiners' list price was 18/9 a cwt, sugar was being sold retail in London and other areas at 2d a lb—equivalent to 18/8 a cwt. In the evidence before the Greene Committee it was maintained that at such a wholesale price a retail price of $2\frac{1}{4}$d per lb was the minimum which would actually cover costs. At a price of 2d a grocer buying on the most favourable terms would have shown a very small gross profit, insufficient to cover a due share of overhead expenses, and the majority of grocers, who are unable to buy on the best terms, would have shown more or less substantial gross losses. Even at a price of $2\frac{1}{4}$d per lb there would be very little net profit.

Until the most recent tax changes retail prices were at a much lower level than between 1920 and 1930. The average retail price per lb was about 7d just after the last war, and remained as high as 3d or $3\frac{1}{2}$d until about 1928, since which date it has fluctuated between 2d and 3d. Part of the reduction in price was due to a lower effective rate of tax, part to a fall in the price of raw sugar—which stood at 25/9 per cwt (excluding duty) in 1923 and at 4/9 in 1934.[1] Since then the weekly price of raw sugar has varied between 4/- and 8/6.

War Conditions

With the outbreak of war came a deliberate attempt to restrict the amount of sugar eaten. The purpose of sugar rationing—as the Ministry of Food explained in its official statements—was not to share fairly a food which was short but rather to reduce imports which had to be paid for in foreign exchange. This is the explanation of the paradox that after millions of pounds have been spent on building a sugar beet industry in the United Kingdom sugar is rationed after three months instead of as in the last war after three years. Shortage of supply and heavier war time taxation on sugar had the effect of raising its retail price by 49% between 1 September and 1 December 1939.

With the war came still greater strengthening of the position of Tate and Lyle, and still closer relations between this firm and the government. One of the directors of the company was made Assistant Sugar Controller in the Ministry of Food and it seems that the sugar division of the Ministry ran itself most efficiently, apparently through the machinery of Tate and Lyle. Accordingly, at the annual meeting in December 1939, Sir Leonard Lyle was able to describe the situation as follows :—

> Shareholders will be aware that the business of providing the necessary raw sugar for our refineries has been transferred, for the period of the war, to the Food Minister. We are glad that

[1] Annual average of prices of foreign raw sugar 96°.

his task at the inception of control was made easier for him than it might have been by the fact that we had entered into contracts for the purchase of abnormally large quantities of sugar.

The money we have spent in the last few years in perfecting our arrangements for the distribution of our sugar and syrup products has indeed been well justified. The coming of control found us with an up-to-date and reliable system of distribution, and it is a source of great satisfaction to us that our policy both in regard to our expenditure on our factories and on our distributive system has enabled us to place a most efficient service at the disposal of the nation during the present emergency.

Conclusions

There are, it is true, small economies which might be made in the British sugar beet industry. There is, for example, a good deal of waste in the transport of beet, and each season there are a number of prosecutions for careless loading of lorries which lead to the beet falling on to the roadway and causing danger as well as waste. More serious is the fact that despite the elaborate 'control' to which the sugar industry is subjected there has never been any real planning, particularly so far as the siting of factories is concerned. The one Scottish factory—at Cupar—has a minimum economic throughput which is just twice as large as the largest sugar beet crop which has ever been grown in Scotland. But at the same time, even if small economies could be effected, there would be fundamental weaknesses in the industry. The sugar beet produced in this country costs the Exchequer about 3/4 per cwt in direct assistance, quite apart from the rebates in taxation which have been granted to encourage the industry. This could be reduced slightly by a revision of the 1936 Sugar Industry Reorganisation Act and the transformation of the British Sugar Corporation into a government department relieved of the obligation to pay 4% on its capital; but even this would not bring the cost of producing beet sugar down to that of producing cane sugar abroad and transporting it to London. There do not, however, appear to be any reasons for expecting extensive reductions in the costs of beet sugar production [1] whereas

---

[1] 'No revolutionary developments in its technique or revolutionary changes in its costs may be expected.' Majority Report of the Greene Committee, p. 94.

by better organisation, particularly at the factory stage of production, it might well be possible to lower the cost of cane sugar.

The British beet sugar production is divided up between eighteen factories which worked an average of 73 days each in 1937-8 season.[1] Clearly a processing industry organised in units of this size and with so short a season is not likely to be efficient and economical even when the factories are also used as refineries in the off season. As a result of this use of factories in the off season, the United Kingdom has a refining capacity which amounted in 1934 to 3,887,000 tons annually and is probably much the same to-day. The refineries proper accounted for about 60%, and as a result of the existence of the factories the country now has the capacity to refine far more sugar than it consumes or is ever likely to consume.

The form and organisation of the British Sugar Corporation and the Sugar Commission is quite compatible with the gradual disappearance of the sugar beet industry. Expense to the Exchequer can be reduced year by year without the factories in which a good deal of capital has been sunk, and which are politically not uninfluential, being a penny the worse. The shareholders presumably still receive their 4% dividend so long as the present scheme remains in operation, even if no more than one ton of sugar is produced. In fact, the quantity of sugar produced has declined each season since 1936 and is now just two-thirds of the maximum quantity which might be produced under the provisions of the Reorganisation Act.

No tears need be shed over the British sugar beet industry. It has been exceedingly expensive to establish and is defensible only on the ground that it is of benefit to agriculture. A programme for agriculture based upon the increased production of the protective foods would remove that argument. There remains the defence argument; but this can be met by a policy of storage of stocks of sugar.

---

[1] The number of days worked had been 97 and 98 in the two preceding seasons. The factory season begins in September or October and lasts until the new year.

The expensive establishment and maintenance of a British sugar industry is particularly difficult to justify in view of the increase in production of cane sugar and the difficulties which have arisen in the West Indies. It would seem that if and as the British sugar industry declines further, preference should be given to the West Indies. The situation there, as a result of distress, has changed greatly, and the growing Labour movement is demanding public control of the sugar factories; so that any increased demand for West Indian sugar would probably stimulate trade union activities to ensure that the workers secured a larger share of the income of the industry.

The refining business in this country is a different question. Here the refiners in peace and war make very large profits indeed from their monopoly position. Here is an opportunity for the extension of real public control over a highly organised industry which profitably controls an article of everyday consumption. The public control at present exercised—by the Ministry of Agriculture—over the refining margin is thoroughly inadequate. The 13/- per cwt agreed upon, subject to adjustment as costs of refining rose (but not apparently as they fell), secures—if profits are any criterion—a very ample margin.

11 BRITISH AGRICULTURE AND FOOD SUPPLY

A fair proportion of the total supplies of the essential foodstuffs were in peace time produced in the United Kingdom itself. All the milk, 60% of the eggs, almost all the potatoes, 90% of the fish, more than 40% of the meat, 10% of the butter, 25% of the cheese, 80% of the vegetables, 25% of the sugar and probably some 15 to 20% of the flour annually consumed in the United Kingdom were home produced. Thus in any consideration of prices and supplies there must be some discussion of the complicated issues of farming practice and policy.

The Character of British Agriculture

British agriculture has changed a good deal in the last hundred years. The gloomy prophecies of the Protectionists in the forties of last century, who declared that the ruin of agriculture would follow the repeal of the Corn Laws, have not been fulfilled. It was not until the '70s when the development of railways opened up the prairies of North America for wheat production that the British farmers felt the severe competition of imports. This led to greater attention to livestock; but when the use of refrigeration made possible the supply of meat also from overseas, British agriculture found itself in difficulties. A solution to these difficulties was sought in concentration upon high quality products for a necessarily comparatively limited market and, later, upon the production of milk, vegetables, fruit and eggs, which had to be got fresh to the consumer.

The character of British agriculture has continued to change since the end of the last war. The figures for gross returns to British agriculture published annually must be used with caution, for a particular farming product may be essential but, having no cash realisation value, may not feature in the return.[1] Nevertheless they show what

[1] Thus grass, which A. G. Street describes as ' by far the biggest and most important crop in British agriculture ', is rarely sold off the farm and so scarcely appears in these figures.

agriculture is providing in the way of food for the rest of the community, and the amount of money which is being paid over to the farmers for these supplies. The total return for Great Britain is about £260 million annually. Livestock and livestock products account for nearly £170 million of this, whereas wheat accounts for £7 million worth and fruit and vegetables (including potatoes) together for £42 million. If the livestock figure is analysed further it shows a return of £64 million in respect of milk and £18 million in respect of eggs as against £86 million in respect of meat. Livestock is in fact the basis of British agriculture; and if the protective foods—milk, eggs, vegetables (excluding potatoes) and fruit—are taken together they account for no less than £109 million, which is more than 40% of the total income of British agriculture.[1] These commodities have increased in importance to the farmer in the past twenty years.

Since 1918 the concerns engaged in processing and distributing the products of agriculture have grown in size. In part this was the consequence of the experience of war time, when companies were encouraged to cooperate with one another and when a consequent stimulus was given to combination; but in greater part it has been due to the general tendency towards the concentration of capital and the attempt to secure monopoly in a profit making society, and has in some cases been fostered by the Government. In 1916 the United Dairies was set up; five years later the firms of Tate and Lyle combined; and in 1929 the Millers Mutual Association came into existence. In part the organisation of agricultural producers and the regulation of marketing, as envisaged by Addison when he introduced the 1931 Agricultural Marketing Act, were intended to strengthen the farmers in face of those who were buying their produce.[2]

---

[1] Farm crops, including cereals, sugar beet, straw and potatoes (which alone account for £17 million) bring in by contrast only 18% of the income of agriculture.

[2] A. W. Street, then Principal Secretary of the Ministry of Agriculture, opening a discussion on *Agricultural Organisation To-day and To-morrow* at the 1935 Conference of Agricultural Organisers, put the matter in this way. He cited the example of American monopolies which cut down growers' prices and maintained consumers' prices. ' Great as is the

Marketing organisation and regulation developed considerably between 1931 and the outbreak of war. The elaborate milk scheme, administered by a board elected by registered producers, was set up; a potato scheme, administered in the same way, limited the acreage and regulated the marketing by use of the riddle and by authorisation of merchants; the National Farmers' Union negotiated with the British Sugar Corporation the price to be paid for beet; a restriction scheme for hops was introduced; and a persistent endeavour was made to organise the bacon industry under boards representative of pig producers and bacon curers, with a Development Board to supervise the industry and to administer a scheme giving a guaranteed price to the farmers and a guaranteed margin to the curers. At the same time a Wheat Commission, representative of all interests involved, secured to farmers a price for wheat from funds derived from a levy on flour, and a livestock commission was appointed to survey and regulate local markets, to set up three experimental slaughterhouses and pay a subsidy on fat cattle. This appointed commission is assisted by advisory committees representative of the trades concerned.

Despite this organisation of marketing mostly by organisation of the producers themselves, the processing and distributing concerns enjoyed very great prosperity. United Dairies have made profits of more than £600,000 a year for several years; the cheese factories have been able to pay 20-25%; the head of a firm of bacon curers—a private company which is reputed to control 40% of the bacon output—left a fortune of half a million; the brewers' profits remained undiminished although the barley growers were in difficulties.[1] In the case of milk, the retail margin

difference in degree, let us not forget that the milk situation as we knew it a year or two ago was, in certain respects, fundamentally similar to the tobacco situation in America—the almost complete powerlessness of the individual primary producer in face of the gradual emergence of immensely wealthy and powerful combines.' He then went on to say that the positive and constructive side of organised marketing was even more important.

[1] An interesting comment upon the condition of agriculture is made by a writer in the *Journal of the Institute of Bankers* (1936) who proposes a Rural Investment Trust. ' The basis of trust securities would be carefully selected holdings of farm lands and buildings supported and balanced by

increased steadily. Nor does there appear to be any prospect of the Government reducing distributive costs—if the abortive Milk Bill, published and withdrawn in the autumn of 1938, is any guide. That provided for an independent Milk Commission which would have been able to make regulations about the number of deliveries and the size of bottles; but it would in addition have enabled the milk distributors to set up a scheme covering the whole country, or part of it, under which they could have consolidated their own power, limited the expansion of the cooperatives, and taken over the functions of the Commission relating to distribution. There would in fact have been no guarantee that milk would be any cheaper.

The Farm and the Labour

The £260 million worth of agricultural produce of Great Britain is provided by some 300,000 farmers working nearly 30 million acres of land and employing between them some 740,000 workers. Their holdings vary a good deal in size and may be divided as follows :—

Size group	No. of holdings	Percentage of total agricultural acreage in this group
Over 300 acres .	14,000	26
150–300 ,, .	41,000	27
50–150 ,, .	110,000	35
Under 50 ,, .	134,000	12

Thus, practically 50% of the agricultural land in Great Britain is in holdings under 150 acres each. The overwhelming majority of the farms are not specialised; and the fact that a particular crop may be grown not for its own sake but because of its use in the general running of the farm makes statements of farm costs sometimes misleading. There has, it is true, been some development of specialised poultry and fruit farming in the last twenty years; but on the

holdings of shares in companies concerned with the processing and distribution of agricultural produce—for example fruit canning factories, bacon factories and—to name an individual company—United Dairies Ltd. The vertical structure would secure for an agricultural investment a share in the relatively high profits of the allied distributing companies. Companies formed solely to hold land may, however, offer some attraction to a limited special public.'

other hand it has become clear that vegetables fit exceedingly well into the routine of the general farm, and it would in fact be difficult to find evidence for the view that there is a definite tendency in British farming towards specialisation. The imagination of some has been caught by the large scale collective farms of the Soviet Union which make the fullest use of modern machinery; and it is suggested that such methods might well be used here for the cultivation of wheat on the same scale as in the United States or Canada. There is little doubt that technically it would be possible to lower the cost of wheat production in this country in this way. But there seems to be little point in making such a break with the established methods of British farming and changing so completely the appearance of the countryside. Britain has not the wide plains of North America or of the Soviet Union; and it would seem to be best to maintain substantially the present balance of British agriculture rather than to attempt in an altogether artificial way to turn Britain into a corn producing land.

Two to three hundred acres is stated by experts to be the smallest unit of arable land on which modern machinery can be efficiently used[1]; and there seems to be no case on economic grounds for units much larger. Especially is this the case if livestock is the foundation of farming in the district. The economies which can be made in the purchase of fertilisers and feedingstuffs are available to the man who works on a comparatively modest scale and give him an advantage over the smallholder. But the reductions in costs which can be effected by casting farm to farm are not large; and except in arable farming the advantages of the producer on a really large scale—say 500 acres or more—arise rather in marketing or in securing credit than actually in production.[2]

Moreover it is not always easy to increase the size of a

---

[1] See *British Agriculture*, Chapter XIX, for a discussion of the question of farm sizes.

[2] The output per £100 worth of total equipment, horse and labour costs, rises with size from £110 per annum in the case of 20–50 acre farms to £144 in the case of farms over 300 acres. After that the increase is very slight. This was the conclusion of R. Carslaw and C. Culpin in an article, 'Labour Power and Equipment in Arable Farming,' in the *Journal of the Royal Society of Agriculture*, 1936.

farm even when the farmer concerned has the necessary resources. There must be land adjacent which is suitable for the purpose required and which is available for purchase or for rent. These conditions are often not fulfilled, so that the farmer who wants to expand will be compelled to take another farm at a distance, perhaps in another county; and clearly the technical economies which can be effected under these conditions are not large.

If then the basis of any increased production is to be an agriculture which in its broadest outlines resembles the present system, the next point is to consider how production may be stimulated and costs lowered. A total increase of about 50% in the present production of milk, 40% in the production of eggs, 25% in the production of meat and 50% or so in the production of vegetables is what is required in terms of present home production if imports are maintained at their present level. These are the foodstuffs of which Britain at present produces a considerable share and which she is by natural conditions well suited to produce.

The well-being of British agriculture depends directly upon the home market for foodstuffs. Since this was not expanding as rapidly in the past twenty years (and particularly during the period 1929 to 1935) as in the decades before 1914 difficulties were likely to arise. These were made more certain by the general expansion in distributive margins which has been going on since the war, for this expansion has decreased the share actually paid to the farmer of the total expenditure on home grown food. At the same time the government was unwilling to see the amount of money paid for imported food decreased, because this would react upon the industrialist exporter and the investor who draws an income from abroad.[1] Since the market—comparing the last two or three years with 1927-9—has not expanded, any increase in home production (unless accompanied by a reduction in prices) was bound to mean a reduction in imports. The main hope of British agriculture lies in fact in an attack upon malnutrition and in a consequent revival in the demand

---

[1] This difficulty from the Conservative point of view is put very clearly in the first chapter of *British Agriculture*.

for home grown foodstuffs. In the absence of a programme to effect this all that was offered to agriculture was a series of subsidies granted in response to political pressure by the farmers. Agriculture is in fact existing on a Speenhamland system; its earnings are supplemented by public doles. The consequence is a lack of any spirit of enterprise and an inability to use present technical resources to the full.

Since the last war the productivity of labour in agriculture has been rising; and there is no question at all that, given the necessary time, far larger quantities of food could be produced on British land at reasonable prices. In recent years the output per worker has risen by about 4% per annum; although the tendency for specially skilled workers at special rates of pay to form a large proportion of the total has meant that output per £100 spent in wages has not risen so sharply. At the same time the agricultural worker still remains very poorly paid, and is forced to endure bad housing conditions and a lack of the social amenities taken for granted by the town dweller. A better standard of living for the agricultural worker should be a first charge upon a revived agriculture; and it is a charge which must be met. The Fordson Estate, for example, where vegetables and fruit are cultivated on a large scale and are marketed in large quantities, is able to pay wages which are 25% above the county minimum; but even these wages are below those which workers of comparable skill secure in urban occupations.

The share of labour in total costs varies with the commodity produced. Labour accounts for the greater part of the costs in the case of fruit and vegetables; about 25% in the case of milk; about 16% in the case of egg production on the battery system. But owing to the prevalence of general farming these calculations do not carry us very far. The best indication of the importance of wages as an agricultural cost is the total wage bill for agriculture. It amounts to £50–51 million [1]—to be set against a total value of agri-

---

[1] This is based on Colin Clark's estimates, in *National Income and Outlay*, 1937, of the average annual income of various types of agricultural worker. The average wage of a regular adult worker he reckoned at £91·2 per annum in 1930–1. Wages for casual and women workers were a good deal lower. It is necessary to add 10% to cover wages advances since 1931.

cultural output (which is of course not the same as total cost) of some £260 million. This figure of £50 million includes only payments actually made to hired workers—it does not include any allowance for family labour which is of great importance to British agriculture.

The Farmers' Costs : Feedingstuffs and Fertilisers

This calculation shows that wages are not the largest single item in agricultural costs; feedingstuffs cost the farmer as much and call for special consideration.[1] Since livestock and livestock products account for some two-thirds of the total value of British agricultural production, the question of feedingstuffs required for the animals is clearly of key importance. It has been estimated that nine-tenths of the agricultural land and one-half of agricultural labour is used to provide feedingstuffs; and particularly in the winter months the actual purchase of feedingstuffs is a very large item in the expenses of the livestock farmer. Probably the best estimate that can be made of the actual cash expenditure on feedingstuffs by the farming community is £50 million although the true figure may be 10% higher.

Animals are inefficient machines for converting feedingstuffs into foods; and indeed Colin Clark has gone so far as to argue that from the point of view of national defence agriculture is more of a liability than an asset.[2] Not more than 2,278,000 tons of meat and livestock products, he argued, were produced as a result of an import of 8,936,000 tons of fodder. This argument certainly brings out very clearly the extent to which farming in this country has become a processing industry dependent on the use of raw materials from overseas.

It seems at first sight as though animals will eat anything—fish meal, the leafy tops of sugar beet, the molasses which remain after the sugar has been crushed out, potatoes and

---

[1] It is difficult to arrive at a satisfactory estimate because calculations usually quoted are concerned with the total value of feedingstuffs used, in terms of money. This includes a good deal consumed on the farm where it is produced, which cannot therefore fairly be set against the output of agriculture.

[2] Article in *The Spectator*, 23 April 1937. His calculations were based on 1934 figures.

any surplus vegetable stocks—all of these, the standard books on agriculture assure us, can be fed to livestock. But that is not to say that an animal can be fed indiscriminately on any of these that happen to be to hand; the diet of a cow must be planned and balanced carefully if the best results are to be obtained. Not only must the animal take protein and starch and vitamins; it must have some bulky food such as straw, as well, to give it warmth and satisfy its hunger.

The available supplies of feedingstuffs are made up as follows[1]:

	Total Supplies	Available nutrients (000 tons)		Percentage of nutrients supplied by each class	
	(000 tons)	Protein equivalent	Starch equivalent	Protein equivalent	Starch equivalent
Home production.					
From arable land	14,571	1,165	7,473	33·8	35·3
From permanent grass	18,163	1,348	8,910	38·9	42·0
From by-products	275	77	154	2·2	0·7
Total home produced	33,009	2,590	16,537	74·9	78·0
Imported.					
Cereals and cereal products	6,013	526	3,672	15·2	17·4
Oil seed products	1,735	341	989	9·9	4·6
Total Imports	7,748	867	4,661	25·1	22·0
Total Supply	40,757	3,457	21,198	100·0	100·0

This brings out very clearly the importance of grass as a food for cattle compared with imports or home arable as a source of fodder. In recent years a good deal more research and attention has been devoted to grass growing[2]; although it does not appear that the results of the research have yet been widely applied. It has been shown that young grass is richer in protein than old grass; and that there are varying types of grass, each with its own characteristics and uses. Two million acres of land in England and Wales are already under cultivated grass. Results of research suggest that the

[1] Based on a table relating to 1935 figures in Norman C. Wright, *The Importance of Home Produced Feeding Stuffs*, reprinted from *The Transactions of the Highland and Agricultural Society of Scotland*, 1938.
[2] On this, see, for example, D. H. Robinson, *The New Farming*, 1938.

capacity of these pastures and of the millions of acres of rough grazing could be increased. Grasses have been developed which come to maturity at different times of the year, so that all-the-year-round grazing is a possibility.

This suggests one approach to the problem of winter grazing—which is obviously a difficulty in the way of completer reliance upon grass for fodder. Normally the dairy farmer who depends upon grass to feed his cows in the summer has to buy comparatively large quantities of imported feedingstuffs during the winter. It seems possible that the more careful cultivation of grass may enable cattle to be pastured throughout the winter; or alternatively the process of drying grass may be cheapened and so supplies of winter feed ensured.

This artificial drying of grass by the use of machinery is more efficient than the natural drying method—that is, by haymaking. In the case of hay, grass is cut at its least valuable period and much of its food value is lost. Grass for drying can—and indeed must—be cut at the right moment. All forms of stock can take it as a food; and there is no reason why a milch cow for example should not be maintained upon fresh grass in the summer and dried grass in the winter, except that it would under present conditions be rather expensive. The prospects for dried grass have been summed up as follows:—

> The main virtue of dried grass, however, is as a protein and mineral food and a possible substitute for imported feedingstuffs. The economic value of the process will depend mainly on whether it will be found possible to produce sufficient quantities of good dried grass at a price which will compare per unit of value with other foodstuffs. There seemed every reason to suppose that this was possible at 1937 prices, while, should the prices of other feedingstuffs rise, the incentive to produce dried grass will thereby increase. In 1937 the cost of grass drying under favourable conditions seemed to work out at about £5 per ton of dried grass at 1937 prices, and assuming a reasonably high protein content, this would be very profitable, and we may reasonably expect to see a considerable increase of production.[1]

[1] From *British Agriculture*, Chapter IV. Early in 1939 a grass drying machine costing only £450—considerably cheaper than any that had previously been available—was put on the market.

AGRICULTURE AND FOOD SUPPLY

Apart from grass British livestock is fed mainly upon the produce of arable land, either in Britain itself or overseas. According to calculations of the Food Defence Plans Department, a total of 3,440,000 tons of wheat and wheat offals are required for feeding British livestock. Some of the wheat is of course consumed actually on the farms where it is grown—although since the Wheat Act the proportion used in this way must be very small; some of the wheat and wheat offals are for farm use, but most of the wheat offals are available to farmers as a by-product of the milling industry, which is highly organised. Inasmuch as the supply of wheat offals is derived from this source it does not vary much from year to year; for it must bear a constant relation to the amount of flour, for which demand is fairly stable. Consequently the price of wheat offals rises sharply as demand increases; under the influence of an advertising campaign the price index of milling offals rose from 97 in 1933 to 140 in 1937 and 123 in 1938. The greater part of the increased price must have gone to the millers, since where agents handled these feedingstuffs and the farmers did not deal direct, competition kept the margins down.

The Food Defence Plans Department calculated that the average consumption of maize and maize meal was almost as high as the consumption of wheat—3,215,000 tons, all of it imported. The maize is imported untreated or in the form of ready manufactured maize meal; most of it comes from the Argentine. It is used only for cattle feed, so that the demand for it is purely agricultural. Prices show a four year increment corresponding to the pig cycle, and since 1935 prices have risen steadily (in 1935 the index number was 74 and in 1938 it was 115).

Compared with wheat and maize the quantity of barley used for cattle is small, and about two-thirds of the supply is brought in from overseas. Most barley is fed in the form of meal, and whether home produced or imported passes through the hands of the millers. Its price has fallen over the last ten or fifteen years as a whole; but in the last three or four years the trend has been upward, as has been the case with other feedingstuffs (barley has risen from 79 in 1935 to 102 in 1938).

The principal remaining feedingstuff is oilseed cake and meal, all of which is imported, although the greater part of it goes through a manufacturing process in Britain. ' The quantities of cake consumed in this country,' it has been said, ' seem to depend chiefly on the state of prosperity of British farmers, not on the numbers of the livestock population nor much on the price of the cake.' [1] Generally speaking there is a greater demand for cake in the winter than in the summer, so that prices rise in the autumn and fall in the spring ; although recently this seasonal movement has been less marked than a few years ago. The total expenditure of the farming community upon this type of feedingstuff is about £12 million annually.

The question of feedingstuffs is clearly one of the most difficult in any discussion of British agriculture from the point of increased production. Cereals, sugar beet tops, small potatoes and all the other feedingstuffs which are used up on the farm where they are grown and which consequently do not figure in accounts of gross output, have nevertheless a very definite cost of production and are used by the farmer because it is cheaper for him to produce them than to buy manufactured cake. Any changes in relative price, particularly any lowering of costs of imported feedingstuffs, might have the most far reaching effects upon British agriculture—might make it more of a processing industry than ever. At the moment the situation is that grass is the standby for livestock feeding during the summer, and that during the winter the farmers use more cereals and cake. The tendency has been for a good deal of bargaining to take place in the trade in feedingstuffs. The large farmer who can buy in large quantities direct from the mill if need be, can get better terms than the small man who buys from agents in the local market working on a margin of 5/- to 7/6 a ton. Recently the tendency has been for farmers to buy readymade feeding mixtures rather than to make up their own mixtures, although there is little doubt that they could save money by the latter

[1] *British Agriculture*, Chapter VII.

course. Cooperatives for the preparation of these 'balanced rations' have been set up in some parts of the country, usually deriving supplies from the CWS; and this seems to be a way in which this important item in farmers' accounts can be reduced.

As far as increasing the production of feedingstuffs is concerned it would seem that the first step must be improved grassland—secured by ploughing up and planting with grass as proposed by Stapledon, a course which would probably cost about the £2 an acre already allowed as ploughing up subsidy—and the development of grass drying. At the same time the establishment of farmers' cooperatives should strengthen the hand of the buyers against the agents and the large concerns which mill cereals and manufacture cake, and so should make it possible to reduce the total feedingstuffs bill which the farmers have to pay.

In addition to feedingstuffs, fertilisers, seeds and store cattle are an appreciable item in the farmer's costs. Colin Clark estimates these at £17 million for 1930-1, but this may well be too high a figure.

The principal artificial fertilisers used in British agriculture are nitrates, superphosphates and potassium compounds, and as far as can be discovered from the inadequate figures available, the British farming community pays about £8 million a year for them. Imports of fertilisers are valued at about £2¼ million. Taxation on these raw materials of agriculture amounts to nearly £200,000 per annum (at the rate of £4 per ton on compound fertilisers and 10/- per ton or 20% ad valorem—whichever is the greater—on superphosphate of lime), and the distribution probably costs another £300,000, meaning a cost to the farmer of £2¾ million in respect of these imported requirements.

The 1937 Agriculture Act provided for a subsidy to farmers buying lime or basic slag to enhance the fertility of their land. The subsidy for lime is 50% of the cost of buying and carting (but not of laying) it and for slag 25%. In the first year of the scheme the Government paid a little over £1 million for fertiliser in connection with the scheme.

The Farmers' Costs: Land and Working Capital

The farmer must have land and capital with which to work; usually he has to pay heavily for both of them. Tenant farming has long been held to be the characteristic of British farming; but since the last war owner occupiers control a much larger proportion of the land. After 1918 many landlords wished to dispose of their lands for ready money, and the amount of agricultural land worked by its owner is reckoned by the Ministry of Agriculture to have risen from 10 to 30%. Under such conditions the farmer has to perform those functions which involve sinking large sums of money in the land for long periods, and which traditionally were performed by the landlords. Even where a man still holds a farm as a tenant he may well find that the landlord cannot or will not afford to do what his predecessor did.[1] Nobody knows precisely who owns the land of the country, except that some 3 million acres of it [2] (of which perhaps 1½ million acres are agricultural) is owned by public bodies including the Ministry of Agriculture, the Commissioners for Crown Lands and the Universities. It is calculated, however, that some £25 million are paid out annually in rent.[3] This seems an unduly low estimate when compared with that of Colin Clark based on the Inland Revenue statistics and covering rent and tithe. He reckons these at £38 million.

The failure of landlords to perform their traditional functions, and the growth of owner occupancy, makes the question of adequate provision of cheap credit particularly acute. At present farmers are provided with the credit

[1] Addison quotes Lord Hastings speaking in the House of Lords on the contribution which the State was to make towards manuring of land. 'What a ghastly confession it is to those who were brought up in the strict tradition of land ownership which prevailed universally not more than thirty years ago! It is positively shocking to think of the need that a Bill should be introduced into Parliament including a land fertility clause. In those days it was the proudest boast and first duty of every landowner to make himself responsible for that fertility. In those days he had the power to enforce it, and in the main he had the means to make his essential contribution to it. To-day he has neither the power nor the means.' (*A Policy for British Agriculture*, p. 29.)

[2] Addison, Appendix IV.

[3] D. R. McMaster, in *Journal of Institute of Bankers*, 1936, calculates that the total amount of 'landlords' capital' is £815 million and that the return on this is at the rate of about 3%.

necessary for carrying on farming by the banks, the merchants with whom they deal and by certain special corporations set up to finance them. It is, it has been said, a question of 'financing individuals, usually with small capital, engaging in a business offering considerable risk and limited financial returns', and as such is not a very favourable proposition. The most important of these special agencies is the Agricultural Mortgage Corporation, which was set up under the 1928 Agricultural Credit Act. This Corporation has lent some £10 million to farmers. Most of this has been for land purchase—the Corporation will not lend more than two-thirds of the value of the land which the borrower wants to buy. Bank advances have varied from time to time, but probably stand to-day at £60 million. If 4% is being paid on these loans, an additional £3 million a year must be set down to the costs of agriculture.

The result of inadequate facilities for cheap credit under government auspices has forced the farmer to seek relief from the merchants with whom he deals or to set up with insufficient resources. Consequently it is reliably reckoned that so much of the land of the country is badly drained, badly fenced, and has such unsatisfactory buildings that an average of £10 an acre must be spent on such items by a farmer who wishes to bring average land up to first class condition.[1] There is in fact an opportunity in agriculture for the investment of anything between £100 and £200 million.

The only satisfactory way in which the problem of capital for agriculture can be settled is for the State to assume the functions of landlord. The lines of this far reaching proposal have been worked out by Lord Addison [2]; but the essential points as far as the production of food is concerned are that more capital would be easily available for long term investment in State controlled land; and second, if this were combined with a settlement of the tithe question, it would lighten the

[1] This is the estimate of a farmer who has increased his holding gradually to 2,000 acres and has found it necessary to spend this amount of money per acre to bring up land in average condition with usual equipment to the level that he believes necessary for efficient farming.
[2] In *A Policy for British Agriculture*, Chapter VIII and Appendix III.

burden in respect of rent which falls upon the agricultural producer. The objective of the compensation should be to safeguard as far as possible the position of the owner occupier and to decrease the income derived from agriculture by such property owners as are functionless.

The main charges of British agriculture, necessary to secure £260 million worth of agricultural produce, are as follows :—

	£ million
Wages	50
Feedingstuffs	50–55
Rent and tithe	38
Interest to banks, payments for credits from merchants, etc.	8
Fertilisers, seeds, etc.	14
	£160–165

In addition to these sums farmers have to make a number of miscellaneous payments, depending on the part of the country and the type of farming. Transport, depreciation on implements and machinery, fuel and power, tackle hire—all these and others must be included in the farmers' costs; probably £20–30 million is a reasonable estimate for them.[1]

If the annual outlay of British agriculture is in the neighbourhood of £200 million, it should not impose an impossible burden on the industry to advance agricultural workers' wages all round by 20%. If a reduction of the expenditure on feedingstuffs can be effected and the farmers relieved of some of their payments to the landlords, the tithe-owners and the banks, there need be no increase in agricultural costs as a result of the improved standard of living. The balance of £60–70 million which represents the return to the farmer cannot be said to be excessive since it is divided between some 300,000 farmers and is remuneration not only for their own labour but often for that of their families as well. It is true that some farmers make a very good living—but these are the exception and often they derive their income not from the actual farming operations but from acting as middlemen buying the produce

---

[1] This is based upon the figures of farm expenses collected by the Cambridge Department (*Changes in the Economic Organisation of Farming 1937 and 1938*), and by the Bristol Department of Agriculture. It is necessarily an extremely rough estimate.

AGRICULTURE AND FOOD SUPPLY

of their neighbours and selling it in the wholesale market. At present many farmers do find themselves in difficulties, if the surveys conducted by University Departments of Agriculture are any indication. To take a particularly serious case—the Eastern Counties—a survey [1] has revealed that of 200 farms 46 made a loss in 1937 and 65 in 1938, while only 57 made good profits (more than £300) in 1937 and 38 in 1938. In other parts of the country losses have not been so numerous, but they have been too heavy to be explained away as occasional examples of incompetent management. Unfortunately it is not the custom of those who prepare these figures to relate the figures of profits and losses to the size of the farm or to give any such indications which might be valuable in discussions of policy.

The Expansion of Agriculture

So much for the expenditure side of British agriculture. It should be possible to effect reductions in some items, but the claims of the agricultural workers mean that little reduction in the aggregate costs can be expected. What is needed in order to revive agriculture is neither lower costs nor subsidies —but an assured market. The reason that British agriculture remained in existence at all during the nineteenth century was because industry was expanding, and with it the demand for the products of British agriculture. That market is no longer expanding, so that the potentialities of British agriculture which arise from mechanisation cannot be realised ; men leave the land and the industry decays.

No less important than increasing the market for agricultural products by reorganising distribution and if necessary subsidising consumption is guaranteeing a fair price to the farmer. As Addison points out,

> it is not so much higher prices that need to be aimed at as stability of price. Many prices are high enough now to provide a good living for an efficient producer if he knew that he could rely on them.[2]

[1] *Changes in the Economic Organisation of Farming 1937 and 1938*, published by the University of Cambridge Agricultural Department Farm Economics Reports, No. 27.

[2] *A Policy for British Agriculture*, Chapter XIII.

All those who propose policies for agriculture are now talking in terms of this guarantee of prices. The National Farmers Union has demanded ' (a) . . . price insurance plans to operate wherever unduly low price levels are shown to exist, and (b) the enforcement of effective regulation of food imports from overseas. . . .'[1] In the debate that followed the appointment of Dorman Smith as Minister of Agriculture it seemed that this principle found general acceptance; but it has different meanings to different people. To the Government it means ' putting a bottom in the market ', to some at any rate of the rank and file farmers it means a definite price, guaranteed by the Government and fixed high enough to cover costs of production and a reasonable profit.

The background to peace-time discussion of price insurance is a static British agriculture. While the market for foodstuffs is limited, any expansion of home production must mean a reduction of imports; and this will upset the export trade and the return on British capital invested abroad.[2] Consequently, British agriculture must be discouraged from expansion unless the market is expanded too.

If, however, the objective of policy is precisely this expansion of production so that British agriculture may provide as much as possible of the additional quantities of food required, then the whole background of agricultural price policy is different. A policy of guaranteeing a price based on that of the preceding years and not much above the current market price (similar to the policy being followed for sheep prices) will be as attractive to the farmers as one of arriving at a price by estimating costs of production and adding a margin of profit in the present conditions of restricted production.

The methods used for different commodities may vary in detail. In the case of fruit and vegetables local producers' organisations which paid an average price for a particular commodity (with bonuses and deductions according to quality), which graded and marketed the produce and had

[1] *British Agriculture 1938* : Views and Recommendations of the National Farmers Union.
[2] See the introductory chapter of *British Agriculture*.

AGRICULTURE AND FOOD SUPPLY

available storage space to prevent really severe slumps in price, could do a great deal. They would have to be supplemented, however, by some government agency which operated in the central markets and had the duty of putting a bottom into the market whenever necessary. In the case of milk, arrangements for the collection of milk and payment of producers similar to those operated by the Milk Marketing Board should continue. The Wheat Scheme should be continued, although with the old restriction upon the total acreage in respect of which full subsidy should be paid and with the assistance paid from the Exchequer. A varied policy has already been applied to livestock. Beef, mutton, lamb, pork and bacon account between them for one-third of the money returns to British farmers. Before the war a subsidy was given on every head of fat cattle sold, there was a guaranteed price averaging 10d per lb for sheep, and the Bacon Industry Scheme secured a guaranteed price for bacon pigs, based on the cost of feeding. These measures, however, were unsatisfactory. The bacon scheme has come into notorious confusion, and has benefited the curer rather than the farmer, while much of the subsidy on fat cattle has gone to benefit dealers instead of farmers. The subsidy on sheep was introduced only in June 1939, so that there was before the outbreak of war little experience of its working; but the Minister of Agriculture in introducing it emphasised that it was not intended 'that these price-insurance proposals should lead to an expansion of the United Kingdom production of mutton and lamb beyond the capacity of the market to absorb home killed sheep'. It was in this light that he defended the plan for a limit on the number of sheep on which the subsidy was payable.

The subsidy scheme proposed for sheep would be fairly satisfactory if expansion of the total production were to be encouraged under it. The limit now imposed is in the case of sheep a far more serious discouragement to agriculture than that applied to wheat. For livestock, since it is now the basis of British farming, the guaranteed price should be on an unlimited quantity. With this important modification the guaranteed price method is a far better expedient than the subsidy method used for cattle, which does not guarantee anything to anybody—except a good margin for the dealer. Cattle production should be expanded by the securing of an annual average price, fixed on the basis of farmers' prices in the last few years.

To sum up, the part which British agriculture can best play in ending malnutrition is that of providing the additional quantities of milk, eggs, vegetables and of certain kinds of fruit required. Already home agriculture provides a large share of the British demand for these foods; and there is every reason to believe that if cheap capital were available to agriculture and some kind of security given to farmers by a guaranteed price scheme production could be increased at competitive prices. To increase the output of milk by 30%, fruit and vegetables by 40% and eggs by 33%—quite apart from an increase in the production of meat—would mean that at pre-war prices agriculture was producing an additional £40 million worth of food a year.

12 THE PROBLEM OF DISTRIBUTION

Between 1918 and 1939 there was a very considerable expansion of distributive costs and services. One indication of this was the growth of the number of insurably employed men and women listed as distributive workers; and these, when combined with the comparatively large number of proprietors of wholesale and retail businesses, make up a formidable section of the total population. Such a distributive industry is indispensable; but the number of those who gain their livelihood by the handling of foodstuffs is so large that any adequate description of the food supply of the country must include an examination of the chances of simplifying this machinery. The total amount paid by the consumer for food is well in excess of the gross output of agriculture plus the value of net imports of food stuffs.

The most striking change in the food trades considered as a whole is the emergence since the last war of large scale distributing and processing concerns which absorb a very large share of the market. Tate and Lyle now control a very high percentage of the sugar refining of the country; Marsh and Baxters are reliably said to cure 40% of the bacon produced; the milling firms and tea blending firms, few in number, control their respective trades almost completely and are in fact challenged only by the coops; in milk distribution United Dairies control directly and indirectly a large share of the trade in London; a few importers handle all the meat imported from South America. These concerns are naturally in a very powerful position, since (with the exception of the millers) their position has in each case been secured and guaranteed by a government scheme of tax preference, agricultural marketing or import regulation. They are able to use their power despite the government scheme; and there does not exist a single case of a well organised and profitable concern in the food trades which suffered in any way as a result of state intervention. On the one hand they are able to secure advantageous terms from the producer. On the other they have reduced many small retailers to the position of virtual agents, and are able within limits which vary according to the commodity to determine the price which the consumers pay.

The Effects of War Time Control

The operations of the Ministry of Food during the last war, which were gradually extended until they touched in greater or less degree 'everything that man could eat without being poisoned', assisted the early growth of these large, would-be monopolistic enterprises. Although the food control machinery implied government trading with profit on some lines and loss on others, the customary channels of distribution continued to be used. The Ministry had a costings department which was to calculate prices which would cover the costs of the traders concerned and allow them a fair profit. Some difficulty arose, however, because of the wide differences between the costs and profits of different firms in the same line of business whose books they examined to arrive at a margin. Cooperation between firms was insisted on and this, combined with the fixing of margins which by the Ministry's figures were below the costs of some of the firms concerned, meant that the larger units in the food trades went through a period of hothouse growth and the whole trade learnt by experience the economies of combination.[1]

This can be illustrated from the history of a number of powerful concerns in the war and post-war years. Union Cold Storage, which before 1914 was linked with a number of other companies handling South American meat, increased its capital from just over £2 million to just over £4¾ million in 1920 and had profits rising from £105,000 in 1913 to £248,000 in 1919.[2] United Dairies, founded by the amalgamation of a number of firms in 1916, expanded its capital from under £1 million to nearly £2½ million in 1919 and showed

---

[1] For a comprehensive description of the operations of the Ministry see Sir William Beveridge, *British Food Control*, 1928.

[2] The Board of Trade made one contract which ran from July 1916 to three months after the end of the war for the delivery of 50,000 tons of South American meat per month ' at prices not quite double the equivalent pre-war rate' (*British Food Control*, p. 11).

THE PROBLEM OF DISTRIBUTION 241

profits which rose over the same period from £66,000 to £230,000. Lever Bros developed from a combine of 40 companies with a capital of £30 million in 1913 to a group of 140 companies with a capital of £100 million in 1919. The large flour milling firms such as Joseph Rank Ltd and Spillers Ltd did well enough during the war to absorb rival firms and open new mills in 1920.[1]

By contrast, the cooperative movement did not show a growth between 1914 and 1919 comparable with that in other countries—in France, Germany, Belgium or the United States, for example—and if allowance is made for the rise in price on the one hand and the shrinkage in the aggregate supply of certain commodities on the other 'the volume of business shows a genuine increase in quantity in the course of five years of no more than 3%'.[2] The failure of the British movement to expand was directly due to the discriminating manner in which the wartime regulations were operated. First the method of allocating supplies by reference to a datum period hit the coops specially hard. Not only sugar but pretty well every essential food was at some time or another distributed by the government on this basis.

It suited most shopkeepers who had lost custom by the enlistment of men and the migration of working class women to the industrial areas where munitions were made; and suited particularly well the retail grocery chains who counted as one unit and could manipulate their supplies to follow the demand; but it bore very heavily on cooperative societies who served the working class in the industrial areas where population was increasing and which in any case had a growing membership. Second, the Government, at any rate during the first two years of the war, put no cooperative representatives on the trade advisory committees, and in 1916 appointed as the first Food Controller Lord Devonport who had made his fortune as a wholesale grocer and retained, while he held this office, an interest in the multiple shops

---

[1] Based on F. Le Gros Clark and R. M. Titmuss, *Our Food Problem* 1939, pp. 76–7.
[2] S. and B. Webb, *The Consumers' Cooperative Movement*, 1921, p. 238.

which government policy was held to favour. Third, and 'even more bitterly resented', to quote Sidney and Beatrice Webb,[1]

> was the unfairness with which the movement seems almost constantly to have been treated in the allocation of supplies so that it frequently happened in many towns that it seemed to be the cooperative household that obtained the least sugar, butter, margarine, coal, potatoes, or whatever was in short supply. Cooperators were accordingly driven literally by hundreds of thousands (as was subsequently proved by the statistics of butter and sugar registration) to resort to shopkeepers for the goods that their own societies were prevented by the Government from supplying.

This was not all. Cooperative societies were harshly treated by military service tribunals and key men drafted into the army; while later the societies, which did not trade for profit in the ordinary sense, were subjected to the Excess Profits Duty.

The effect of this treatment was to rouse the cooperative movement to a political consciousness which it had never shown before. Cooperative representation in the House of Commons was needed to defend the movement against the Government, and the Cooperative Party was founded at a Special National Conference in 1917. The new Party had some successes and entered into alliance with the Labour Party. The cooperative movement drew closer to the industrial working-class movement too, for both movements felt themselves threatened by 'the activities of organised capital'.[2]

After the Armistice there was indeed some opposition to decontrol because it would give the strengthened combines a free hand. J. R. Clynes who had been associated with the Ministry foresaw this in a speech in the House of Commons in May 1919[3]; and the representative Consumers' Council which had been part of the machinery of the Food Ministry protested against decontrol with the support of a number of local Food Committees. By the middle of

---
[1] *The Consumers' Cooperative Movement*, p. 255.
[2] See a pamphlet 'The Union of Forces' published by the United Advisory Council and quoted in *The Consumers' Cooperative Movement*, pp. 277-8.   [3] See *British Food Control*, pp. 280-1.

THE PROBLEM OF DISTRIBUTION 243

1919 it seemed that this pressure was having its effect; the Government announced that the Ministry of Food would remain in existence. Despite this and despite a Profiteering Act (succinctly described by Sir William Beveridge as 'window-dressing'), food prices went up in the winter of 1919-20 and the use of the Ministry during the railway strike of 1919 made it clear that—

> Desire to be prepared for industrial emergencies was probably a consideration that in time had turned the scales and led the Government to decide for recontrol.[1]

Retail Distribution since 1918

The most obvious change which has come over the retail trade in food stuffs since 1918 is the increase in the importance of multiple shops, often linked with powerful manufacturing or importing concerns. Vesteys meat combine controls more than 2,000 shops run under a variety of names; and United Dairies handles a large share of the milk trade of London. The growth of multiple shops, however, has been most marked in the case of grocery and provisions which are handled not only by such firms as Sainsbury and International Tea, primarily retail distributors, but also by the concern linked in the gigantic Lever Bros and Unilever combine. Chivers, van den Bergh (margarine manufacturers), Home and Colonial Stores, Allied Suppliers (with which are linked among others Pearks Dairies, Meadow Dairies and Liptons) are among the three hundred subsidiaries of Unilever. Practically all the country's soap and margarine (except the cooperative supplies) are manufactured by the combine. Firms linked together control margarine, to take one example, from the time when the raw material is bought from the native producers on the West Coast of Africa to the time when the finished article is sold over the counter in London or Manchester. The range of the activities of Unilever is enormous and includes not only trading in groceries on a very large scale, but trading in fish through the extensive MacFisheries group.

Despite the part played by the multiple shops and the

---

[1] This verdict of Beveridge is given on p. 291 of *British Food Control*.
Page 243, line 23. *For* Chivers *read* F. Chivers & Co. Ltd.

manufacturing and importing combines which stand behind them, the retail trade in food is still almost entirely in the hands of a large number of small tradesmen only very few shops and usually only one. Even in the case of foods where the multiples are most important there are small retailers in plenty to whom the consumer may go; in the fish trade MacFisheries is the only multiple shop of importance, while fruit, vegetables and bread are handled almost entirely by small retailers. Even the development of food retailing by chain stores which built up their reputations on altogether different lines of goods has not changed this picture.

While the small shopkeeper succeeded in keeping in business—or at any rate did until the coming of a new war added still further to his difficulties and handicaps—he lost a great deal of his independence and became more and more an agent selling the packeted and often priced goods supplied by the large firms. This is clearest in the grocery trade. The outstanding characteristics of the trade have been the passing away or absorption of the inefficient one-man business and the growth of direct dealing between the retailer and the manufacturer without the intervention of a wholesaler. The independent grocers who remain no longer blend their own tea or weigh out and pack sugar, butter and the other groceries. Instead they take their supplies from the tea blenders, from the manufacturer of breakfast cereals, or from the sugar refiners; the number of articles for which they can fix their own prices is small. Eggs and sugar are perhaps the most important, and in both these cases the tendency is to sell on a low margin (often, with sugar, below cost) in an endeavour to attract custom and so expand the sale of branded goods on which the margin is fixed. A similar tendency is at work in the case of the meat retailer; he has often ceased to be in the proper sense of the word a butcher, and has become to a far greater extent a retailer who buys joints from an importer or a jobber and sells them to the consumer. Sometimes large food distributing firms will sell to the public both directly and indirectly, as is the case of the United Dairies group, which not only maintains roundsmen and retail shops but wholesales milk

THE PROBLEM OF DISTRIBUTION 245

to dairymen. These dairymen work on what is for practical purposes a fixed margin, since they cannot sell at a higher price than U.D. In the case of the bread trade the millers by means of a resale clause enforce the minimum prices prescribed by local bakers' associations.

The fixing of retail prices whether by branding of goods (and advertisement by the manufacturers which so often goes with this) or by marketing schemes (as in the case of milk) or by local agreement enforced by heavy sanctions (as in the case of bread) has been followed very understandably by competition between retailers in the form of additional services instead of price cutting. Money is spent on advertisements, expensive shop fronts, roundsmen and errand boys who take goods in response to telephone orders; and this expenditure becomes in its turn a ground for increasing the margin still further. This can be seen to be the case where retailers have to justify increases in the margin before some kind of public committee (as in the case of bread). The retailer in fact is on the one hand reduced to the position of an agent for a large firm and on the other forced by competition to cut his net margin finer and finer while the gross margin expands.

Retail margins tend to be high in the case of foodstuffs compared with other goods. They amount to 25% of the sale price in the case of fish, 30% with meat, more than 30% with vegetables and fruit. With groceries the margin is usually lower, although it varies from commodity to commodity (for example 16% or so on tea). Compared with the furniture trade, for example, or the retailing of wireless sets, the value of the average purchase is small, but there is not the same need for a large stock or for so much consultation and comparison in the sale of foods. This would seem, especially when combined with the growth of packeting, to make it likely that the small independent shopkeeper would be replaced completely by the chain store employing assistants to receive cash and prevent petty larceny in the same way as, say, Woolworths do at present. But such a forecast would leave two factors out of account—one the opening which the food trades offer to the working class family which has got together a small sum and believes that shop-keeping offers a chance of independence and fortune; the other the value of that individual attention which the small shopkeeper claims as his particularly strong suit. Usually this attention has nothing at all to do with any special knowledge or with any proficiency which a reasonably experienced employee in a large store could not equally display—rather it amounts to the generally pleasant personality of the successful small shopkeeper, his willingness to give credit for short periods, his attention to messages sent by children, and so on.

The second principal development in food distribution in the last twenty years has been the growth of cooperative trade. The share of the coops in milk distribution has increased to about 25%; they bake more than 10% of the bread and distribute 20% of the tea, 20% of the cheese, nearly 40% of the butter and over 20% of the sugar consumed in the country. They do not handle so large a share of other foodstuffs; thus, no more than 10% of the bacon, 5% of the meat, and 8% of the eggs are handled by the cooperatives, and their share of the trade in vegetables, fruit and fish is negligible.[1] This trade of course is organised primarily by the local consumers' societies under direct democratic control, and yielding a return to members in the form of a dividend representing that element in the price which in a normal trading concern would go into the pocket of the entrepreneur as a net profit. The local societies draw a large part of their supplies from the Cooperative Wholesale Society and the Scottish CWS also run on a non-profit basis. Thus there does exist a democratically controlled organisation through which a large section of the working class draws its supplies of food and other essentials; and such an organisation clearly has a very big part to play in any campaign to improve nutritional standards. The cooperative movement has already, in the hundred years of its existence, done a great deal to improve the quality and lower the price of the food which the working class eat.

[1] See George Walworth on 'The Organisation of the Cooperative Movement' in *Public Enterprise*, edited by W. A. Robson, 1937.

The existence of fixed retail prices, as well as encouraging the growth of distributive services and costs, has given an advantage to the cooperative stores; and it is indeed surprising that not more has been done by the competitors of the coops to give coupons and cash vouchers as a reply to the divi. The cooperative movement does at the same time constitute a protection against excessive margins in the retail trade and against the consequences of private monopoly, for example in the milling industry. The British Cooperatives have never shown the aggressive spirit of, for example, the corresponding movement in Sweden, which regards itself as the guardian of all consumers whether cooperators or not, and has carried on energetic campaigns to break the monopolies in margarine, goloshes and electric light bulbs [1]; but there is no doubt that their existence has provided a most valuable safeguard for the British consumer. Any proposal which would have the effect of limiting the power of the cooperative movement to expand— such as the licensing of shops or the zoning of distribution under a committee made up of the members of the trade [2]— might have the most serious consequences for consumers as a whole and open the way to a further increase in retail margins.

The foodstuffs of which the coops handle a very small share—fish, greengrocery and meat—are also those in which the retail distributive margin is high. Most of the supply of these foods is distributed through comparatively small, independent shops. The figures of average annual turnover for shops handling different commodities are approximately as follows [3]:—

[1] See for a fuller account of this R. W. B. Clarke on 'Industry' in *Democratic Sweden*, edited by Margaret Cole and Charles Smith, 1938.
[2] Such as was foreshadowed in autumn 1938 in the abortive Milk Bill.
[3] Meat and Greengrocery figures are for England and Wales for 1931 and are taken from H. Smith, *Retail Distribution*, 1937. Fish and Poultry is calculated from more recent figures of aggregate retail value (given by Feavearyear) and number of shops (White Fish Commission). Grocery and Provisions is by far the roughest estimate; it is secured from Henry Smith's estimate of the number of grocery shops in England and Wales (corrected for U.K.) and the value of retail trade as calculated by Feavearyear. For comparative purposes it may be added that the comparable figure for the boot and shoe trade according to Henry Smith is £4,940.

	£
Meat	2,880
Greengrocery	1,910
Grocery and provisions	2,200
Fish and poultry	1,750

Generally speaking, costs per £1 worth of goods distributed fall with the size of turnover; but the question of the optimum turnover for shops retailing different commodities is too large a one to be briefly examined.

The Reduction of Distributive Charges

An analysis of the costs of handling fish, greengrocery and meat indicates that a large amount of the margin is accounted for by delivery expenses and by waste due to perishing. The dealer in provisions and grocery clearly does not have the same risks of waste; nor does he lose in breaking bulk, as does for example the greengrocer, who cannot possibly weigh out a cwt of potatoes into twenty-eight 4 lb lots; nor, it seems probable, does he have quite such difficulties with delivery expenses as do shopkeepers who have to make sure of getting their orders delivered in time for a particular meal.

Some of the items, then, in the higher costs of the greengrocer, the butcher and the fishmonger are inevitable; but some could be reduced. For example it should be possible to reduce the loss due to deterioration. The butcher has already done this by use of refrigeration; and in greengrocery the loss is less heavy in the case of a shop with a large turnover and a fairly assured clientele. Further it should be possible to reduce the waste due to loss of packages. The annual cost of this has been calculated for the fish trade as being a very appreciable part of the retail margin; a great deal could be done to save this money by some standardisation of conditions and fixing of responsibility, so that the merchant who sought to secure a deposit on his packages was not penalised by loss of business. A large increase in turnover should have the effect of reducing costs per £1 worth of goods distributed. There would, it is true, be the possibility that any such increase would encourage more shops to be

THE PROBLEM OF DISTRIBUTION 249

opened, and so retail margins would be kept up. This, however, would depend upon general economic conditions. There seems to be no ground at all for stating that this would inevitably follow from increased turnover; particularly if cooperative societies gave a lead—as they would be likely to—by lowering their prices or raising their dividends.

The costs of delivery, which account for so considerable a part of the distributive margin, are particularly important in the case of milk and bread, for these foods more than any others are handled by roundsmen. The present method by which milk distribution is organised has been shown again and again to be thoroughly uneconomic. Proposals for zoning, however, such as have been put forward in some quarters, would not necessarily reduce prices, and would have the effect of making rigid the present balance of the trade as between private and cooperative enterprise. A much better course to follow seems to be that of giving the cooperative movement a monopoly in those towns where it already possesses a considerable share of the trade, compensating the displaced dairymen (some of whom would probably be absorbed by the new organisation). Where the cooperative movement has not a large share of trade, milk seems to be sufficiently important, and the economies to be effected by a unified distributive system run without profit sufficiently large, to justify putting the milk supply under municipal control.

To emphasise the development of large processing and distributing firms, and to show how these have made the retailer their agent, is to emphasise the new factors in the situation to the exclusion of the background. In the case of a number of important commodities produced at home the machinery of marketing and wholesale distribution remains as it was as far back as 1914. It has not been gradually moulded round some powerful and highly capitalised firm which has secured a very large share of control at one stage of distribution but on the contrary has remained almost entirely in the hands of small scale enterprises. The gap between the farmers' price and the retail price is no less than it is in the cases where some large firm is paying large dividends; indeed it may well be greater. The methods of wholesale marketing of eggs, fruit and vegetables and meat on a national scale have grown up to dispose of quantities surplus to the needs of the producing district; they still bear the mark of their origin and are not well adapted to handling a large supply in the most economical manner. Prices fluctuate from day to day, and even from hour to hour, as varying supplies are cast on the local or the wholesale market; such a system almost inevitably leads to waste of goods and to risks and uncertainties which provide a justification for high margins. Neither the consumer nor the producer gets the best service from such a system; and the small producer who cannot run his own lorry, get cheap rates on the railway or maintain a stall in the wholesale market, is at a special disadvantage.

Much could be done in the case of eggs, fruit, vegetables and fish by extending the organisation of producers, and putting under their control the first stage of marketing. Cooperatively owned packing stations for eggs should be encouraged and given a monopoly of collection over a particular area (as proposed by the Reorganisation Commission); local cooperative associations of producers might well be set up to maintain agencies in the wholesale fruit and vegetable market; and for white fish the best solution might well be a national marketing board representative of the trawler owners but supervised by an independent government commission.

Transport accounts for a large share of distributive costs. How much it is not possible to say, because there do not exist any figures of the total amount paid for the transport of goods by road as there do for transport by rail. It is possible, however, by using the average cost by rail as a basis, to make some very rough calculation of the costs of road transport. If generally speaking the tendency is for loads to go long distances by rail and short distances by road, the transport costs in respect of fish, for example, must amount to about £2 million, in respect of potatoes to at least £1¼ million and of other vegetables and fruits to nearly £750,000. The total transport charges on milk were

£5,593,000 in one year.[1] These examples illustrate the importance of transport charges in distribution.

At present railway rates per mile vary not only from commodity to commodity but even from town to town, there are so many special rates applicable for specific journeys. These seem to be determined not by costs but almost solely by the degree of competition existing on that particular route and by what the traffic will bear. Transport facilities might be made a useful weapon of a planning authority which desires to give encouragement to some particular district. Certainly, to take one example, the improvement of railway services and lowering of charges would benefit the distressed Highlands of Scotland.[2]

Distribution is probably the most difficult part of the food supply problem. So much of the distributive expansion since 1918 has been unnecessary that clearly reductions ought to be effected; but no government can easily embark upon a programme which may deprive a large number of people of their means of livelihood, even if the programme has the effect of lowering food prices. It is in fact practicable to carry through a far reaching scheme for shortening the distributive chain in the case of essential foodstuffs only during a period of intense economic activity, produced by public spending, in which it is possible for displaced wage earners to find employment.

The problem is made particularly difficult by the poor conditions under which many retail distributive employees have to work. Hours, although they have been shortened considerably, are still too long; and pay is often poor. Much of the retail and wholesale trade is carried on by small businesses which are fairly efficient and yield a reasonable though not excessive return.

Competing with this private trade is the vast cooperative organisation; and particularly if the approach to distribution is made through the food trades, the importance and

---

[1] This figure for 1937–8 is taken from the Milk Marketing Board Five Years' Review. As has been explained in the section on Milk, it is larger than the sum which transport in practice costs.

[2] See David Keir, *Desolation of the Highlands* 1938, and Report of the Herring Board, 1938.

possibilities of this movement are very clear. Some local societies have pursued a policy of absorbing small retailers' businesses and leaving the former owners as managers. It seems that that is a policy capable of extension; and especially as the power of the large combines in the food trades increases further the small shopkeepers may find themselves driven to some kind of joint action through their trade associations in self defence, and may themselves make an approach to the established cooperative movement.

That movement has already established good conditions for its workers and high standards of quality for its products. It has very great advantages over private trade in its scale (although this is offset to a large extent by the high degree of autonomy possessed by local societies compared with the branches of a chain store), its dividend system and its assured clientele. At the same time the organisation and tradition of the movement has tended to make it conservative. It shows a very understandable tendency to concentrate upon the quality of its goods to the neglect perhaps of flavour and appearance; and there tends to be a suspicion of unfamiliar lines of business which involve a risk. These weaknesses have prevented the cooperative trade from growing more rapidly.[1] But the movement is fundamentally a democratic movement responsive on the whole to the wishes of its members; in any reorganisation of food distribution to secure a reduction of margins it has an essential part to play just because its past development makes it able to give such an influential lead.

[1] These points are discussed fully in *Consumers' Cooperation in Great Britain*.

13 FOOD PROBLEMS IN WARTIME

War conditions give a special urgency to the problems of food supply. On the face of it what appears to be happening in the present war is that the lessons which the last war taught and succeeding events have re-emphasised are being applied. Superficially the control organisation for foodstuffs established on the outbreak of war resembles that which had grown up by the end of 1918. But a closer examination reveals a difference of setting and a difference of objective between food control in the last war and in this.

Food Control in the last War

In the Great War state control of food supply and distribution gradually became complete. At the beginning of the war there was a shortage of sugar, for before 1914 supplies had been drawn very largely from Central Europe, and before the end of August 1914 a Sugar Commission with executive powers had been set up, which drew supplies from the East and West Indies. But so far as civilian food supplies were concerned nothing more of substance was done for nearly two years. During this time the State was buying large quantities of food for the Army; the Board of Trade negotiated with South American meat companies and with other suppliers for the quantities required by the Services, and where—as in the case of New Zealand and Australian meat—the whole trade was carried on through the government department, the surplus was turned over for the civilian population at home. In October 1916 an executive commission was set up to secure supplies of wheat; but it was June of the following year before there began, with the appointment of Lord Rhondda as Controller, what has been called the 'heroic age of food control'.

By then retail food prices were just double what they had been in July 1914,[1] and as they had risen working class

[1] According to the monthly index of retail food prices quoted in Beveridge, *British Food Control*, p. 322.

discontent had risen too. The appointment of Lord Devonport as the first Food Controller in October 1916 had more or less been forced upon the government by the pressure, but his unambitious plans had not stopped the steady rise. His successor, Lord Rhondda, emphasised from the beginning the dependence of price regulation on control of supplies. He told the House of Lords,[1]

> My policy, broadly stated, is to fix the prices of those articles of prime necessity over the supply of which I can obtain effective control, at all stages from the producer down to the retailer. Such prices will as far as possible be fixed on the principle of allowing a reasonable pre-war profit for those engaged in the production and distribution of the particular commodities. Indeed the policy in effect will be one of determining profits at every stage though it will take the form of fixing prices. Every effort will be made to prevent speculation and unnecessary middlemen will be eliminated. Existing agencies—I make a strong point of this—will be utilised for the purposes of distribution under licence and control and under the supervision of local food committees to be appointed by the local authorities.

The food controls which were established in the succeeding months were certainly comprehensive. In the case of a number of essential foods—including bread and flour, meat and canned meat, sugar, tea, cheese, margarine, dried fruits, condensed milk, imported bacon and imported butter—the Ministry of Food controlled prices throughout, acting as the importer in the first place or buying from the producer or manufacturer. All other foods of any importance except bananas, oranges and fresh vegetables were subject to a greater or less degree of control in respect of import, manufacture, wholesale and/or retail prices.[2] The control of prices enabled the government to exercise some influence over the use of available resources ; thus, to take one example, the price of home produced butter was fixed so low as to prohibit the manufacture of it and to encourage the marketing of the available milk in a liquid form.

When Lord Rhondda took the post of Food Controller he found already drawn up a scheme of sugar distribution which he operated without any substantial changes. The

---

[1] 26 July 1917, quoted by Beveridge, p. 56.
[2] See Beveridge, pp. 163-4.

need for such a scheme arose from the shortage of supplies of sugar which had become apparent in 1916. First an attempt was made to deal with the problem along the line of 'datum-period' distribution; supplies were divided up among wholesalers in proportion to the quantity they had handled during a datum period when conditions were comparatively normal—in this case the period was the year 1915—and the wholesalers were instructed to supply the retailers who bought from them on the same principle. The method of allocating supplies had serious drawbacks— it did not take account of the considerable shift in the population to centres of munitions manufacture; it preserved all the wastefulness of the old system; it gave no complete security of supply to any individual consumer; and in any case an exactly proportionate reduction in the consumption of rich and poor alike would be extremely inequitable.[1] In an endeavour to overcome these disadvantages the new scheme put into effect by Lord Rhondda was devised in the first half of 1917. It was based on the registration of consumers with retailers and the distribution of supplies arranged so as to allow each retailer to provide the ration of eight ounces for each customer who had registered with him. The scheme involved too the setting up by local authorities of nearly 2,000 Food Control Committees which were in the first place to supervise the registration of consumers for sugar, and as the system of control of food supplies developed had additional responsibilities imposed on them. The committee in each locality was intended to be representative of all the interests involved—consumers, traders and farmers.

This sugar scheme actually came into operation on the last day of 1917; and events in the early part of the following year forced an extension of the rationing principle. Control of prices meant that shortage of available food did not lead to price rises which would have adjusted the demand to the supply; and as a result the working class housewife had to make sure of getting her jam, margarine, cheese or whatever it was by queuing up outside the grocer's shop. This

[1] See Beveridge, pp. 184-6.

became indeed the only way of getting some necessaries, and on each of four successive Saturdays in the first two months of 1918 a total of half a million people, it was estimated, stood in queues in London alone. The workers in some districts left the munition works to take their share of the standing in the cold, and soldiers at the front were said to be talking of doing the same.[1] A device had to be found which would end the queuing—it was found in an extension of rationing. The queues in fact were 'abolished by organisation, not by an increase of supplies'.

The control of foodstuffs—taking this in its widest sense, to include the attempts made by the Ministry of Agriculture to expand home production—had some profound effects on the diet of the population. The figures of total consumption of certain essential foods in the war and pre-war years are shown in the accompanying table (pp. 258–9). If the figures of weekly consumption per head are compared it is clear that the population relied to a very considerable degree on bread, bacon and ham, margarine, lard and potatoes. The consumption per head went up in the case of these foods by about 40%, whereas it went down by about the same percentage in the case of butcher's meat, butter and sugar. Milk consumption went down by about 25% in the course of the war.[2] Meanwhile far greater demands were made upon the working class than had been the case before 1914—wives and mothers in far larger numbers had to perform arduous factory work and to maintain nutritional standards there would have been need of an actual improvement in working-class diet.

Between Two Wars

Up to September 1939 the problem of war-time food supply appeared to have three main aspects. The first of

[1] This nearly frightened the government out of its wits. Sir William Beveridge describes a meeting with 'the Prime Minister himself with Mr. Bonar Law and the Quartermaster-General in a state of agitation about the queues, and Lord Rhondda rather like a schoolboy under examination as to what if anything he was doing to end them' (*British Food Control*, p. 204). It was about this time that Lord Rhondda told his assistant, 'It may well be, Clynes, that you and I at this moment are all that stand between this country and revolution' (J. R. Clynes, *Memoirs*, 1869–1924, p. 234). [2] Beveridge, p. 319.

these was the supply of food from overseas. The amount of food brought by ship to Britain in wartime depends partly on strategical considerations—upon the extent to which Britain is master of the seas—and partly on the respective importance attached to foodstuffs and war materials by the authority responsible for allocating shipping space. Closely associated with the shipping space problem is that of the foreign exchange available—and here again the amount of food brought from abroad as compared with the amount of munitions and industrial raw materials will depend on the policy of the controlling authority. Again purchases of foodstuffs by a belligerent in modern warfare are bound to be affected by political considerations—the desire to buy the staple exports perhaps of a potential ally.

The second aspect was home production. The degree to which the Government must in war rely upon the resources of its own country depends directly upon the amount which can be brought in from abroad, so that an expensive policy of agricultural expansion cannot be finally decided upon until there is some indication of how the war at sea is likely to turn out. The problems of home production are complicated by the imports of feedingstuffs and fertilisers which in peace time at any rate play so large a part in British agriculture; and by the fact that any adaptation of an agricultural system is bound to take so many months if not years to accomplish that it cannot be embarked upon lightly.

The third aspect was the processing of the foodstuffs available and their distribution to the consumer as quickly and cheaply as possible, and it involved the question of ensuring a fair share—and, what may be a different thing, an adequate diet—for the working population.

On the outbreak of the present war the position was worse than in 1914 in respect of each of these aspects of the food problem. As compared with 1914 there were $2\frac{1}{2}$ million acres less under arable cultivation and a quarter of a million less men on the land. In peace some two-thirds of the country's food supplies were imported. Even such home production as there was depended entirely, it seemed, upon

Estimated Annual Consumption of Some Principal Foodstuffs in the United Kingdom

	Home	1909–1913 Imported	Total	Home	1914 Imported	Total	Home	1915 Imported	Total
Wheat as Grain	1,210,000	5,070,000	6,280,000	1,200,000	5,100,000	6,300,000	1,355,000	4,795,000	6,150,000
Wheat as Flour	870,000	3,650,000	4,520,000	865,000	3,670,000	4,535,000	975,000	3,455,000	4,430,000
Beef and Veal	753,000	488,000	1,241,000	789,000	487,000	1,276,000	789,000	430,000	1,219,000
Mutton and Lamb	322,000	265,000	587,000	283,000	257,000	540,000	282,000	228,000	510,000
Bacon and Hams	125,000	234,000	359,000	120,000	249,000	369,000	130,000	313,000	443,000
Pork	224,000	33,000	257,000	194,000	56,000	250,000	227,000	19,000	246,000
Eggs	140,000	140,000	280,000	140,000	132,000	272,000	140,000	93,000	233,000
Fresh Fish	694,000	91,500	785,500	662,000	87,500	749,500	377,000	68,500	445,500
Milk	4,510,000	—	4,510,000	4,630,000	—	4,630,000	4,565,000	—	4,565,000
Butter	126,000	203,000	329,000	126,000	193,000	319,000	126,000	163,000	289,000
Margarine	60,000	55,600	115,600	78,000	76,400	154,400	115,400	100,400	215,800
Fruit	365,000	879,000	1,244,000	405,000	871,000	1,276,000	365,000	894,000	1,259,000
Potatoes	3,610,000	260,000	3,870,000	4,420,000	165,000	4,585,000	4,630,000	110,000	4,740,000
Other Vegetables	800,000	429,500	1,229,500	800,000	425,000	1,225,000	760,000	416,000	1,176,000
Tea	—	131,000	131,000	—	142,000	142,000	—	141,000	141,000
Sugar	—	1,535,000	1,535,000	—	1,600,000	1,600,000	—	1,680,000	1,680,000

	Home	1916 Imported	Total	Home	1917 Imported	Total	Home	1918 Imported	Total
Wheat as Grain	1,405,000	4,925,000	6,330,000	1,185,000	4,505,000	5,690,000	1,205,000	3,585,000	4,790,000
Wheat as Flour	1,010,000	3,550,000	4,560,000	—	4,930,000	4,930,000	—	—	1,385,000
Beef and Veal	773,000	372,000	1,145,000	831,000	324,000	1,155,000	557,000	381,000	938,000
Mutton and Lamb	304,000	160,000	464,000	318,000	113,000	431,000	218,000	82,000	300,000
Bacon and Hams	136,000	328,000	464,000	108,000	278,000	386,000	71,000	417,000	488,000
Pork	228,000	16,000	244,000	134,000	9,000	143,000	65,000	5,000	70,000
Eggs	140,000	67,000	207,000	125,000	56,000	181,000	115,000	50,000	165,000
Fresh Fish	320,000	31,000	351,000	349,000	33,000	382,500	430,000	50,000	480,000
Milk	4,190,000	—	4,190,000	3,825,000	—	3,825,000	3,325,000	—	3,325,000
Butter	125,000	121,500	246,500	114,000	94,500	208,500	103,000	73,500	176,500
Margarine	128,900	130,400	259,300	181,700	74,200	255,900	235,700	—	235,700
Fruit	330,000	805,000	1,135,000	400,000	350,000	750,000	270,000	281,000	551,000
Potatoes	4,220,000	90,000	4,310,000	3,980,000	80,000	4,060,000	5,490,000	50,000	5,540,000
Other Vegetables	780,000	420,000	1,200,000	770,000	361,000	1,131,000	830,000	382,000	1,212,000
Tea	—	135,000	135,000	—	125,000	125,000	—	135,000	135,000
Sugar	—	1,280,000	1,280,000	—	1,050,000	1,050,000	—	975,000	975,000

Figures in tons. Based on Table XX in Beveridge, *British Food Control*.

enormous imports of feedingstuffs and fertilisers.[1] The government had refused to accept the threat of war as an argument for any special planning of agriculture. Mr. Chamberlain in his celebrated Kettering speech had deprecated the part which agriculture might play in the event of war; and a favourite sentiment of Mr. W. S. Morrison while Minister of Agriculture was that the government would look very silly if it prepared for a war which did not happen. Moreover since 1919 distributive costs and services had undergone very considerable expansion, and would constitute a proportionately heavier burden upon the consumer in the event of rises in the price of imports or of agricultural products. Entrenched in the food trades were a number of powerful and profitable monopolies whose interests could not lightly be disregarded. Partly as a result of their activities the storage of food stocks in the country was normally at the principal ports and especially in London, which would be highly vulnerable from the air. Most of the commercial tea stocks were carried in London warehouses; nearly half the cold storage capacity of the country was concentrated in London, and there were other plants at Hull, Southampton, Liverpool and Bristol. No preparations had been made by improvements of harbour and storage facilities and of communications with the main centres of population to enable the smaller west coast ports to be used for the landing of cargoes of food. Perhaps most serious of all, as Lloyd George pointed out, the carrying capacity available was 6 million tons lower than in 1914, and only 2 million tons higher than at the end of the last war.[2]

No serious attempt had been made to remedy this situation by storage of quantities of essential foodstuffs. Wheat, whale oil (for margarine), animal feedingstuffs and sugar had, the government declared, been purchased—but this method of storage through the agency of private firms meant that these government-financed stocks were held in lieu of private stocks normally held, and consequently did not

[1] See the figures of Colin Clark quoted on page 226.
[2] House of Commons, 25 January 1940.

increase the total reserve of foodstuffs which in the ordinary course of trade would be held in the country.[1]

The Character of War-time Control

Although the government had declared before war began that stocks had been stored and a department of the Board of Trade had been for two years occupied in making plans for food control in the event of war, the first few months after the outbreak of hostilities were characterised by frequent and drastic changes of plan. Nothing in the first months seemed intended for the duration; but what was done and left undone gave some indication of the principles underlying policy; there was no lack of straws to show which way the prevailing wind was blowing.

Since in normal times two-thirds of Britain's food supply is imported, the organisation of war-time purchases from overseas is of first rate importance. In September 1939 licensing of imports was introduced and world freight rates stood at practically 100% above the figure of two or three months before. Import licensing placed a practical ban on the import of some foodstuffs—certain fruits regarded as luxuries, for example—and imposed limitations in the case of others. Emergency legislation gave to the Ministry of Food wide powers to fix by order retail and wholesale prices, to requisition stocks and to control the manufacture and distribution of food.

This Ministry grew out of the former Food (Defence Plans) Department of the Board of Trade—a shadow ministry which had been preparing against the eventuality of war for more than two years. As the brief reports which the Department issued before September 1939 show, the food traders were very willing to co-operate in the drawing up of schemes and placed their trade organisations at the disposal of the Department. The working of this is shown by the personnel of the Ministry at present; in each section the executive positions are held by men who previously had prominent posts in the private firms in the trade. The only

[1] A detailed plan of food storage had been advanced by J. M. Keynes in an article in the *Economic Journal*, September 1938.

exceptions are where the controllers have come over from the marketing boards which previously handled the commodity and are now more or less absorbed into the Ministry of Food; in this case their assistants or advisers are representatives of the big combines. The Bacon Controller is a representative of Marsh and Baxter [1]; the Assistant Sugar Controller is a representative of Tate and Lyle [2]; the Chairman of the Cereals Imports Committee is also the Chairman of Ranks, Ltd., the big milling concern [3]; the Assistant Director of Imported Meat Supplies represents Union Cold Storage.[4] But the most remarkable section of all is that dealing with Oils and Fats (including margarine, which is apparently to play so large a part in war-time diet) where there are eleven individuals performing administrative work. One (the worst paid by the way) is a civil servant; one was formerly occupied running his own business; and of the remaining nine who came from large private firms, seven were previously employed in the firm of Lever Bros. and Unilever Ltd, or one of its subsidiaries.[5]

Many of these gentlemen are in a most public-spirited way giving their services without remuneration; as *The Economist* points out :—

> There is no need to assume any deliberate partiality; unquestionably all the controllers are deeply anxious to serve the public interest. But they have an unavoidable bias towards seeing things through the particular spectacles of the interest from which they come. There are a large number of instances where the controller's power has been used to enforce changes in process or in trade practice (such as terms of contract, etc.) which whether or not that was their purpose in the controller's mind have undoubtedly had the effect of benefiting the section of the industry from which he comes at the expense of its customers.

Such a control system was not likely to show itself well disposed towards the small trader, for whom the war brought special difficulties. War regulation involving sudden fluctuations in the supply of goods passing through the normal

[1] J. F. Bodinnar, chairman of C. and T. Harris (Calne), which is linked with Marsh and Baxter.   [2] C. J. N. Lyle, director of Tate and Lyle.
[3] J. V. Rank, chairman of Ranks Ltd.
[4] H. Jones, director of W. Weddel, part of the Union Cold Storage Group.
[5] Reply to a question in the House of Commons, 6 December 1939.

channels of trade are bound to affect the large concerns less adversely than the small, which often have not the reserves or the credit to carry them through the difficult period. Import licensing has probably driven out of business already some of the smaller firms which maintained a precarious position in the import trade; while in the case of bacon curing a more direct method was used and the smaller curers were flatly forbidden to engage in the trade—until their general indignation forced a partial revocation of the ban. While as for the small retailer of foodstuffs there can be no doubt that his position as against the multiple has been worsened since war began.

In the first few days of war the government assumed control of the supplies of butter, bacon and sugar and made allocation to retailers on the basis of a datum system; retailers were entitled to a percentage—the same for all of them—of the quantities which they had handled during a previous datum period. This system of allocation did not take account of the very considerable changes in the distribution of population which followed the outbreak of war; it was advantageous to the large retail chain which could switch supplies from place to place as demand varied and disadvantageous to the small shopkeeper (who in the reception areas could not get extra supplies to meet the increased demand) and to the cooperative societies (who because they were expanding organisations would be hit by any scheme which based their quota of supplies on a period in the past).

The cooperative movement has found the assistance which it unstintingly offered the Food Defence Plans Department ungenerously refused. It is a curious fact, for example, which may be set down to coincidence or which may have other causes, that when a ministerial order requisitioned certain stocks of butter the method adopted meant that the cooperative movement lost a far larger share of its total stocks than did private traders—because its supplies were less dispersed. Thus in the first few weeks of war the cooperative societies were less able to supply customers with butter than were the private traders. The cooperative press has been full of examples of difficulty in getting sufficient quantities of food. On 21st November for example a meeting of cooperative general and grocery managers gave evidence of widespread difficulties. One representative said that societies were losing prestige because of lack of supplies; another pointed out that they were suffering in many ways in which private shops were not. The CWS, it was pointed out by the chairman, was not like the multiples; it could not allocate supplies to societies as it pleased. A CWS director replying to the discussion agreed that the movement was going through a difficult time. Membership was increasing but the Ministry of Food still stood firmly by the datum principle.[1]

Cutting Down Food Consumption

The registration of consumers carried out towards the end of November showed that despite the embarrassments which faulty allocation of supplies had caused and the campaign against the coops in the Beaverbrook press the movement retained an immense share of working class custom. Registrations were made separately for bacon, butter and sugar so that the three totals were not the same. Generally, however, the registration for all three commodities were about twice as large as the purchasing membership of the retail societies. The allocation of supplies on the basis of registration introduced in the case of butter on December 4, and in the case of sugar on December 11, meant some improvement in the situation for the coops. It amounted to rationing, however, since the formula was that no retailer might receive more butter than was needed to supply each of his registered customers with 4 oz per week, or more sugar than was needed to supply 1 lb per head per week and in many parts of the country before the end of November even rationing along these lines was being carried out by retailers.

Such was the general character of the control established

[1] *Cooperative News*, 25.11.39. A. V. Alexander declared on November 8 that one of the leading civil servants in the Ministry of Food, deputising for the Minister in discussing the situation with trade representatives, had admitted that as a result of evacuation and the billeting of troops the datum principle had broken down.

on the outbreak of war; but it soon became clear that an overriding consideration was the need which the government envisaged to cut down civilian consumption in order to liberate resources—labour, raw material, shipping space and foreign exchange—for war purposes.[1] The working class, however, were not prepared to countenance the direct reductions which in the view of the government were necessary.[2] The rise in the prices of essential foods due to increased freight and insurance as well as by shortage of supply helped towards the desired reduction of consumption. The government itself through the trading operations of the Ministry of Food did something to increase the price rise. As Sir George Schuster, the President of the Home and Colonial Stores, pointed out in the House of Commons, gently rebuking the Ministry,[3]

> It is a remarkable fact that whenever the Ministry of Food has commandeered stocks they have always managed to sell them back at a price which represents a rise of anything from 25 to 50% on the prices at which they were taken over. We find it extremely difficult to understand why that has been done. Let me take the case of butter for example. ... At the time when the butter stocks were taken over it is fair to say that the average price at which they had been bought was something like 118/- a cwt, when the price at which the butter would be released was fixed it was fixed at 145/- a cwt.
>
> Then one may turn to dried fruits as another example. Here we were already buying the new season's crop at a price which, allowing for duty and landing charges, represented 31/- a cwt. There was no difficulty about continuing to make purchases at that price. But the stocks have been taken over by the government and sold back to us at 49/- a cwt.

Rationing of food, too, made its contribution to this reduction of civil consumption, for the case for rationing did not rest

---

[1] This point was very explicitly put by *The Economist* (21.10.39): 'If the Government is not going to raise the resources it needs either by taxation or by the borrowing of genuine savings then a rise in prices is the only way in which the consumption of the people can be reduced to the extent necessary to set labour, materials and capital free for the purposes of war.'

[2] To quote the Chancellor of the Exchequer: 'I have never concealed my view and I have taken many occasions since the war began to proclaim it, that we shall carry through this tremendous struggle to a successful issue only if every person, other than the poorest of the poor, will recognise that there must be for the time being, a certain reduction in standards' (House of Commons, 8.2.40). [3] In the debate of 8 November 1939

upon an actual shortage of food. As Sir George Schuster expressed it,

> The justification for rationing may arise not only because it is physically impossible to get certain foodstuffs here but also because it may be economically desirable to curtail the consumption of particular articles in order to release purchasing power for things more vital for our war effort.

The rise in the price of foodstuffs which amounted by the end of 1939 to 3/4 in every 20/- led to pressure from the working class, particularly the organised section of it, for increases in wages. Hence the government's endeavour to restrict working class consumption had to become an endeavour to prevent the pressure from being effective, and the government announced that so far from making profits on the foods which it handled it was spending £1 million a week in subsidy to keep the cost of foodstuffs down. In the Commons debate on 8th February 1940 Sir John Simon particularised ; £480,000 was being spent on bread, £235,000 a week on milk, £320,000 on home grown meat, and £80,000 on bacon, with the object in each case of preventing retail prices from rising too far above pre-war levels. Sir John Simon put it very frankly that what he was concerned to do was to stop the Ministry of Labour Cost of Living Index from rising and so to stem the demand for higher wages. For he declared that the subsidy had prevented a rise of 12 points in the index, whereas the taxes on tea and sugar, which were taking from the population a sum which was half as large as the subsidy, had raised the index by only two points. As he engagingly replied to A. V. Alexander, who cross-examined him on the point, ' It is according to the subjects which you take.'

This extremely astute move, however, only opened up new difficulties. For what if lower prices should mean a bigger demand ? Or to put it in Sir John Simon's own words :—

> There are two fundamental difficulties in applying the policy of controlling prices. One is that, unless arrangements are made which will prevent it, if you keep prices down you may diminish supplies and you may get into a situation in which you do more

harm than good. So far we have been careful in our price policy to keep this first difficulty in mind.

There is a second difficulty, again the application of a very simple economic law, which is that if you take artificial steps to keep prices down you may, as I have said already, so stimulate demand that you may actually encourage unduly the consumption of what may be a commodity which you do not wish people who can afford it to buy to an excessive extent.

Later in his speech Sir John Simon gave the answer. Controlled prices could only be prevented in one way from ' to a certain extent defeating our own aim by enabling the cheaper price to attract a larger consumption '—that way was by rationing wherever necessary.

Home Production in War

On the other side of the problem—home agricultural production, the beginning of the war was marked by an ambitious and comprehensive programme of expansion. The basis of it was to be the ploughing up of $1\frac{1}{2}$ million acres before the harvest of 1940.[1] The Minister of Agriculture announced three weeks after the beginning of war that the ploughing up subsidy of £2 per acre would be extended to cover land put under the plough before 31st March 1940; livestock farmers would be guaranteed a market for cattle, sheep and pigs which would be bought by the Ministry of Food when food rationing commenced; prices paid for cattle would be announced later, would vary according to killing out percentage and would be modified according to season; prices for sheep would be raised when the Minister of Food took control to an initial figure of $11\frac{1}{2}$d per lb with the purpose of ensuring an average over the year of 1/- per lb for fat sheep.

Sufficient and suitable labour was essential to the programme. Agricultural workers were reserved so that their skill would not be wasted in the Army; and their unions by pressure in local wages committees were able to get all-round increases in wages during the first few months of war, so that in one district at least, early in 1940, a minimum of

[1] $1\frac{1}{2}$ million acres in England and Wales and half a million in Scotland and Northern Ireland.

40/- per week was reached. A central wages board with powers to fix a national minimum was established; and the government refused to accept the proposals of the National Farmers Union for linking wages in one way or another with the prices which agricultural products realised. Local committees remain in existence and may fix county minima above the national figure—and even, after special consultation with the Central Board—below it. The available agricultural labour is to be eked out by the Women's Land Army whose members will normally undertake lighter and less skilled farm work.[1]

By far the weakest spot in the agricultural programme was the shortage of feedingstuffs. Wheat was the only cereal stored before war broke out and the supplies of offals available for agricultural purposes were completely inadequate. The largest item in the increased agricultural costs of which farmers complained was due to this shortage; and in many cases farmers could not get the feeding stuffs they wanted at any price. Early in October 1939 an order was made by the Ministry of Food which was intended to stabilise feedingstuff prices roughly at pre-war levels and it was announced that the government would release the stocks which it had accumulated. Complaints grew rather than diminished and during November the farming press was full of complaints that it was impossible to buy feedingstuffs at the published price or anything like it and often difficult to get anything at all. In the following month the Minister of Food was compelled by pressure of farming opinion to promise that greater efforts would be made to enforce the prices which the government was announcing.

The Conseqences of Control

The war-time controls extend over practically the whole field of British food supply. Home-grown fruit and vegetables are almost the only essential foods which are marketed and distributed in the same way as before the war, with no government regulations. The varied controls which have

[1] The rate of pay prescribed for this Army, 28/- per week plus full board, is not likely to encourage farmers to use them to undercut male workers.

been imposed are likely to have far-reaching and permanent effects. All the small shopkeepers, small importers and the rest who have been put out of business cannot be put in business again by an Act of Parliament; and, as in the last war, probably much of the administrative machinery announced as being 'for the duration' only will prove to suit the traders concerned so well that it will become part of the permanent organisation of the industry. The effect of the control system and of the general conditions of war-time trading is to accelerate the tendencies at work in the food trades in peace time. The large bacon curers and the large milk distributors have increased their share of their respective fields, while the position of the combines which operate at the processing stage of foodstuff supply—the flour millers, sugar refiners, etc.—have had their positions confirmed. The same is true of the large South American meat importing interests. In other cases—and here imported bacon is the clearest example—the effect of war conditions has been to promote a new company for which those formerly in the trade act as agents on a fixed commission. Such import monopolies may well spread as a permanent feature of the economic system.

Control in wartime in fact reveals the same characteristic as control in peace—it does not imply the subordination of the food trades to popular wishes but the encouragement of monopolistic elements in the trades and the entrenchment of the monopolies which already exist. Such control is not likely to prove beneficial either to the small units at the processing, importing or retailing stages or to the cooperative movement. The cooperative movement is mainly a retail distributing agent; the production and processing carried on under its auspices, although fairly substantial, are not comparable with the activities of the retail societies; whereas the most powerful private concerns in the food trade do not carry on any retail distributive business at all or at any rate subordinate it to their manufacturing or importing. Consequently any regulations which limit and reduce distributive margins, although they will harm the small shopkeeper and the cooperatives, will not involve the flour millers, the bacon curers, the food importers or the rest of the concerns which are so well represented in advisory and executive positions at the Ministry of Food, in any serious loss.

Control of prices carried with it another especial danger for the cooperative movement—a ban on the dividend on purchase which distinguishes cooperative from private trading. The Petroleum Board has already refused supplies to a cooperative society unless a pledge is given that no dividend will be allowed. The coops do not sell much petrol; but the principle if upheld here might be applied with disastrous effect to all foodstuffs subject to price regulation. The dislocation of cooperative supplies at the beginning of war and the press campaign waged against the movement at that time did not prevent the early registrations for foodstuffs from proving on the whole very satisfactory to the coops, but the machinery of control may well be applied in such a way as to hamper cooperative trade during the war and place it at a disadvantage compared with its private competitors when peace returns.

14 THE IMPROVEMENT OF NUTRITION

'Do not trouble your head about social problems; what is wrong with the poor is poverty....' Bernard Shaw wrote this a quarter of a century ago, but there could be no better summing up of the problem of malnutrition. Even in peace time the scales of benefit and assistance on which the families of unemployed men had to live were too low to provide an optimum diet and so could not secure full health and vitality; at the same time the authorities charged with the administration of these scales were forced up against the fact that wages in many industries were so low that it makes no improvement in a family's condition, or very little, for the wage earner to be employed. This is not only the case in occupations where the wages are traditionally low, such as agriculture, or in industries which are declining, such as the cotton industry; but also in prosperous trades where the labour is unskilled and unorganised.

War has made the situation desperate. The first four months of war saw a rise of nineteen points in the Ministry of Labour cost of living index and this probably underestimated the increase in the cost of the working class food budget. At the same time it became established as a principle of government policy that total working class consumption must be reduced by taxation, higher prices and rationing. In an unequal society a call for sacrifice in the common good means a deliberate and calculated attempt to make the poor poorer. As G. K. Chesterton wrote in another connection: 'The little professional politician threatens to make the poor poorer than they can possibly be without starving in the street or falling back into another form of support by the State. People who are already clinging with their teeth and finger nails to the edge of the chasm are to be formally and legally kicked into it.' It is probable, unless marvels of wastefulness are being performed, that a fair proportion of the conscripts are better fed than they would be if they remained civilians. That circumstance, however, does not offset the fact that, because of evacuation expenses, heavier indirect taxation, the inadequacy of state allowances and pensions and the failure of the trade union movement to secure wage advances to compensate for the increased cost of living, the 'war for democracy' was in the first few months at any rate waged at the price of forcing tens of thousands of families below the level at which their diet is sufficient to maintain them in health and strength. The population will be less resistant to disease, shorter lived and of less efficiency, there will be more rickets, a higher death rate in childbirth and all the wretched consequences of dietary deficiency unless a battle or two is fought for democracy on the home front.

The consequences of underpayment and underfeeding on national health in peace and war are clear enough; what remains is to discuss how to raise the standard of living. One side of this is the reduction of prices by the improvement of organisation, the increase of supplies, and the public control of those profitable concerns which have got a large share of the trade at one of the 'bottlenecks'—the flour milling stage, for example, or the sugar refining. The other side is the promoting of measures for increasing working class purchasing power and the organisation of any special feeding services.

The basis of any improvement in national health must be an allround increase in wages. Such an increase can have its origin, as all similar movements in the past have had their origin, only in the organised pressure of the working class. Combined with that there must be some kind of provision for the as yet unorganised workers who are receiving in many cases less than a living wage. New minimum wage legislation and a minimum wage commission, to ensure that no adult male worker in any industry shall be employed at less than, say, 50/- a week, has been proposed; and combined with this has gone a plan for family allowances for the third and subsequent children.[1] There is clearly a case for such

---

[1] This proposal has been advocated by G. D. H. Cole in his pamphlet, *Living Wages*.

THE IMPROVEMENT OF NUTRITION

measures in view of the especial poverty of large families [1] and the effect which this is likely to have on the physique of a large proportion of the rising generation. But there is some opposition to such a plan from working class quarters; and if adopted it would have to be carefully worked out so that it was not a device for making the childless working class family contribute to the support of the larger family. This need for higher wages and a national minimum (appropriately higher because of increased costs) is as great in war as in peace. The profits of the food trusts are a luxury which a democratic society cannot afford under war conditions; nor can such a society without jettisoning its principles maintain a tiny class of wealthy men and women by making inroads on the standards of the workers.

Such questions extend far beyond the scope of a discussion of food policy; but if statecraft is the best utilisation of available resources, the problem of underfeeding is not one which can be abstracted from the social structure and contemplated in isolation. Apart from a general advance in working class wage standards, there are certain special measures which may be taken to improve nutrition. These, incidentally, could be put into effect immediately and would not in any way cut across a subsequent more general programme.

A Surplus Commodities Corporation?

In several countries already the existence of stocks of food which farmers hold off the markets for fear of destroying prices has contrasted with the real need in which many people live. This is a situation which seems to call for a direct solution failing an overhaul of the distributive system; and in the United States a special body has been set up to administer a solution. It is the Federal Surplus Commodities Corporation, and its purpose is to put a bottom in the market for primary products. If the price of a particular foodstuff seems likely to collapse the Corporation brings relief to the farmer by buying up supplies. As a buyer it

---

[1] According to *The Standard of Living in Bristol*, to take one example, a quarter of the families with three children and half of those with four children or more were below the poverty line.

acts upon the advice of the Secretary of Agriculture. Usually the first suggestion of a purchase by the Corporation comes from the growers themselves or from some others engaged in the trade who notify the Marketing Division of the Agricultural Adjustment Commission, who in their turn make a report to the Minister with recommendations as to what should be done. The Corporation, if it finally buys, takes only so much of the crop as is necessary to improve marketing conditions and growers' prices. The supplies which it acquires the Corporation distributes through the welfare agencies in various states. These provide the machinery of free distribution; they maintain in fact a permanent organisation for this purpose.

Certain commonsense safeguards have to be applied in such planning. The food habits of different states to which food may be sent must be studied to prevent waste; care has to be taken that surplus commodities are not sent from one state to another where there is a similar surplus; and precautions by packaging, labelling and imposition of penalties must be taken against resale in competition with goods which have passed through the normal distributive channels.

The system seems to have brought very satisfactory results to growers and consumers. In the year ending June 1938 nearly 50 million dollars, most of which was provided by the income from the tariff, was used by the Corporation. Among the largest purchases were 4 million lb of apples, 4 million lb of butter (bought at about 25 cents per lb) and 10 million barrels of wheat flour—but the total list of commodities handled by the Corporation included every important foodstuff produced in the United States. The Corporation is now initiating a new scheme under which, by an elaborate system of relief checks given to those families receiving incomes from the WPA, the demand for commodities listed from time to time as surplus will be stimulated. This method is being used, it seems, with the full cooperation of the distributive trades.[1]

[1] For a general description of the work of the Surplus Commodities Corporation see its Report for the year 1938, issued in Washington. The new plan for distribution through the normal channels was outlined by the Department of Agriculture in April 1939.

It seems doubtful how far the same organisation could be used in British circumstances even in peace. Although there are from time to time gluts of particular products, they are not on the same scale as in the U.S.A. It seems questionable whether a permanent organisation could usefully be maintained for the sole purpose of dealing with them. There may well be a glut of soft fruits in a summer month and a glut of, say, herring at some stage in the winter; but the UK does not produce a large enough range of foodstuffs or on a sufficiently large scale for an organisation to be employed doing this work of adjustment. It seems better to accept the principle of the American scheme but to apply it to each individual commodity through the marketing organisation or other machinery of government control proposed.

School Milk and School Meals

There is not available in this country the same national welfare machinery for use in distribution of surplus products; the obvious agency would be the local authorities. Already almost all local authorities through their maternity clinics are providing milk free or at a cut price to expectant and nursing mothers; and some of them have made arrangements for meals and milk to be provided for school children.

The provisions for the feeding of school children even in peace time leave much to be desired. As far as free feeding is concerned the local authorities must take the initiative and determine the conditions under which meals and milk may be provided without payment. As a result the proportion of children benefiting varies a good deal from one part of the country to another. Out of a total school population of over 5 million, 560,879 children were given milk free and 151,535 had meals free for some period during the year 1937-8.[1] It has been calculated that the number of children receiving free (solid) meals at any one time must have averaged less than 2% of the school population,[2] and in March 1939 it was pointed out to the President of the Board of Education

[1] Report of the Chief Medical Officer of the Board of Education, 1937-8.
[2] Calculated by the Children's Minimum Council.

that the number of children receiving school meals had declined by 7,000 in the past four years.[1] Generally speaking it is the rural authorities that have been backward in providing meals free, although canteens where meals can be had for payment have tended to develop in large country schools rather than in towns.

The economies which can be made by buying and cooking food in large quantities are quite considerable ; although of course it is not possible to make any valuable or realistic comparison of the cost of preparing and serving a meal for a child in school with the cost at home, where probably food is being prepared anyway for other members of the family. It seems to be the case that as far as buying food in bulk for communal feeding is concerned, the greatest economies can be effected in buying for a hundred. In catering for larger numbers any reductions in cost are due to cheaper maintenance and management rather than to cheaper food.

There is generally a division between the provision of meals for payment and of free meals ; and the method of selection of children to be fed free varies, despite the Board of Education instructions, from district to district. Local authorities providing meals which are a charge on the rates must make a decision to do so ; although in some school canteens free meals are provided without such a decision from the surplus of the payments made by other children taking meals. Where meals are provided free the local authority must ascertain that funds other than public funds are not available in sufficient amount to meet the cost ; but not all authorities provide meals on a simple income test of parents—evidence of malnutrition must be offered by the teacher or the school doctor.

What is required is a system of school feeding which shall avoid differentiation between children who can afford the meals and those who cannot ; and shall be based on sound nutritional knowledge—as much school feeding at present is not. The most satisfactory method would be to make it the rule rather than the exception for children to

---

[1] Deputation organised by the Children's Minimum Council reported in the press, 28 March 1939.

take a midday meal in grant aided schools. Those children whose parents' incomes are shown to be above a certain level should be required to pay, but there should not be any separation between the children who pay and those who are fed free; the feeding should as far as is practicable be done in school or in some well furnished and well appointed centre nearby (so that children would not have to hurry over their meals). Any payment made should be kept as low as possible—at, say, 2d per day.

Children attend school, however, for only part of the year; and although many parents will undoubtedly prefer to feed their children at home during the holidays there is no doubt that many parents would welcome the opportunity for their children to take a midday meal at school outside term as well as during it. Certain minor administrative problems might well arise, but they would not be insoluble. In particular the lack of a suitable room in many of the present antiquated elementary schools might cause difficulties and necessitate the use of a near-by hall.

While the actual feeding should be as decentralised as possible to give the children a real break and rest at midday, the buying of foodstuffs should be done on the largest practicable scale, because of the economies which can be effected. The L.C.C. already makes considerable economies by buying on contract from the producers or the importer; and it has already been proposed that some machinery should be devised for making surplus products available at a special price to feeding authorities. A central bureau under the Ministry of Health should be charged with the duty of advising on buying and on diets so that the schools get the best value for their money.

The feeding of all elementary school children should be made obligatory upon local authorities. Part of the cost would have to be covered by a grant from the Exchequer, but the total cost would not be prohibitive. Mrs Barbara Drake, LCC, has made a calculation based on the Ministry of Education estimate that school dinners, including food and overheads but excluding capital expenditure on buildings, cost 5d per head. This shows that to provide all children in elementary schools with free dinners during term and to give 50% of them free dinners on Saturdays and during the holidays would cost £36 million.[1] If a charge of 2d were made for all meals the cost would be reduced by £13 million. As a temporary measure it might even be desirable to make such a charge (but subject to such an income test that about a quarter of the meals provided were free). This would make income from parents about £10 million and reduce the total cost to £26 million.[2]

That is a large sum of money; but there is no question that it would be well spent. The proportion of children coming from families where the income is not sufficient to cover needs is so large that some counter measure on this scale must be taken. This expenditure of £26 million a year, rising to £36 million a year,[2] by ensuring one balanced and sufficient meal a day to elementary school children would lay a firm foundation for the health of the people in the future.

War time with the evacuation of school children makes the case for an extension of school feeding overwhelming. Quite apart from the direct nutritional advantages of this scheme there are few measures which would ease the working of evacuation of school children more than one which provided for children (country bred as well as evacuees) to have their midday meals at school. The two shift system in the schools throws out the routine of the household which includes some children who attend the first and some who attend the second school.

A Ministry of Food Supply

Such welfare schemes would be useful but they would not go to the root of the matter. What is required as a long term programme is a comprehensive plan for the organisation

---

[1] From a pamphlet, *Nutrition: A Policy of National Health*, 1936.

[2] This estimate of expenditure leaves out of account: (1) The effects of the decline in the birth rate. Even if social changes check this decline it is likely that the present low rate will show an effect on school populations throughout the decade 1940–1950. This, however, may well be offset by changes in the school leaving age. (2) The reduction effected by a more general adoption of bulk buying on the lines suggested or on those already followed by the LCC.

of food supply which shall distribute at the lowest possible prices sufficient food to provide the whole population with a satisfactory diet. Apart from welfare schemes which are in the nature of emergency measures, the first essential would be genuine public control over the ' bottle necks ' of food supply. Already at the strategic points, usually at the processing or wholesaling stage, large concerns have formed themselves and are aiming at monopoly control. Their position enables them within broad limits to dictate their terms to the ineffectively organised primary producers on the one hand, and the ineffectively organised consumers on the other. If the control applied at these strategic points—flour milling, bacon curing, milk wholesaling, sugar refining, and so on—were in the public instead of the private interest, a plan for improving nutrition could be carried out without any other extensions of public ownership in the field of food supply.

These concerns should actually be taken over to be operated by a Ministry of Food Supply whose head would be responsible to Parliament ; but in British agriculture and in retailing, what is wanted is the growth of cooperation among those already engaged. The marketing boards were originally devised by Lord Addison, when Labour Minister of Agriculture, as farmers' cooperatives on a national scale. They should return to that conception, negotiating on behalf of their constituents with the Ministry of Food Supplies and charged subject to the Ministry's approval with spending a proportion of their receipts on schemes for the improvement of the quality of the product which they respectively handle. So far as retailing is concerned, a large share of the trade in food is already controlled by the cooperative movement. That movement would have to be relied upon to make the pace in reducing retail margins ; this would supplement the work of the Ministry of Food Supplies.

This is not a plan for mere state supervision or even state control of food supply. Any comprehensive account of peacetime trade organisation and still more any honest description of war-time food ' controls ' shows that state intervention in a profit-making society is not the antithesis of private capitalism but its most developed and rigid form. Public control of the food trades if it is to be a step to the improvement of the national dietary must be carried out at the same time as public control of key industries by a government which is genuinely concerned with the drastic redistribution of wealth and the establishment of social equality. The political movement which led to such a government in peace or war would be paralleled by an industrial movement for higher wages. This working class pressure on two fronts is the only means by which an adequate supply and an equitable distribution of food can be secured.

What the Present Demands

Present circumstances, however, require an emergency programme for immediate application. War conditions demand the most positive and energetic action in defence of the working class standard of living. One side of such action is the demand for higher money wages to cover the increased cost of living; but in war such agitation is not sufficient. As J. M. Keynes has shown very forcefully, if the proportion of the total resources which is devoted to the production of goods for civilian consumption is reduced and kept at the same abnormally low level throughout the war, then increases in money wages will not make the working class as a whole any better off. So if the working class standard of living is to be maintained and, in the case of that section of the working class whose diet is too poor to ensure health, actually improved, there must be a vocal demand for an increase in the supplies of foodstuffs not less than for a stabilisation of price.

In the local Food Committees established all over the country by the Ministry of Food there are the means for giving such a demand expression. Their constitution provides for the representation not only of retail traders but of consumers as well; but it is clear from the limits imposed on their action that they are intended to have the innocuous function of seeing that the local retailers do not charge more than the prices specified by the government for a restricted number of commodities. By coordinated action, however, backed by an informed public opinion, these committees could gradually extend their functions. They could ensure that every rise in the price of any food, whether subject to government control or not was traced back to its source and publicly justified. For this a National Consumers Council on a representative basis (similar to the Consumers Council which existed in the last war) would be needed. This, working in conjunction with the local Food Committees, should be able to examine the books of any concern in the food trades and make recommendations to the government as a result of its investigations. It should be within the province of the National Council and of local Committees to review the share of national resources—taking that term in its widest sense—being devoted to the supply of foods.

Such reviews are not in themselves sufficient. They should be given the fullest publicity—for the present danger to the people's food supplies does not come from a blockade which might perhaps necessitate a degree of discretion in publicity. Publicity would enable trade unions and other organisations to express public opinion on the subject of the share of national resources being devoted to providing food. Such reviews and such organised public expressions of opinion on them are the only means by which the working class standard of living can be defended during war.

INDEX

In the case of some books to which there are a number of allusions in the text a short title has for the sake of convenience been used in all footnote references except the first. In such cases the short title appears in the index with an indication of the page on which particulars of the book will be found.

Aberdeen, 131, 134, 137; Fish Trades Association, 137; Steam Trawling and Fishing Co Ltd, 140 n.
Addison, Lord, 31, 70, 76, 85, 109, 111, 220, 232 n., 233, 235, 279
Agriculture, Act 1937, 231; British, 219–238; character of, 219; expansion of, 236; farmers' incomes, 234; guaranteed prices, 236–8; holdings, size of, 222; labour conditions, 225; labour in wartime, 267–8; land, 232–3; land capital, 233–4; livestock, importance of, 81; main charges on, 234; marketing organisation, 221; monopolies, 220; and national defence, 226; productivity of labour, 225; proportion of food provided by, 219; specialisation, 222–3; subsidies, 225, 231, 235, 237; wage bill in, 225–6; wages in wartime, 267–8; wartime, 257, 260, 267–8
Agriculture, Council of, 111
Agriculture, Ministry of, 10, 26, 92, 158, 162, 210–12, 218, 232, 236, 237, 260, 267
Agricultural Adjustment Commission, 274
Agricultural Credit Act (1928), 233
Agricultural Marketing Act (1933), 158, 220
Agricultural Mortgage Corporation, 233
Alexander, A. V., 106, 264 n., 266
Allied Suppliers, 198, 200–1, 243
Anglo–Argentine Meat Trade, Joint Committee of Inquiry into (1938), 93 n., 95; Trade Agreement (1933), 26, 92
Anglo–Danish Commercial Agreement (1933), 70 n.
Aplin and Barrett Ltd. 51, 52 n.

Apples, see Fruit
Argentina, 25, 26, 90, 92–4, 207, 229
Armours Ltd, 93, 94
Assam, 193–4, 196
Associated Fisheries, 141
Auckland, 58
Auctioneers, District Chairman of, 107
Australia: Apples imported from, 178, 179; butter imported from, 49; eggs imported from, 70; and international sugar agreement, 206–8; meat imported from, 90, 92, 93, 96–8, 253; wheat acreage, reduction of, 26; wheat imported from, 24, 25

Bacon and Ham, 114–128; consumption of, 4, 114, 258–9; contract system, 117–119; curing, 115, 117–123, 126, 221; guaranteed prices, 120–1; imports, 114, 116, 117, 120, 125, 126, 128; offals, 127; pig cycle, 115, 127; pre-war supplies, 13; production costs, 116, 126; quota prices, 120; Reorganisation Commission for Pigs and Pig Products, 1932 (Lane-Fox Commission), 114–16, 119, 123, 126; retail trade, 124–6; retail price, 13, 82, 114, 118, 122, 123, 127; sales quotas, 122–3; subsidies, 266
Bacon, Industry Development Board (1935), 116, 119–121, 122; Industry Act (1938), 119; Industry Scheme, 116–123, 237; Importers' National Defence Association, 125
Baking, 15–20; conditions of labour, 15, 19; costs of production, 16–18; distribution, 16–19; Joint Price Committee

INDEX

(London), 18; London scales, 16; modernisation, need for, 19–20; Night Baking, Report of the Departmental Committee on, 15 n.; retail trade, 15, 16, 18; standard prices, 17–18, 19; Trade Board, 15, 19; wages, 15, 19; wholesale trade, 15–18
Barley, 221, 229–230
Barrow in Furness, 8
Battery system, *see* Eggs
Beef and veal, *see also* Meat and Livestock, 4, 13, 41, 79, 90, 91, 92, 98, 100, 107, 108, 258–9
Beilby, O. J., 68
Beveridge, Sir William, 243, 256 n.
Billingsgate, 137, 138
Bishop Auckland Experiment, *see* Vegetables
Bloomfields Ltd, 140, 145, 145 n.
Bloomfields Overseas Ltd, 145 n.
Bodinnar, J. F., 125, 262 n.
Brazil, 90, 92
Bread, 14–31, *see also* Baking, Flour, Millers, Milling, Wheat; brown and white, 14–15; consumption of, 4, 14, 29; delivery expenses, 16, 17 n., 19, 30; maximum prices, 18–19; retail distribution, 14–16, 18, 30, 245, 246; retail prices, 16, 29; subsidy, 266
Brenner and Co, 145 n.
Brewers, 221
Bristol, 7, 21, 142, 260
British Agriculture, 115 n.
British and Argentine Meat Co Ltd, 93 n., 94
British Beef Co Ltd, 93 n.
British Food Control, 240 n.
British Medical Association, 3, 4 n., 6
British Sugar Corporation, 209, 212, 213 and n., 216, 217
British Trawler Owners Federation, 134
Brooke Bond Ltd, 198, 199, 200
Butter, 48–54; consumption, 4, 12, 34, 258–9; costs of production, 50; distribution, 49, 50; factory produced, 51; farm produced, 50, 51, 53 n.; Government control of, 265; imported, 39, 48, 49; Milk Products Marketing Board, 54; pre-war supplies, 13; profits made, 52 and n.; retail prices, 49, 53; subsidy, 53

Canada: apples imported from, 178, 179; cheese imported from, 49; egg consumption, 64; meat imported from, 92; wheat imported from, 24, 25
Cardiff, 33, 136
Caroni Ltd. 209
Cattle, 79–87; disease, 34, 35, 62; dressed carcase weight, 87; farmers' costs, 83; feedingstuffs, *see* separate heading; herd replacement, 37, 62 and n.; imported, 81, 85; marketing 83–90; rearing and feeding, 79–80; slaughtering, *see* separate heading; subsidy, 83, 84, 85, 237; transport, 86; wartime prices, 106–7, 109, 267
Central Milk Distributing Committee, 39
Cereals, 229, 230
Ceylon, 193, 195, 196
Chadbourne Agreement, 206, 207
Chamberlain, Neville, 199, 260
Cheese, 48–54; bonus on, 53; Cheddar, 54; consumption, 4, 34, 48; distribution, 49; factory produced, 51–2; farm produced, 50–1; imported, 39, 48, 49; Milk Products Marketing Board, 54; pre-war supplies, 13; profits made, 52 n.; retail price, 54; subsidy, 53
Chicago, 88, 93
Chile, 90
China, 14 n., 64, 193, 195
Chivers Ltd, 243
Churchill, Winston, 199
Clark, Colin, 5, 16 n., 179 n., 225 n., 226, 231, 232
Clynes, J. R., 242, 256 n.
Collective farms, 223
Committee against Malnutrition, 9 n.
Conscription, 2, 271
Consumers' Co-operation, 23 n.
Consumers' Council during last war, 242
Cooperative Movement, 241–2, 246–8, 251–2; baking, 30, 246; canning factories, 185; feedingstuffs, 231; margarine, 243; meat, 94, 106, 113; milk, 43, 44, 46–7, 57–8, 246; milling, 21, 23, 29; Scottish, 21, 246; Swedish, 48, 247; tea, 198, 200, 246; war conditions, 263–4; Party, 242
Corporacion Argentina de Productores de Carnes, 94
County Durham, 33

INDEX

Covent Garden, 162, 172, 174-5
Cow and Gate Ltd, 51, 52 n.
Crawford, Sir William, 5, 6 n., 11, 14, 33, 34, 64, 114, 129, 142, 157, 182, 192, 203
Cream, 38
Cripps, John, 46 n., 47, 48
Crown Lands, Commissioners for, 232
Cuba, 204, 205, 206
Cupar, 216
Cutforth Commission, see Milk

Dairymen's Associations, National Federation of, 38
David Greig and Co Ltd, 65, 72
Deficiency diseases, 2
Denmark, bacon, 116, 120, 126; eggs, 65, 70 n., 72, 75; milk consumption, 33, 49
Devonport, Lord, 1 n., 241, 254
Distribution, see under separate commodities, also 239-252, 274; conditions of labour, 251; delivery, 249; increased cost of, 239, 260; retailers, 240; small shop-keeper, 241, 244-6, 262-3, 269; waste, 248
Dorman-Smith, Sir Reginald, 236
Drake, Mrs. Barbara, 277
Duncan and Jamieson Ltd, 145 n.
Duncan Commission, see Fish
Durham, 9

East Anglia, 31, 147, 235
East Indies, 193, 195, 253
Education, Ministry of, 276, 277
Eggs, 64-77, 220, 238, 246, see also Poultry; battery system, 68, 69 n., 74; consumption, 64, 70, 258-9; cost of production, 68-9, 225; feeding-stuffs, see separate heading; imports, 64, 65-71, 72, 75; increase in home production, 64, 65-71, 73, 74, 219; labour costs, 68-9; London Egg Exchange, 72; manufacturing, 64; National Mark Scheme, see separate heading; National Mark Egg Central Ltd, see separate heading; pre-war supplies, 13; producing areas, 70; Reorganisation Commission for Eggs (1934), 66 n., 73, 74, 75, 76, 77; retail distribution, 65-6, 75, 244, 250; retail price, 65, 66, 70, 75; specialised production, 67, 68; wholesale distribution, 71-4

Eire, 79, 92
Eldorado Ice Cream Co Ltd, 93 n.
Elliott, Mr. Walter, 10
Elder and Fyffe Ltd, 180
Estonia, 146
Evacuation, 42, 43, 264 n., 272, 278
Excess Profits Duty, 242

Family allowances, 272-3
Feavearyear, 13 n., 14, 64, 75, 129, 155, 192
Federal Surplus Commodities Corporation, 273-5
Feeding-stuffs, 223, 226-231, 234, 257, 260, see also Cereals and Grass; cattle, 35, 37, 38, 41, 62, 81, 82, 83, 109, 161; cereals as, 229-230; dried grass as, 228; oil-cake as, 230; pigs, 81, 82, 115, 117, 120, 127-8; potatoes as, 166-7; poultry, 67-9; shortage of, 268; total cost of, 226
Fertilisers, 109, 169, 190, 223, 231 n., 234, 257
Finland, 146
Fish, 4, 12, 13, 129-154, 219, 258-9; see also Sea Fish Commission, etc.
White fish, 131-142; auctions at port, 136; chief landing ports, 131; consumption, 129; fishing fleet and fishermen, 131, 132-5; fried fish trade, 129, 138, 139-140, 148, 166; imports, 131, 137; landing restrictions, 133-4; price at port, 132, 135, 142; refrigeration, 151; retail distribution, 138-142; Royal Commission Report on the White Fish Industry (Duncan Commission), 130 n., 134, 135, 136, 138, 139, 141, 142; transport, 136-7; White Fish Commission, 138; wholesale distribution, 132, 135-6, 137, 139, 140-2
Herrings, 142-9; canning, 153; consumption, 142, 143, 148, 149; curing, 145, 146, 147, 148; exports, 143, 145-8; fishermen, 144, 147, 149; fleet, 143, 145; Herring Commission (1935), 144, 145, 146, 147, 148, 149; Herring Industry Act, 144; home market, 148-9; imports, 148; landing restrictions, 147; price at port, 142, 143, 146; producers' price, 142, 148; retail price, 142, 148; total landings, 145

INDEX

Fish Friers, National Federation of, 139, 166–7
Fleetwood, 131, 134, 137
Flour, 15–30, 219, 258–9
Flour Millers' Corporation, 23
Food Committees (in last war), 242, 255
Food Council, 16–19, 38 n., 46, 102–4, 139, 165, 168, 195, 197, 201
Food (Defence Plans) Department of the Board of Trade, 125, 156 n., 158 n., 176, 229, 261, 263
Food Economy Handbook, 1 n.
Food, Health and Income, 5 n.
Food, Ministry of, 42, 43, 105, 106, 107, 125, 126, 149, 215, 243, 261, 262, 265, 267, 268, 270, 280; in the last war, 240, 254; wartime controls, *see* separate heading
Fordson Estate, 225
France, 25, 32, 33, 241
Frigorifico Anglo, 94
Fruit, 155–7, 176–191; apples, 156, 157, 176, 178; bananas, 156, 176, 180–2; canning, 157, 177, 182–5; cold storage, 184; consumption, 155, 156, 157, 182, 236, 238, 258–9; cost of production, 225; distribution, 177, 185, 191, 245, 246, 247 n., 248, 250; dried, 265; farmers' prices, 156; home production, 156, 176–8, 220; imports, 157, 176, 178, 179–182, 183; producing areas, 177; retail price, 157, 177; seasonal supplies, 178–9; specialist production, 177; transport, 181, 184, 250

George, R. F., 6, 7
George Green Ltd, 145 n.
George Munro and Co Ltd, 174
George Williamson and Co, 193
Germany, 33, 145, 146, 153, 206, 241
Glasgow, 49, 138, 139, 164
Glebe Sugar Refining Co Ltd, 209
Grass (as feeding-stuff), 227–8, 230, 231
Great Yarmouth Ice Co Ltd, 145 n.
Greene Committee, *see* Sugar
Grigg, *see* Milk (Re-organisation)
Grimsby, 131, 134, 136, 142

Hall, Sir Daniel, 109
Ham, *see* Bacon
Harris, C. and T. (Calne), Ltd, 125 n., 262 n.

Hastings, Lord, 232 n.
Health, Ministry of, 56; Advisory Committee on Nutrition, 3, 10, 32, 54, 185, 203
Herring Industry, *see* Fish
Holland, 65, 145, 146
Home and Colonial Stores Ltd, 65, 198, 243, 265
Hops, 221
Hornimans, 200
Housing, 8
Hull, 131, 132, 134, 136, 142, 260

Import Duties Act, 52 n., 91
Import licensing, 261, 263
Imports, *see under* separate commodities; *also* 258–9
Incentive Agreement, 213
India, 14 n., 25, 193–4, 195, 207, 208
India Tea Association, 193
International Beef Conference, 92
International Sugar Council, 207, 208
International Tea Co Ltd, 243
Ireland, Northern, 81, 159
Islington, 98

Jam, 4, 177, 203
Jamaica, 180, 182
Jamaica Banana Producers' Association, 180–2
James Finlay and Co, 193
James More Ltd, 145 n.
Java, 205, 206
John Walker and Co Ltd, 209
Joint Industrial Council, 24
Jones, H., 105, 262 n.

Keeble, Sir Frederick, 109
Keynes, J. M., 280

Labour Legislation, British Association for, 9 n.
Labour, Ministry of, Cost of living Index, 122, 130 n., 266–7, 271
Lamb, *see* Mutton
Lane-Fox, *see* Bacon (Re-organisation)
Lard, 4, 256
Lever Bros, *see* Unilever
Leverhulme, Lord, 140, 141
Linlithgow Report (*Report of the Departmental Committee on the Distribution and Prices of Agricultural Produce* 1923), 21 n., 50, 51, 155, 170, 172, 174, 175, 176, 177
Liptons, 198, 243

INDEX

Littleton and Badsey Growers Ltd, 172
Liverpool, 7, 21, 138, 260
Livestock, 220; marketing, 83–90, 109–111; rearing and feeding, 79–81; slaughtering, 86–90, 107, 110–12; *see also* Cattle, Pigs, Sheep
Livestock Industry Act (1937), 85, 89, 111
Livestock Commission, 85, 87 n., 89, 221
Lloyd George, D., 1, 260
London: as flour port, 21; milk, 32, 42, 47 and n.; provision exchange, 49; Social Survey of, 7; as tea market, 196–8, 201
London County Council, 142, 277, 278 n.
London Egg Exchange, 72
London Retail Meat Trade Association, 105
Lyle, C. J. N., 262 n.
Lyle, Sir Leonard, 209, 210 and n., 215
Lyons, 198, 199, 200

MacFie and Sons Ltd, 209
MacFisheries, 140, 141, 145, 243, 244
Maize, 229
Malnutrition, 1, 7, 9, 224, 238, 271–3
Manchester, 21, 49, 138
Margarine, 4, 34, 42, 52 n., 243, 254, 258, 259, 262
Market Plans Committees, *see* Potatoes under Vegetables
Market Supplies Committee, 54, 158
Marks and Spencer, 176
Marsh and Baxter, 123, 125, 239, 262 and n.
Martineau Ltd, 209
Mauritius, 204, 207
Maypole Dairies, 198 n.
Mazawattee, 200
McGonigle, G. E. M., 8, 9
Meadow Dairies, 198 n., 243
Meat, 78–113, 219, 220, *see also* Livestock, Slaughter-houses, Beef, Mutton, Pork; consumption, 78–113, 219, 220; costs of production, 82–3; home production, 79–90; imports, 78, 79, 90–8, 100, 101, 105, 108, 219; livestock, *see* separate heading; maximum prices, 106; offals, 87, 88, 89, 90; pre-war supplies, 12; refrigeration, 93, 219; retail trade, 100–4, 105, 108, 112–13; slaughtering, *see* Livestock; subsidy, 266; war conditions, 105–7, 269; wholesale trade, 98–100, 106, 108, 110
Meat Importers' National Defence Association Ltd, 105
Merseyside Survey, 33, 34, 114
Midland Marts Ltd, 84
Milford Haven, 131, 134
Milk, 32–63, 219, 220, 238; accredited producers, 35; attested herds, 35; in B.M.A. minimum diet, 3; 'Certified,' 35; cheap milk schemes, 55–7, 275; Committee of Investigation for England, 38 n., 43, 46, 47 and note, 52 n.; condensed, 4, 33, 42, 66; consumption, 4, 6, 12, 33, 38, 40, 41, 42, 45, 59, 258–9; cost of production, 36, 37, 62, 225; delivery, 43, 46, 47; distributive costs, 46–8, 57, 63; dried, 56, 60; 'Grade A,' 35; manufacturing, 38 and note, 39, 40, 41, 42, 45, 50, 51, 52, 59, 60; pool prices, 40, 41, 42, 43, 45, 51, 53; pre-war supplies, 13; producer retailers, 39, 40, 43, 58; Re-organisation Commission for Great Britain, 1936 (Cutforth Commission), 38 n., 44, 45; Re-organization Commission for Milk, 1933 (Grigg Commission), 38 n., 39, 51, 52; retail distribution, 40, 43–8, 59, 222, 249; retail prices, 32, 41, 42, 43, 45, 46, 47, 57; subsidy, 43, 266; summer and winter prices, 38, 59; transport, 39, 40, 44, 45, 59, 250–1; Tuberculin tested, 35; war conditions, 269; wholesale distribution, 36–43; wholesale prices, 38, 41, 55; yield per cow, 35, 37, 38, 61
Milk Bill (1938), 57, 222
Milk Commission, 57 n., 222
Milk-in-Schools schemes, 55–6
Milk Investigation scheme, 36
Milk Marketing Board (1932), 34, 35, 37–43, 44, 45, 50, 51, 53, 54, 55, 57, 221, 237
Milk Products Marketing Board, 54
Millers' Mutual Association (1929), 21, 22 and note, 23, 220
Milling, 20–4; concentration at ports, 21 n.; costs, 23; distribution, 239–241

Morrison, W. S., 260
Mortality rate, 10; infant, 8 and note, 9, 11; maternal, 8, 9
Muirhead and Willcocks, 140 n.
Mutton and Lamb, 4, 13, 78-80, 90-2, 100, 108, 258, 259

National Canning Co, 184
National Farmers' Union, 38, 158, 213, 221, 236, 268
National Food Canning Council, 184
National Mark Egg Central Ltd, 73
National Mark Scheme, 73, 185
National Poultry Council, 69
Nevilles Ltd, 15
New Zealand, 58, 60; butter imports from, 49; cheese imports from, 49; meat imports from, 90, 92, 96-8, 108, 112, 253; milk consumption in, 33; organisation of fruit trade in, 191
New Zealand Meat Producers' Board, 96, 97, 105
Norfolk Cold Storage and Ice Manufacturing Co Ltd,
Nutrition, Advisory Committee on, see Health, Ministry of, 145 n.

Octavius Steel and Co, 193
Oilseed Cake, 230
Orford Oysterage Ltd, 140 n.
Orr, Sir John, 5, 6, 8 n., 10, 11, 13, 34, 171
Ottawa Agreements Act, 25, 67, 91, 92, 94

Palestine, 179
Pasteurisation, 46, 47, 48, 58, 59
Pearks Dairies, 65, 198, 243
Petroleum Board, 270
Pigs, 79, 81, 115, 121, 122, see also Bacon; curers' prices, 122; marketing, 83-90, 116; pig cycle, 115, 127; producers' prices, 116, 117, 125; production areas, 81; subsidy, 236; wartime prices, 106
Pig Industry Council, 116 n.
Pig Marketing Board (1933), 116, 117, 118, 120
Plymouth Food Control Committee, 17 n.
Poland, 146, 206
Policy for British Agriculture, A, 31 n.
Pork, 13 n., 79, 81, 90, 114, 115, 118, 125, 127, 258-9

Potatoes, see Vegetables
Poultry Diseases, Committee on, 69
Poultry Bill (1939), 75
Poultry Board, 76
Poultry Commission, 76
Pouparts, 174
'Poverty line,' 6, 7
Primary Products Marketing Organisation, 49
Profiteering Act, 243
Purchase Finance Co Ltd, 22 n.
Pure Ice Co Ltd, 93 n.

Railway transport, 137, 162, 172-3, 250-1
Rank, J. V., 262 n.
Ranks Ltd, 22, 241, 262
Rationing, 215, 256, 264-7
Refrigeration, 93, 151, 219, 260
Reorganisation Commission for Eggs; see Eggs for Great Britain; see Milk; Milk, see Milk; Pigs and Pig Products, see Bacon
Rhondda, Lord, 253-6
Rickets, 9
Rowe, White and Co, 193
Royal Commission on the Fish Industry, 130 and note; Food Prices, 102; the West India Sugar Industry, 205, 206
Rumania, 25
Russia, 26; see also USSR.

Sainsbury, 72, 243
Salmons, 200
Sankey Sugar Co Ltd, 209
Sansenina, 93, 94
Schools, cheap milk scheme, 55-6; medical examinations, 9; meals, 275-8
Schuster, Sir George, 264, 265, 266
Scotland, 43, 52, 53, 130, 144, 148, 216, 251
Sea Fish Industry, Royal Commission on the (Duncan Commission), 130 and note. (For Reports see Fish)
Sea Fish Industry Bill, 150; Order, 133
Sea Fishing Industry Act, 130 n., 151
Sheep, 79-82; dressed carcase weight, 87; marketing, 83-90; subsidy, 237; wartime prices, 106, 267
Shreeve Ltd, 145 n.
Simon, Sir John, 43, 266, 267

INDEX

Slater Ltd, 145 n.
Slaughter-houses, 87, 88 n., 89, 107, 111
Slaughtering, *see* Livestock
Slaughtering of Livestock, Report of the Committee on the, 87 n., 88, 111
Smithfield, 98, 99, 105
Smithfield and Argentine Co Ltd, 93, 94
South Africa, 70, 92, 179, 207
South African Sugar Association, 207
South America, 92–6, 98, 167; *see also* Argentina
South American Meat Importers Freight Committee, 94
South Wales, 8 n., 9, 214
Southampton, 7, 260
Spillers, 22, 241
Standard Fruit Co Ltd, 180–1
Standard Price, Report of the Committee on the (1935), 27, 30
Stapledon, Sir R., 231
Stiebeling, 3 n., 5
Stockton-on-Tees, 8, 9
Subsidies, *see* separate commodities
Sugar, 13, 203, 218, 219, 244; beet, 204, 205–6; consumption, 4, 203, 206, 212, 258–259; costs of production, 213; distribution, 214–15, 246; growers' prices, 206; industrial uses, 203; in last war, 253, 255; international restrictions, 205–208; refining, 204, 208–210, 216, 218; sources of supply, 204; taxation, 203, 204, 205, 215, 216; transport, 216; U.K. industry, 208, 210–13, 216–17; U.K. Sugar Industry, Committee of Enquiry into (Greene Committee); use as feeding-stuff, 230; war conditions, 215–16, 269
Sugar Commission (1914), 253; (1936), 213, 217
Sugar Industry Reorganisation Act (1936), 207, 213, 216, 217
Sweden, 11, 32, 48, 153, 247
Swifts and Wilson Meats Ltd, 93, 94
Switzerland, 33, 48

Tate and Lyle Ltd, 209, 210, 212, 215, 220, 239, 262
Tea, 13, 192–202; blending, 199–201, 239; conditions of production, 193–4, 201; consumption, 4, 192, 258, 259; imports, 193; international control, 194–6; London market at Mincing Lane, 196–8, 201; prices, 192–6; re-exports, 197; retail distribution, 199–201, 246, 246; tax, 192–9, 202
Tea Control Committee, 201
Trade, Board of, 17, 20, 52 n., 90, 91, 94, 120, 133 n., 158–9, 176, 240 n., 253, 261
Transport, 234, 250–1, *see also under* separate commodities and Railways
Tuberculosis, 10, (cattle) 35

Unilever, 140, 198 n., 241, 243, 244, 262
Union Cartage Co Ltd, 93 n.
Union Cold Storage Co Ltd, 93, 94, 95, 100, 240, 243, 262
United Dairies, 44, 45, 46, 47 and note, 54, 220, 221, 239, 240, 243, 244, 245
United Fruit Co, 180–1
USA: apples imported from, 178–9; egg consumption, 64; herring exports to, 153; large scale vegetable production, 190; milk consumption, 33; slaughter of livestock, 88, 89; wheat imported from, 24, 25
USSR, 25, 145–6, 153, 197; *see also* Russia
Uruguay, 90, 92

Van Den Bergh, 243
Vegetables, 12, 14, 155–176, 236, 238, *see also* Littleton and Badsey Growers; consumption 4, 155, 156, 157, 258, 259; cooperation of growers desirable, 188; distribution, wholesale, 169–175; distribution, retail, 170, 171, 176, 245, 246, 247 n., 248; farmers' prices, 156; home production, 156–169, 220; imports, 156, 157; in general farming, 169; large scale market gardener, 169; large scale production in USA, 190; producing centres, 169, 170, 174; quota regulation of imports, 157; small growers handicapped, 173–4; transport, 171–3, 175
Potatoes, 13, 158–169; Bishop Auckland Experiment, 165–7, 186; consumption, 4, 155–6, 158, 166, 258, 259; costs of production, 225; disposal of surplus, 167; distribution, wholesale, 161,

162, 163, 164, 167; distribution, retail, 161, 164, 165–7, 168; exemption from marketing scheme, 160; farmers' prices, 156, 158, 159, 162, 167–9; home production, 159–160, 161–9; imports, 158–9; Importers' Association, 159; marketing scheme (1933), 155–8, 159–169, 185, 186, 221; Market Plans Committees, 164, 165; Potato Exchanges, 165; Price Recommending Committees, 165; producing centres, 161; quota regulations of imports, 159; 'riddle,' 159, 160; transport, 162, 250; yield per acre, 158

Vestey Bros, *see* Union Cold Storage

Walter J. King Ltd, 145 n.
War-time control by the Ministry of Food, *see* separate commodities; *also* 105–107, 253–270; Bacon Supplies, Controller of, 262; Cereal Imports Committee, Chairman of, 262; Imported Meats Supplies, Director of, 105, 262; Oils and Fats Division, 262; Sugar Controller, Assistant, 262

Weddel Beef Co Ltd, 93 n., 105, 262 n.
Welfare schemes, 6, 56–7, 60, 275–8
Westburn Sugar Refineries Ltd 209
West Indies, 205, 206, 208, 209, 218, 253; Sugar Co Ltd, 209
Weston Ltd, 20 n.
Wheat, 24–31; as feeding-stuff, 229–230; home-grown, 20, 26, 28, 31, 220; imported, 20, 24–6; offals, 21, 28, 62; standard price, 27; subsidy, 27, 28, 30–1
Wheat Act (1932), 26, 27, 28, 31, 229
Wheat Commission, 20, 24, 237
White Fish, *see* Fish
William Low (Fraserburgh) Ltd, 145 n.
Williams, Lady, 9
Wisbech, 162, 167, 184, 185
Women's Land Army, 268
Works Progress Administration (WPA), 274

For Product Safety Concerns and Information please contact our EU representative GPSR@taylorandfrancis.com
Taylor & Francis Verlag GmbH, Kaufingerstraße 24, 80331 München, Germany

www.ingramcontent.com/pod-product-compliance
Lightning Source LLC
Chambersburg PA
CBHW071158300426
44113CB00009B/1243